Amish Education in the United States and Canada

Mark W. Dewalt

ROWMAN & LITTLEFIELD EDUCATION
Lanham, Maryland • Toronto • Oxford
2006

Published in the United States of America
by Rowman & Littlefield Education
A Division of Rowman & Littlefield Publishers, Inc.
A wholly owned subsidiary of The Rowman & Littlefield Publishing Group, Inc.
4501 Forbes Boulevard, Suite 200, Lanham, Maryland 20706
www.rowmaneducation.com

PO Box 317
Oxford
OX2 9RU, UK

British Library Cataloguing in Publication Information Available

Library of Congress Cataloging-in-Publication Data

Dewalt, Mark William
Amish education in the United States and Canada / Mark W. Dewalt.
p. cm.
Includes bibliographical references.
ISBN-13: 978-1-57886-446-1 (hardcover : alk. paper)
ISBN-10: 1-57886-446-1 (hardcover : alk. paper)
ISBN-13: 978-1-57886-447-8 (pbk. : alk. paper)
ISBN-10: 1-57886-447-X (pbk. : alk. paper)
1. Amish—Education—United States. 2. Amish—Education—Canada. I. Title.
LC586.A45D49 2006
371.071'973—dc22 2006001183

™ The paper used in this publication meets the minimum requirements of American National Standard for Information Sciences—Permanence of Paper for Printed Library Materials, ANSI/NISO Z39.48-1992.
Manufactured in the United States of America.

Contents

Acknowledgments

Writing a book of this nature is not an easy task without the help and encouragement of many individuals. I must first acknowledge all of the Amish and Mennonite people who have provided information, reviewed sections of this book, and invited me into their homes and their shops. Without the assistance of these faithful people this book would not be as accurate as it should be. I must also acknowledge the numerous neighbors of the Amish people who have provided contacts with the Amish community or provided tidbits of information about Amish education and life in general.

Partial funding for the travel and time needed to write this book was obtained from research and sabbatical funds at Winthrop University. I must also thank the faculty and staff in the College of Education at Winthrop University. Many of them have provided feedback on topics for this book, reviewed chapters, and generally encouraged me to pursue its completion. It is also important to note that early in my career as I began this research in earnest, I received financial support and encouragement from faculty and staff at Susquehanna University.

A special thank you to Bonnie Troxell for her insight and expertise related to Old Order education in the United States. Her knowledge and assistance over the years were significant contributions to the data collection and writing of this book.

Illustrator Tim Stiles is an accomplished artist with a pottery studio in Gastonia, North Carolina. Tim is a graduate of Winthrop University and an art teacher at Ashbrook High School in Gaston County.

I must also thank Amanda MacDermaid (graduate assistant) for her diligent assistance in many aspects of the library research, data collection, and proofreading of this document.

Finally and most important, I must thank my wife, Carolyn, and my family for their wonderful support throughout this project. They have been most supportive in every aspect of the lengthy research process and the writing of this book. I cannot thank them enough for their tireless support.

Introduction

> Although Amish children do not study religion in the classroom, they learn a great deal about their religion.
>
> —Hostetler, 1989

This book is an ethnographic description of Amish education in 21st-century America. The book is not an attempt to compare Amish education to other types of private or public education, nor is it an attempt to say that public schools should adopt some of the teaching methodology of Amish schools. It is my earnest desire that by the time the reader finishes the book he or she will have a very good picture of the Amish educational system. Because the Amish culture is steeped in tradition and a faith that is in action seven days per week, it is necessary to take some time to describe to the reader that tradition and faith system. Amish schools are based on this tradition and faith and would be difficult to understand without this background.

Research procedures used in collecting information for this book are found in Appendix A and Appendix B. The setting for the book is the Amish communities in the United States and Canada, and Appendix B briefly outlines all of the communities that I have visited. While making the visits to Amish communities, I have always been struck by several things. First, Amish students and teachers enjoy school. Second, Amish parents and teachers hold students accountable for their own learning, especially learning in reading, writing, and mathematics. Third, Amish schools build community by stressing group achievement rather than individual achievement. And the Amish appreciate and value their right to have their own parochial school system.

I have chosen to tell the story of Amish education for several reasons. First, it is a remarkable story and one that has garnered my interest for several years. It is a story of humility, determination, remarkable achievement, funny events, and anguish. It has not been easy for the Amish to establish their own schools, and as we will see they faced many hardships along the way.

Second, writings by Egerton (1967), Fuller (1982), Grove (2000), Gulliford (1984), Hughes (1986), Sherman (1998), Snyder (1987), and Snyder and Huffman (1995) have chronicled the public country schools in the United States but provide little to no information on Amish country schools. As I have studied rural education and one-room schools in particular I have found that the Amish are in some ways preserving many of the teaching styles and patterns utilized in the thousands of public one-room schools that once dotted North America. There were many positive components to that system of education, and the Amish have continued to utilize the strengths of the one-room school concept.

Third, there are many misconceptions about Amish education. Telling this story will help the reader gain a thorough and accurate picture of Amish education. In doing so, we will better understand the Amish but also better understand our views of education.

Before we go further, a note about terminology is in order. I will on occasion use the term "scholars" in place of students. On numerous occasions I have read in Amish periodicals and have heard the Amish refer to students as scholars. One will also see the term "frolic." To the Amish the word frolic means a work event that involves a group of people working together to complete a task. While the task is completed, fun, fellowship, and food will be shared. The term "Plain People" will sometimes be used to refer to all Old Order Amish and Old Order Mennonite peoples. Lastly, the Amish use the term "English" to refer to anyone who is not Amish. I will use that term in several places in this book as well. It should be noted here that I will define literacy as the ability to read and converse in English and German as well as the ability to understand and apply mathematical thinking to home and vocational trades in areas such as quilting, running a small business, furniture making, and farming.

It is important to note here that while this book is not about the Old Order Mennonites, much of the information about Amish schools will apply to Old Order Mennonite Schools. Both groups have similar school buildings, use similar textbooks, attend the same summer teacher meetings, and use the same teaching methodology.

Each chapter will begin with a quote that relates to the content of the chapter and/or an aphorism or maxim that has been posted in an Amish school. As we move through each chapter in this book we will further explore the notion of community, literacy, and responsibility. It is my hope that you will enjoy the trip as we explore Amish education in the 21st century.

1

An Overview of Amish Education and Culture

> We are known by our actual deeds and not by what we boast that we can do.
>
> —Aphorism posted in an Amish school in Pennsylvania (Hostetler, 1989)

Our story begins in the southeastern corner of Minnesota, a good stone's throw from the Iowa border and not far from a tiny town of perhaps ten houses. West of the town lies a school nestled in the gently rolling hills that looks much like that used by our forefathers throughout much of the rural history of North America up until the 1950s. This school is located at the intersection of two dirt roads that is situated at the edge of about 15 acres of cropland that leads to a farmstead and then to a small creek/river at the base of a tree-covered hill to the south and west. Standing on the dirt road to the north of the school, as one gazes south on this cloudy and very cold day in February of 2005, are the red-painted barn and shed that stand in vivid contrast to the snow-dusted corn fields. Also visible are the fields of tan corn stubble, the white-painted school, the white horse shed, the white outhouses, the two silver/white silos, and the two corncribs filled to the brim with the straw-colored dried corn on the cob. The schoolyard is bare except for the three old tires that most likely serve as bases for games of tag or softball as the weather permits. This school serves the Amish children who live on farms within walking distance of the school.

The story of the Amish parochial school in the 21st century includes the rural environs of Pennsylvania, Ohio, Indiana, and Illinois—each state a traditional home for the Amish—as well as Tennessee, Kentucky, and Montana, all states not often associated with the Amish. These parochial schools do not want public funding or public recognition. Neither do they desire fancy buildings, large libraries, spacious sports facilities, elaborate auditoriums, or state-of-the-art cafeterias. The community that supports these schools simply seeks to educate its children for a disciplined life within its close-knit society. The following sections will describe typical Amish schools, provide a brief history of the Amish break from public schools, and explore the growth of Amish education. While not all Amish groups have the same way of doing things, a common bond among the Amish is that the school is small in size and is located in a rural setting, free of fancy architectural details and shrubbery.

In Pennsylvania, Amish parochial schools are generally one-teacher schools; however, not all Amish schools are one-teacher schools. For example, many schools in Ohio, Indiana, and Illinois have two teachers in one building. One school in Ohio is a typical example. The school, which is located on a rural blacktop road, is larger than most one-room schools and has a full basement. The school has white vinyl siding and white vinyl windows. Across the front of the room is a green chalkboard with cabinets and bookshelves underneath this board. Each teacher has a desk that is placed in the front of the room facing the students. Beside each teacher's desk is a table where instruction usually takes place. Student desks are arranged in rows, and students are seated in groups associated with their grade. If the number of the pupils in the school is fairly evenly divided by grade, one teacher instructs grades 1 through 4 and the other grades 5 through 8. This school has a chain link backstop for use when the students play softball at recess.

Amish schools are typified by being situated in a rural setting, away from busy roads, and near the farm of an Amish family. The schools are usually small frame structures with wood, aluminum, or vinyl siding. On occasion there is a brick school, a cement block school, a stone school, or a stucco school. White is the predominant color used for the exterior, although some tan or gray schools exist as well. Amish schools do not have shrubbery around the foundation of the school or cement walkways from the street to the school. The absence of shrubbery and sidewalks provides insight into the Amish culture. Shrubbery serves no functional purpose and would make the schoolyard more difficult to keep up in the summer. Sidewalks are not needed since students walk through fields, on dirt roads, or along the sides of a blacktop road; a sidewalk would serve no purpose since one's boots or shoes are already dirty from the walk to school. Many schools will have visible bell towers, while in schools without a bell tower the teacher utilizes a hand bell to announce the start of school or the end of recess. The school and curriculum, regardless of the specifics, reflect the values of the Amish community that has joined together to build the school.

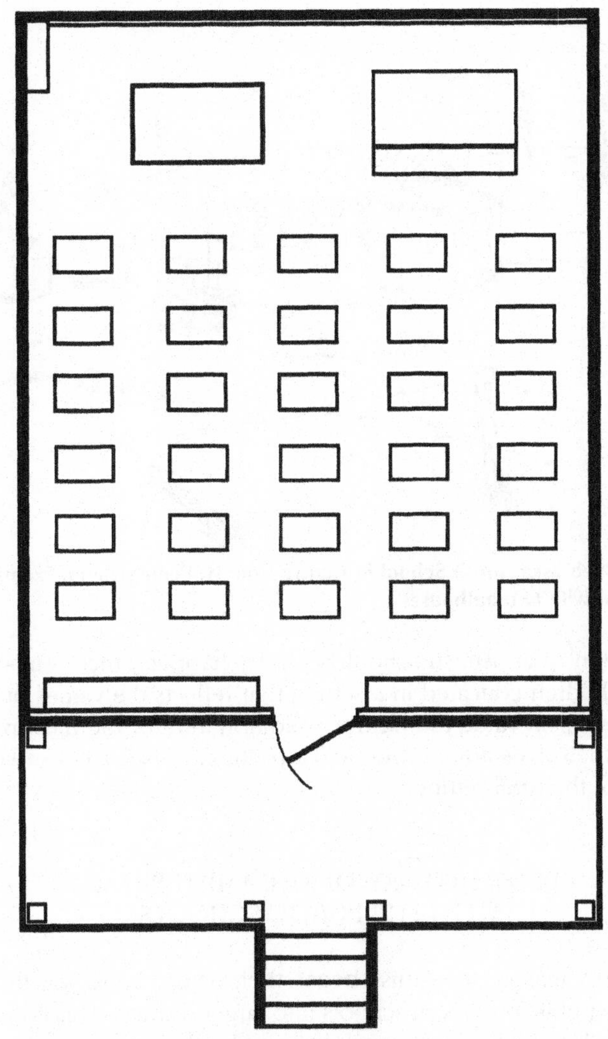

Figure 1.1. One-teacher school with porch, 30 student desks, and teaching table

Figure 1.2. Nebraska Amish School in Centre County, Pennsylvania. Example of one-teacher school with two outhouses.

The location of an Amish school is not by happenstance; Amish parents want their children educated in a setting that reflects the values of the community. The Amish value the farming tradition and for the most part prefer to conduct their lives among the fields, pastures, small creeks, woods and farm yards of the rural setting.

BRIEF HISTORY OF THE AMISH BREAK WITH THE PUBLIC SCHOOLS

One of the key reasons the Amish began their own schools was the consolidation of the public one-room schools into larger districts. This consolidation required pupils to be bused to much larger schools in towns and cities away from the rural setting. For most of their history in North America, Amish children attended public one-room country schools alongside children of their English neighbors. The Amish were perfectly happy with the curriculum and teaching methods used in small country schools and did not support the closing of these schools. They thus set about the difficult task of beginning their own schools once public school consolidation efforts began in earnest. William Lindholm (1989), a Lutheran pastor, further notes that the Amish utilized public schools for over 100 years and only organized their own schools because they feared the new education policies of a rapidly changing and materialistic culture. They did not start their own schools for religious instruction but rather as a place for children to learn their Amish identity.

The Amish have been peacefully protesting school attendance laws, writing school rules, building schools, and creating textbooks since the beginning of the Amish school movement. Lapp (1991) has collected and reprinted over 300 pages of newspaper reports that chronicle the court cases and imprisonment of Amish parents from 1950 to 1956 in Lancaster County, Pennsylvania. Numerous parents were arrested, fined, and sometimes jailed for refusing to send their children to consolidated high schools. These struggles eventually led to the vocational plan in Pennsylvania that allowed high school–age students to participate in an Amish-run educational system instead of attending a public high school. For over 60 years Amish leaders have attended numerous meetings on the local, state, national, and international level, produced numerous textbooks and workbooks, met with public school officials, organized summer teachers' meetings, designed curriculum appropriate for Amish students, designed several monthly publications devoted to educational issues, and built or remodeled over one thousand schools!

The Amish have also been active in recording their community and school history. Booklets such as *The 40th Anniversary of Woodside School*, a 52-page history of this Indiana school, and the *25th Maple Grove School Reunion Booklet*, a 50-page booklet produced in 1993 for another Indiana school, point to the value the Amish place on their heritage and schools. Numerous other Amish-authored books such as that by Kauffman, Petersheim, and Beiler (1992) record the history of specific communities. Schools will almost always be mentioned in these historical accounts. The fact that these histories are recorded attests that the Amish value literacy and community and that they take seriously their responsibility to provide a good education for their children.

The community that supports a new school will elect a building committee and a school board, and the first task of the school board is to determine how the school will be funded. The building committee's responsibility is to determine a timetable for constructing the school because the Amish do not employ contractors to build the school. The actual building of a school is not an easy task, for it requires the building committee to decide on the type of structure to be built and to acquire the appropriate building permits once the site of the new school is determined. Once this is accomplished the committee buys the materials and transports them to the building site. Then the committee determines when the members of the community will convene to build the school. Simultaneously, the school board will be searching for furniture and educational materials for the school. It also has to employ a teacher for the school.

Establishing a New School

- Elect school board
- Elect building committee
- Determine funding
- Select site
- Secure building permits
- Determine date of frolic to build the school
- Obtain building materials
- Select teacher
- Build school
- Collect school furniture and supplies
- Open school

TYPICAL AMISH SCHOOL DAY

In most instances an Amish school day is composed of about two 75–90 minute blocks of instruction in the morning and two 60–90 minute blocks of instructional time in the afternoon. These instructional times are divided by morning recess, the noon lunch break and recess, and the afternoon recess. Teachers work with one grade at a time, and this instructional time will be about 10–15 minutes in length for each subject at each grade level. Students then return to their desks where they will complete their assignments for the day. All students are expected to do their work in an accurate manner without interrupting other students or the teacher. Schools nurture the values of the Amish culture, values such as humility, patience, the joy of work, cooperation not competition, and taking personal responsibility for one's learning.

My observation in an Amish school in Dover, Delaware, in January of 2005 is illustrative of the Amish teaching style. The school, which was heated by a coal stove, was nice and warm compared to the cold and snowy weather outdoors. After the opening exercises for the day the students began their schoolwork without any verbal directions from the teacher. The teacher then stated, "First grade students, please remember to write your names in your tablets. Third grade arithmetic." The third graders proceeded to the front of the room in an orderly fashion and sat around the table in front of the chalkboard. The teacher then used the chalkboard to illustrate how to solve a division problem in which three digits were divided by one digit. After giving the students three examples, she called the students two at a time to the board. She then stated a division problem, and each child had a chance to do a problem on the board with teacher assistance as needed. After each child was successful he or she went back to their desk to complete the work for the day. This entire arithmetic lesson was completed in about 10 minutes, and then the teacher walked around the room giving students individual assistance as needed. It is important to note that as the teacher was working with the third graders on arithmetic all of the other students in the class were engaged on their morning work. As one can see from this example, an Amish teacher gives instruction on a new skill and then has the students practice that new skill at their desks while she is working with another grade level.

All instruction in Amish schools is primarily conducted in English except when teachers teach children to read and speak German. Subjects taught in Amish schools are reading, arithmetic, English, penmanship, health, history, geography, phonics, spelling, art, and German. Students do not receive instruction in music, physical education, or science. Physical education classes are perceived to be not needed because students get plenty of exercise each day at recess, getting to and from school, and completing their chores at home. Students sing each day at school, and many have an opportunity to color or draw as well. The primary language of most Amish homes is Pennsylvania Dutch (a dialect of German); thus many children come to school speaking minimal English. For this reason, teachers will spend extra instructional time with the first graders at the beginning of the year.

Contrary to popular opinion, Amish schools do not assume the responsibility of the teaching of religion, as this is the purview of the church and the home. Amish schools do begin the day with religious activities such as singing, the Lord's Prayer, and the reading of a chapter or a story from the Bible. There is no discussion, however, of the Bible reading.

Amish textbooks and aphorisms posted on the walls of the school and bulletin boards emphasize the virtues of hard work, humility, kindness, and caring. Many schools post the Golden Rule: Do unto others as you would have them do unto you.

Amish students attend school until they complete eighth grade. At this point their formal classroom-based education ends, and they work with their parents to learn the skills that will enable them to take part in the work economy of the settlement. In Pennsylvania, Amish students participate in the vocational school plan until their 15th birthday; a detailed description of the vocational school plan will be found in chapter 6. This system seems to be working well; in my travels to Amish communities throughout the United States and Canada I have been unable to find an instance where an Amish adult is unemployed.

IDENTIFYING AMISH CULTURE

The Amish first came to America in the 18th century and settled in Pennsylvania. Since these humble beginnings they have established numerous communities in Canada and over 20 states in the United States. The Amish are a

Christian people with their roots firmly planted in the Anabaptist traditions of 16th-century Europe. Other Anabaptists with similar roots in 16th-century Europe are the Mennonites and the Hutterites. In the United States there are many groups of Mennonites, from those that are very similar to the Amish (such as the Old Order Mennonites) to the less conservative groups that drive cars but still retain some distinctive forms of dress. The Hutterites are a communal people who have several colonies in the United States and Canada. While the Amish and Hutterites are quite different in use of modern farm equipment and dress, they both retain the use of German Bibles and the use of the German language in church services. The Amish are often confused with, but are not related to, the Quakers, Shakers, Moravians, and the Inspirationists of the Amana colonies in Iowa. The Amish and the Amana colonies are often confused as being the same or related groups for three reasons: 1) Amish and Amana are similar words, 2) both groups have a German heritage and utilize German in their church services, and 3) the Amana colonies are in close proximity to the Amish settlement in Kalona, Iowa.

Key components of the Amish culture include the wearing of plain clothing, the use of Pennsylvania Dutch as the primary language of the home, travel by horse and buggy, the use of horses in the fields rather than tractors, the use of homes for worship services, the use of German Bibles, no modern electrical appliances, no participation in sports leagues, and a limit of formal education to the eighth grade. The Amish culture stresses kindness, humility, and the importance of the group rather than the self. Furthermore, the Amish value and enjoy manual labor and the agrarian lifestyle. Key tenets of the Amish faith include adult baptism, church services held in homes rather than churches, religious leaders who are chosen by lot and serve for life with no financial remuneration, and pacifism.

Key Amish Cultural Values

- Modest dress
- Kindness
- Humility
- Group more important than self
- Enjoy manual labor

As of the 2004–05 school year there were 1,345 schools scattered in 24 states in the United States and the province of Ontario, Canada (*Blackboard Bulletin*, 2005). The states with the largest number of schools were Pennsylvania with 387 schools, Ohio with 286 schools, Indiana with 153 schools, and Wisconsin with 134 schools. Table 1.1 lists the number of schools per state.

The Amish were involved with German schools prior to 1924, but the primary purpose of these schools was religious in nature (Lapp, 1991, p. 128).

Table 1.1. Number of Amish Schools in the United States and Canada as of the 2004–5 School Year

State	*Number*
Colorado	1
Delaware	10
Illinois	28
Indiana	153
Iowa	51
Kansas	2
Kentucky	34
Maine	1
Maryland	8
Michigan	52
Minnesota	23
Mississippi	2
Missouri	60
Montana	5
New York	53
N. Carolina	1
Ohio	286
Oklahoma	2
Ontario	29
Pennsylvania	387
Tennessee	19
Texas	1
Virginia	2
West Virginia	1
Wisconsin	134
Total	1,345

These German schools were not designed to replace the role of public schools. Crowded conditions in small one-room schools near Dover, Delaware, in 1924 initiated discussions in the Amish community about how to best address the needs of Amish children as well as the Amish community. These meetings eventually led to the building of the first Amish parochial school in the United States and Canada, Apple Grove School, which began in 1925. In subsequent years Amish schools appeared in Pennsylvania in 1938, Ohio in 1944, Tennessee in 1945, and Ontario, Canada, in 1953. The rapid growth of Amish schools in the United States and Canada is illustrated in tables 1.2 and 1.3.

There are three main reasons for this growth. First, for most of their history, Amish children attended public one-room schools. As consolidation efforts closed these schools the Amish balked at sending their children on buses to schools in towns because of their preference for children to be educated near their home. In response, the Amish bought many of these

Table 1.2. Number of Amish Schools in the United States

Year	*Frequency*
1925	2
1930	3
1935	3
1940	5
1945	8
1950	19
1955	42
1960	88
1965	132
1970	247
1975	319
1980	423
1985	514
1990	708
1995	914
2000	1,157
2005	1,316

Table 1.3. Number of Amish Schools in Ontario, Canada

Year	*Frequency*
1954	1
1960	2
1965	4
1970	10
1975	14
1980	19
1985	20
1990	21
1995	24
2000	31
2005	29

one-room schools and started their own parochial schools. The second key reason for the phenomenal growth is the United States Supreme Court decision of *Wisconsin v. Yoder* in 1972, which acknowledged the freedom of the Amish to maintain their own schools and to limit school-based formal education to eighth grade. This crucial decision has led to the creation of more Amish schools. In fact, during the last three decades the average rate of growth is 40 new schools per year. The third reason for the rapid growth rate of Amish schools is the fact that the Amish have large families. There will thus be a need for more schools to house all of the students. The number of schools in Ohio is an example of this growth with an increase from 86 schools in 1975 to 286 schools in 2005. This is an increase of 200 schools in 30 years, with an average growth rate of 6 new schools per year. Other states have had similar growth patterns.

In the following chapter we will explore Amish history, beliefs, and culture. This exploration is critical to the understanding of Amish education because everything the Amish do is based on their faith and tradition. In subsequent chapters we will explore in detail the curriculum, textbooks, teaching methods, organization, teachers, and students. We will then explore the unique characteristics of many Amish schools and communities and conclude with a discussion of Amish schools in the future.

2

Amish History, Beliefs, and Community

"Amish values of simplicity, humility, and austerity call for personal sacrifices that build commitment to the community."

—Donald B. Kraybill, 1989

Understanding the importance of the Amish school to the Amish community requires knowledge of two things: history of the Amish and beliefs of the community. We will delve into Amish history first and then explore the Amish beliefs that shape contemporary Amish culture. In doing so, we will build a basis for understanding the Amish belief about education which is that education should prepare one for a life of humility and service among a community of believers.

HISTORY OF THE AMISH

A brief review of the history of the Amish will serve as a basis of our subsequent discussion of Amish schools and many of the key components of Amish education. Because the Amish are a branch of the Anabaptists and the Anabaptists sprang from the Reformation, we begin our brief journey through the ages with Martin Luther, who was the key figure in starting the Protestant Reformation.

The story of the Amish begins in the sea change that was 16th-century Europe and the Protestant Reformation begun by Martin Luther. Cary (2004) notes that at this time medieval piety or the devotion to religious duty was focused on the living helping the dead. For example, one could purchase indulgences or a mass for the dead to reduce their time in purgatory and thus ensure their entrance into heaven. These practices were one of the ways the church funded the papacy.

As a Catholic priest, Luther was troubled by these practices and thus turned to extensive study of scripture, prayer, and the completion of good works (Cary, 2004). This study led him to the belief that one was justified by faith alone, and this belief put him in direct conflict with many of the practices of the Roman Catholic Church at that time. In an effort to reform the Catholic Church, Luther posted his 95 theses on the church door in Wittenberg, Germany. Although he never sought to begin a new religion, his extensive writings soon placed him in direct conflict with the pope. In order to prevent him from being captured, a group of colleagues spirited him into hiding at the castle in Wartburg. Here he continued his writing and began the translation of the Bible into German, signaling an important transformation in religious belief—the common man did not require a priest to interpret the Bible. Instead, each person could read and respond individually to the Gospel.

For many peasants in the German and Swiss areas of Europe the Reformation seemed to be a call for the end of feudalism because all men appeared equal in their relationship with God. Since this change was not readily apparent, leaders such as Thomas Müntzer urged the overthrow of the hierarchy of power in the church and state (Gregory, 2001). This belief eventually led to the Peasants' War that began in 1524 but ended in utter defeat for the peasants. Scholars now believe that the results of this war had an impact on future Anabaptist teachings. If the world was going to reject the truth of the Gospel, then small groups of committed Christians would need to live in separatist communities to practice Christian love.

Another important leader of the Reformation era who questioned church practices was Ulrich Zwingli of Zurich, Switzerland (Gregory, 2001). Like Luther, he was a Catholic priest who carefully studied the Bible. However, Zwingli and Luther differed sharply on their view of the holy sacrament of communion. Nolt (1992) explains that by 1518 Zwingli's teaching attracted reform-minded people to Zurich, and these people started meeting in private homes for prayer and Bible study. Eventually many of these people came to the belief that the church consists of a group of individuals who decide to commit to the teachings of Jesus. A clear sign of this commitment to the group and to Jesus is being baptized (Kinney, 1996). Thus, baptism can only be received by those who willfully and consciously elect to become members, as opposed to infant baptism, which requires no consent by the individual being baptized. These groups were the forerunners of the Amish faith and at this time were called Anabaptists. They were widely persecuted for their beliefs. However, in Switzerland, some cantons officially accepted and sanctioned Zwingli's teachings while other territories remained Catholic.

This untenable situation led to war in 1531 in which Zwingli was killed in the Battle of Kappel (Gregory, 2001).

While some principalities in Germany afforded Luther and his followers the luxury of protection from Catholic authorities, the Anabaptists in Europe were often forced to meet in secret or flee to the hinterlands to escape persecution. Their beliefs, which also included a resistance to military service, contrasted with those of both the Catholic Church and most of the Protestant reformers. Despite severe persecution, Anabaptism spread through parts of Germany, Switzerland, and the low countries. Persecuted Anabaptist groups included the Swiss Brethren, the South German/Austrian Anabaptists, and the Hutterites. The *Schleitheim Articles* (1527), written by Michael Sattler, clearly outlines the pacifism of these groups.

In a strange turn of events, a small group of Anabaptists secured leadership of the town of Munster in the low countries and soon began persecuting anyone who refused adult baptism (Nolt, 1992). This faction of Anabaptists was eventually overthrown, and other Anabaptists, such as Menno Simons, denounced this group and its activities. As noted by Gregory (2001), the legacy of the events in Munster caused many in Europe to be even more wary of most Anabaptist groups. Menno Simons, a former Catholic priest, soon emerged as the leader of the Dutch Anabaptists and, as a result, they were eventually referred to as Mennonites.

Persecution endured by the Anabaptists continued, including torture, burning at the stake, imprisonment, and drowning. In 1535 a group of Anabaptists was captured and imprisoned (Nolt, 1992). During their lengthy time in the dungeons of Passau Castle they wrote over 50 songs. By 1564 these songs were collected and printed as a book, and they proved to be well-liked among the Anabaptists. Eventually other songs were added to the collection, and the second printing, including over 130 songs, was titled the *Ausbund.* Another key book of the Anabaptist tradition is the *Martyrs' Mirror. Martyrs' Mirror* is a collection of stories written by a Dutch Mennonite minister in 1660 about the many acts of brutality and persecution of the Anabaptists. Today, both the *Ausbund* and the *Martyrs' Mirror* are key books for the Old Order Amish and Old Order Mennonite groups in North America and help both groups stay connected to their Anabaptist roots.

The Thirty Years' War, which began in Europe in 1618, made life difficult for all inhabitants of the area, including the Mennonites. These events most likely further reinforced the Mennonites' beliefs about pacifism and building a community that was separate from the world. By the 17th century, the Mennonites were faced with a clear struggle between two groups over the practice of social avoidance (shunning) of those who leave the faith. Jacob Ammann was the leader of a group that believed in strict adherence to shunning and separation from the world while Hans Reist was the leader of an opposing group that did not believe in social avoidance (Kinney, 1996; Nolt, 1992). Efforts to rejoin the two groups remained unsuccessful; thus the beginning roots of the Amish were formed. Ammann accepted all the Anabaptist statements of belief, but was adamant in his thought that distinctive clothing, separation from the world, and the use of shunning were defining Amish characteristics. He eventually came to be considered the founder of the Amish church.

In retrospect, it is hard to imagine that Martin Luther could have envisioned the trajectory of different Christian religions that sprang forth as a result of the Reformation. Likewise it is improbable that he could have envisioned the tumult and war that occurred in Europe once the Reformation began in earnest. As noted by an Amish elder in Iowa, it is ironic that even though some Protestants, including Lutherans, participated in the persecution of the Anabaptists, many Amish still read Luther's translation of the Bible into German on a daily basis.

Key Dates in Amish History

1520s	Anabaptist groups start meeting in Switzerland
1525	Swiss Brethren begin adult baptisms
1527	Schleitheim Confession of Faith written
1530	Anabaptism spreads to low countries
1536	Menno Simons switches to Anabaptist faith
1693	Amish split from Mennonites
1700s	Amish begin immigration to Pennsylvania
1719	Big Valley, Pennsylvania, settlement founded
1808	Holmes County, Ohio, settlement founded
1865	Arthur, Illinois, settlement founded
1860s	Splits between Old Order Amish and other Amish begin
1910	Peachey Amish leave Old Order Amish
1925	First Amish parochial school begins in Dover, Delaware
1938	First Amish parochial schools begin in Pennsylvania
1965	Iowa school controversy
1972	*Wisconsin v. Yoder*

AMISH FOUNDATIONS IN AMERICA

The American Amish foundations begin in England with William Penn. William was the son of Admiral William Penn, who had a distinguished career in the English navy (Klein & Hoogenboom, 1973). The younger William's faith journey led him to the Quakers in the 1660s. At that time the Quakers were considered by many as a threat to English society and the established church because their unique belief systems were not in congruence with the beliefs of the Church of England. As a result, many Quakers, including the younger Penn, were jailed for their beliefs. Admiral Penn wrote letters on his son's behalf seeking intercession from both King Charles and James the Duke of York. Both men honored his requests, and upon his death in 1670, the admiral left his son a prestigious name and an inheritance of land and money.

During the decade after his father's death, Penn lived as a missionary for the Quaker faith (Klein & Hoogenboon, 1973). Because of the continued persecution of the Quakers, Penn began to dream of a land in America that would serve as a haven for persecuted people. In 1680, he applied to King Charles II for a grant of land west of the Delaware River for such a haven. Penn's application was granted, and he spent the next year planning for the administration of Pennsylvania. Lapp (1991) writes that Penn termed his work in starting this colony as a "Holy Experiment." Penn set about writing several publicity pamphlets for the new land that were distributed in England and across Europe. In subsequent years, Penn successfully attracted numerous immigrants from a variety of persecuted groups, including the Amish, to Pennsylvania.

Hostetler (1993) records that the migration of German-speaking peoples to America began in 1727, with a large majority of the Mennonite and Amish settling in Pennsylvania. Pennsylvania was also a key destination of many other Protestant groups from Europe, which included adherents of the Lutheran, Church of Christ, Quaker, and Moravian faiths. The two major immigration periods that included Amish families were from 1727 to 1770 and 1815 to 1860. The 19th-century Amish immigrants settled in Ohio, Pennsylvania, Indiana, Illinois, New York, and Ontario.

One group of Amish immigrants attracted to Pennsylvania included those onboard the vessel *Charming Nancy,* which arrived in Philadelphia in 1737 (Hostetler, 1993). The years 1737–1754 saw the significant migration of Amish to the North American continent and the first Amish settlements in Berks, Lancaster, and Chester counties of Pennsylvania. The fact that the Amish would not take an oath of allegiance or join the militia was interpreted by many fellow colonists as an implicit endorsement of the British during the Revolutionary War, and consequently, several Amish were charged and jailed on treason charges in Reading, Pennsylvania.

The years between 1800 and 1865 were years of relative prosperity for the Amish, but differences between groups began to appear (Nolt, 1992). Both Nolt (1992) and Yoder (1991) indicate that by 1865 these differences began an irreconcilable split between traditional-minded Amish (Old Order Amish) and change-minded Amish (Amish Mennonites). Further divisions among the Amish continued over the next 40 years. By the end of the 1800s those who chose the Old Order numbered approximately 5,000 individuals, and they resided in a variety of states. The Old Order groups maintained traditional church discipline, worshiped in homes, and wore plain clothing patterns, which clearly distinguished them from the non-Amish. During this time several Old Order communities were established in Arthur, Illinois; Daviess County, Indiana; and Geauga County, Ohio. All of these Old Order communities currently exist.

The 20th century marked the beginning of rapid technological change, which brought challenges to the Old Order Amish community. For example, a split among the Amish in Lancaster County revolved around telephones in the home, the use of electricity, and one belief system not related to technology, the practice of strict shunning (Nolt, 1992). This split made it very clear to the Old Order group that telephones and electricity would not be permitted. Another decisive division was that of the automobile (Scott, 1981), which accounted for Amish disagreements between the 1920s and the 1950s.

The 20th century was also a time of two devastating world wars that presented numerous problems for the Amish because of their pacifist beliefs. Kraybill (1993) writes that in World War I, most Amish youth who were drafted were able to serve their time as conscientious objectors (COs); however, all COs were sent to regular Army camps in hopes that they would be influenced by the others to take up arms as well. Amish COs faced reduced rations, confinement in military jails, and physical abuse. These acts of coercion did not change the pacifism of the COs since the Amish, as a group, remained true to their beliefs.

The second great conflagration of the century, World War II, initially posed similar problems for conscientious objectors. Members of the Peace Churches (Quakers, Mennonites, and Brethren) remembered the difficulties faced by COs in World War I and were determined to remedy this at the onset of World War II (Kraybill, 1993). The Peace Churches successfully lobbied for a clause in the Draft Bill of 1940 to allow COs to do work of national importance under civil, not military, supervision. As a result, members of the Peace Churches were permitted to work with the Selective Service personnel to design the Civilian Public Service (CPS) program for COs. Most of the Amish who were drafted were able to enroll in this program.

During World War II, a number of Amish communities were the target of derision by some in the English community. Most of the Amish youth at this time attended public schools. Wittmer (2001) writes that very few of the English understood the pressures of an Amish youth in the public schools at that time. Most of these pressures related to the fact that Amish young men were not in military service and facing death like the non-Amish. This provided a foundation for resentment of the Amish. In addition, Amish youth did not recite the Pledge of Allegiance or take part in class pictures or educational films. Some of the classmates of the Amish children chastised and/or laughed at them for these acts of nonconformity. Teachers implied that to be successful, students should aspire to a college education, which was in direct contrast to the Amish belief that formal education should end at grade eight. Wittmer (2001, p. vii) further records some of the acts of hostility against the Amish at that time: "outsiders attacked us and verbally assaulted us when we rode in our buggies. They threw firecrackers, eggs, tomatoes and even rocks." For many of the Amish, World War II was a time of trial because of their beliefs and distinctive lifestyle.

In the latter half of the 20th century the Amish continued to see splits among their group, with the two examples being the Schwartzentruber Amish, a conservative group, and the New Order Amish, a more liberal group. Since World War II, the Amish population has increased at a rapid pace in the United States and Canada. As a result, the Amish have started many new communities and now live in over 25 states in the United States. This rapid population growth, coupled with many new communities, has resulted in the need for many new Amish parochial schools. We will explore the critical issues associated with the beginning of these Amish parochial schools in detail in the next chapter.

AMISH BELIEFS

The Amish view themselves as a Christian community living apart (as much as possible) from the wider world community. Hostetler (1993) states that the Amish use the German word *Gemeinde* or the dialect version *Gemee* to express the meaning of the corporate redemptive community. The church of God is composed of those who have repented, believe, and have subsequently voluntarily chosen to be baptized. The church is separate from the world and is identified by practicing the ordinances of Christ in building a community of believers, which is essential to living one's faith in all aspects of life.

Hostetler (1993) states that the Amish firmly believe they are to be separate from this world. There are two passages in the Bible that are often referred to in sermons to illustrate this belief. The first is, "And be not conformed to this world, but be ye transformed by the renewing of your mind, that ye may prove what is that good, and acceptable, and perfect will of God" (Romans 12:2). The second is, "Be ye not unequally yoked together with unbelievers: for what fellowship hath righteousness with unrighteousness? What communion hath light with darkness?" (Second Corinthians 6:14). To the Amish these passages indicate that one should not dress or conduct oneself like those of the world, and furthermore, one should not marry an unbeliever or even enter into a business with a non-Amish person. This principle of separation and the following of Christ's teaching means the Amish will not take up arms to defend their families or the country in which they live. Furthermore, they will not swear oaths or take a public office. Amish teaching emphasizes self-denial and humility. These beliefs are in clear contrast to a world that applauds and celebrates individual accomplishments.

Membership in the Amish church community is attained by voluntarily choosing baptism (Hostetler, 1993). Baptism signifies redemption and complete commitment to the Amish community and thus adulthood. Kraybill (1994, p. 5) states the importance of this event in this way: "Adult baptism is the singular event in Amish life when members not only make a public commitment to the Christian faith but also vow to uphold the teachings of the *Ordnung* for the rest of their lives." According to Hostetler (1993) this step is not taken lightly, and the Amish provide biweekly instruction to those adolescents who wish to take it. The Dordrecht Confession of Faith is the basis for these preparation classes. Ministers emphasize to the adolescents that it is better not to be baptized than to be baptized and break one's commitment to the community. In the Amish church, members kneel for baptism, and the deacon pours water into the cupped hands of the bishop, which are placed above the head of each person being baptized on that Sunday (Hostetler, 1993).

Social order for the Amish is personified in the *Ordnung* (Hostetler, 1993). The *Ordnung* embodies two types of regulations. First are those that have been discussed and approved at conferences of the Amish that date back to the 16th century. The set of laws agreed upon at the conferences are recorded. The second set of rules to live by are those that spell out the precepts of each individual congregation of believers. Each church discusses these rules in the fall and spring of each year, and the assembled believers must agree on the rules before communion is held at the next service. The rules to live by for each individual church are unwritten but may include such things as the type of equipment permitted in the fields, the use of screens on windows, the type of straw hat men wear in the summer months, and whether the schoolhouse will be large or small.

The *Ordnung* is based on Biblical principles and Amish tradition and defines how the group will be different from the outside world. In the majority of Old Order Amish congregations, the *Ordnung* prohibits telephones in the home, electricity generated by a power company, and ownership of automobiles. Furthermore, the *Ordnung* defines appropriate styles of hair, formal education (limited to eighth grade), and dress. An Amish individual either keeps the *Ordnung* or does not; there is no middle ground. The *Ordnung* stresses community over individual power, prestige, wealth, or status.

Key Aspects of the Old Order Amish *Ordnung*

Plain dress	Married men wear a beard but no mustache
Horse and buggy transportation	Women wear prayer cap
Pennsylvania Dutch language	Worship in homes
No phones in the home	No electricity from utility companies
Eighth grade education	No TV or computers
No automobile ownership	Use of horses in the fields*

*A small number of communities permit steel-wheeled tractors.

Kraybill (1989) and Yoder (1991) affirm that one way to better understand the Amish approach to life and following the *Ordnung* is the German word *Gelassenheit,* which means submission to a higher authority. *Gelassenheit* means that the individuals yield themselves to "higher authorities: the will of God, church elders, parents, community, and tradition" (Kraybill, 1989, p. 25). In addition to a yielding spirit, the Amish rely on divine providence. Because of this reliance on divine providence and the Amish characteristics of humility and meekness, an Amish person would not pronounce that he or she is sure of salvation. This fact, however, does not mean that they do not believe in salvation. Obedience, humility, and separation from the world are other components of *Gelassenheit* and further define how their belief system impacts everyday life. For the Amish religion is not practiced for just one or two hours one day a week but is practiced 24 hours, each day of the week. Another important component of the Amish faith system is the belief that manual labor and being thrifty contribute to a wholesome life (Kraybill, 1989). *Gelassenheit* also means that the Amish respect and value their tradition, a tradition centered on a rural lifestyle and a slower pace of life.

To have an ordered community requires some measure of discipline. For the Amish belief system, the ultimate form of discipline is exclusion from the community. Hostetler (1993) states that persons will be excluded or shunned by the community if they are clearly guilty of living in sin, causing strife or divisions within the group, or teaching a false doctrine. For example, car ownership is not permitted. If a member of the Amish church purchased a car and drove it around town, that would not be acceptable. Elders and ministers in the group urge the persons to repent of their wrongdoing by making a public confession to the church. If they do so they will be accepted

Table 2.1. Amish Church Leaders

Title	*Duties*
Bishop/*Volliger Diener* (Full Servant)	The bishop performs baptisms, marriages, ordinations and will pronounce the shunning of an individual from the group. The bishop provides leadership for each church and will also preach. There is one bishop in each church community.
Preacher/*Diener zum Buch* (Servant of the Book)	The preacher assists the bishop with preaching and assists bishop as needed. Each church usually has two preachers.
Deacon/*Armendiener* (Servant of the Poor)	The deacon collects and disburses the monetary funds of the church and assists the preacher and bishop as needed. There is usually one deacon in each church community.

(Nolt, 1992); (Hostetler, 1993)

back into full fellowship; if not, they will be excommunicated and thus shunned by the community, meaning no member of the community may eat at the same table or engage in business with the offenders, with the hope being that the persons will eventually mend their ways and return to the church. However, if they do not, they will be shunned for life.

Leadership for each Amish church group comes from within the group. Each church has a bishop, deacon, and preacher (Nolt, 1992; Hostetler, 1993). Individuals are nominated for these positions by members of the congregation, and those receiving the most nominations are placed in the "lot." Once nominated, a person may not remove his name from the lot. Those in the lot will then select one of the Bibles or hymnbooks placed before the group. The individual who picks the book with the hidden slip of paper has been chosen. Amish leaders serve for life and do not receive any monetary compensation from the congregations they serve.

Old Order Amish Church Practices

Adult Baptism	Self-examination prior to communion
Meet in homes—no churches	Religious leaders selected by lot
Three or more ministers lead worship	Kneeling for prayer
Worship every other Sunday	Foot washing
Holy kiss	Seating by gender
No instruments of any kind	Singing in unison

Each Amish congregation meets for worship every other Sunday in the home or barn of one of the families. On the off Sunday they may visit the service of another congregation or visit relatives who live a good distance away. Each family takes a turn at hosting the three-hour worship service and the noon meal. Amish worship services do not include many of the religious symbols often associated with worship services of other Christian groups, such as crosses, candles, flowers, flags, altars, pulpits, and robes. Amish worship services are about three hours long and will include two sermons.

Order of Amish Worship

- Several hymns are sung in unison
- Introductory sermon
- Silent prayer—all kneel
- Deacon reads a chapter from the Bible—all stand
- Main sermon
- Remarks by other ministers in attendance as requested by the minister who gave the main sermon

- Closing comments by the minister who preaches the main sermon
- Minister reads a prayer—all kneel
- Benediction—all stand
- Announcements
- Hymn
- Dismissal

(Hostetler, 1993, p. 213)

The final component of the Amish belief system is the importance of tilling the soil (Hostetler, 1993). To the Amish the most wholesome lifestyle is that of farming. It is the goal of many families to be able to help their children find and purchase land so that they can pursue farming. If land is scarce, other occupations that relate to farming or that allow one to work in a rural setting are appropriate choices. The Amish do not see manual labor as something to be avoided but rather something that builds one's enjoyment of life.

The unique Amish belief system, a belief system that shapes all aspects of one's life taken in context with traditions, serves to mold the way they view education. While the Amish realize that reading, writing, and arithmetic are important they believe that a sound education is more than learning the 3 Rs. Education is about preparing one for a life of separation from the world. This is exemplified by a life of humility and service among a community of believers. In our next chapter we will learn why it became necessary for the Amish to start their own schools as we explore the struggles associated with the beginning of Amish schools in 20th-century America.

3

Amish School Origins: Cooperation, Incarceration, and Litigation

"Amish mothers on the porch broke out into loud sobbing."

—Raffensperger (1965), describing the scene at an Amish school near Hazleton, Iowa, just after Amish students ran away from officials attempting to take them to public school.

In chapter 2 we explored the history of the Amish and key tenets of their faith. The focus of this chapter will be on some of the struggles associated with the beginning of Amish schools. In most cases these struggles revolved around two issues. The first issue was mandatory school attendance until the age of 16. Once Amish schools were established, the second issue was the certification of individuals teaching in Amish schools. Efforts by the Amish to establish their own schools have resulted in imprisonments, fines, and confiscation of property in states such as Pennsylvania, Ohio, Iowa, Nebraska, and Wisconsin. In this chapter we will focus on some of these occurrences as well as the peaceful beginning of the first Amish school in America.

In the first half of the 20th century the majority of rural children attended one-room country schools. For example, the National Bureau of Educational Statistics reported that in 1930 there were about 149,000 one-teacher schools in the United States (Snyder, 1987). Most of the schools were within walking distance of the children that attended the school, and in many cases the school was a source of community pride and recognition. Amish parents were happy with these schools, and some parents even took school leadership roles. For example, Fisher (1978) reports that in 1880 the Lancaster County township of Leacock had school board representatives from the Mennonites, the Amish, and the English. These men oversaw a township composed of eleven schoolhouses that served plain and nonplain children in the same schools. Further evidence of the Amish satisfaction with small public country schools was reported by Kauffman, Petersheim, and Beiler (1992), who stated that some of the first Amish residents of southern Lancaster County were treated with respect by their teachers and fellow English classmates. They further report that the English and Amish children often exchanged bologna and cheese sandwiches for apple butter sandwiches. Kauffman, Petersheim, and Beiler (1992) further report that this degree of cooperation was evident in other schools in southern Lancaster County as well.

Stirrings about having their own schools began many years ago. Uriah Byler (1989), a promoter of Amish schools, recalls an Ascension Day talk with Bishop Dan A. Byler that cemented the idea of having their own schools in Uriah Byler's mind. A problem with picture shows in the local school prompted the conversation. Bishop Byler stated, "Do you think it's right for us to tell them how to run their schools? The world won't stop with their big ideas on education just because of a few Amish" (Byler, 1989, p. 133). The elderly bishop further stated, "Let them have their schools. They have their reasons, with their kind of life, to go for the modern things. We shouldn't hinder them, or be a stumbling block" (Byler, 1989, p. 133). Bishop Byler urged Uriah to talk with the younger parents to get them to think about starting their own parochial school system.

As rural communities started emphasizing a high school education, Nolt (1992) writes, while the Amish were not opposed to education they were wary of what they termed higher education. To the Amish, high school was a place that encouraged competition, self-improvement, and individualism. They felt these values were in direct contrast to their belief system based on cooperation, humility, and servanthood.

As public schools began to consolidate and compulsory attendance laws were enacted and enforced with more vigor, the Amish began to seek ways to meet the needs of their children and community within the existing laws. The Amish knew from experience that if their adolescent children were removed from the rural environment and the small country school setting they would be exposed to numerous behaviors that did not match their belief system.

The decision by the Amish to start their own schools was not always an easy one, and many parents needed a rationale for the change (Bontrager, 1989). John Bontrager cited two reasons. The cost of a new modern school in Indiana was one reason. He indicated that a new consolidated school in Indiana would cost $2,500 per child while the Amish could build a new school for 35 scholars for $3,000 with donated labor. Second, a great advantage of having their own schools would be that children could learn to live a Christian life while obtaining a solid basic education.

One of the first school consolidation issues occurred in the Dover, Delaware, community in 1924 and was resolved in a cooperative manner between state officials and Amish elders.

Year of first Amish parochial schools by state or province, prior to *Wisconsin v. Yoder* (1972)

1925	Delaware
1938	Pennsylvania
1944	Ohio
1945	Tennessee
1946	Iowa
1948	Indiana
1948	Missouri
1949	New York
1953	Ontario
1966	Wisconsin
1966	Illinois
1967	Maryland

Luthy (1994); Myers (1993); Dewalt (1997)

THE FIRST AMISH PAROCHIAL SCHOOL

Lapp (1991) and Troyer and Mast (1965) reported that there were two main concerns for the Dover Amish community. First, the state of Delaware decided to reduce the number of public one-room schools, and to limit existing one-room schools to grades one through six. Seventh- and eighth-grade students would now be bussed to consolidated schools in town. In addition, Amish migration into Delaware had dramatically increased the number of children attending Rose Valley School, and public school officials were not interested in adding a room to this school to relieve the overcrowding. The second concern for the Amish was that the public school officials' solution to this school overcrowding was to the bus the children to Dover. In response to these two concerns, the Amish decided to pursue the idea of having their own school.

At the suggestion of Charles Hopkins, a state senator, two Amish elders went to meet with the state superintendent of education, Mr. Holloway. This meeting was fruitful, and both parties agreed to cooperate. Hollaway remarked, "If you take out some of the children it will cost us less money!" (Troyer and Stoll, 1965, p. 38). With the agreement in place a three-man school board was selected to organize all aspects of the Amish school. After some discussion, the site selected for this historic school was in the orchard of Samuel Hertzler.

Construction of this school began in October of 1924 under the direction of Jonathan Beiler, head carpenter (Lapp, 1991; Troyer and Mast, 1965).

Members of the community volunteered much of the labor required to build the school. Amish residents were assessed a fee based on real estate valuation to provide funds for building materials and furniture for the school. In addition, pupils were charged a fee of $1.00 to pay for books. A retired teacher in the area, Mr. Franz Karbaum, assisted with the organization of the new school and accompanied the school board members to Philadelphia to purchase books for the school. He also served as the first teacher and was paid the grand sum of $5.00 per day. Mr. Karbaum was well respected by parents and students alike. Letters from some of his former pupils were published in the issue of the *Blackboard Bulletin* that commemorated the beginning of this school, and many letters praised Mr. Karbaum. One former student wrote, "I can say he was the best teacher I had in my school years" (*Blackboard Bulletin*, 1965, p. 41). Another former student wrote, "He was the best teacher I ever had. When he said something, we all knew that was just what he meant" (*Blackboard Bulletin*, 1965, p. 42).

Other pupils from that first year also described the school itself. One former student wrote, "The school house was roomy, with a furnace in the basement. The two windows on the north side were more like ventilators. But on the south side the whole length was windows. The blackboard ran across the whole front of the room" (*Blackboard Bulletin*, 1965, p. 42). Another former student wrote, "The new school house was a joy to be in. Not drafty, heated well all through, well-lighted even though the windows were mainly on the south side" (*Blackboard Bulletin*, 1965, p. 43).

The first Amish teacher to serve the school was Esther S. Swartzentruber (Troyer and Mast, 1965). She did not possess a teaching certificate, but there was no objection voiced by public education officials. The original name of the school, Apple Creek Mennonite Private School, was changed to Apple Grove School and then to Apple Grove Amish Parochial School in 1964.

In reflecting on this notable school, Troyer and Mast (1965) write that there was little publicity or attention given to the opening of this school by the Amish community at that time. They believe this was due to the fact that there were Amish German schools in existence previous to this date; however, these schools were primarily religious in focus. These schools were a supplement to the rural public schools. Thus having a school was not a totally new concept to the Amish community. What is noteworthy about Apple Grove School is that it was designed to replace the role of the public schools.

Apple Grove School is still in existence and has been moved several times but is located in the same general vicinity as the original site. Today, Apple Grove School has two teachers who share the one-room school. The school is one of the few Amish schools that has a sign inside the building indicating the date of origin. Letters to spell out "Welcome to Apple Grove School" are strung on wire across the room about one foot below the ceiling. The school has a large green chalkboard across the front of the room and has wainscoting about four feet high under the windows on each side of the classroom. The floor is made of plywood and has been painted gray. The school has a large level play area and a variety of playground equipment.

AMISH SCHOOL BEGINNINGS IN PENNSYLVANIA

The beginning of the Amish parochial school movement in Pennsylvania was not as smooth as that in Delaware. Myers' (1980) review of the beginning of the movement reveals some of the dilemmas facing the Amish. The impetus for the Amish schools in Pennsylvania began in 1937 in the East Lampeter public school district in Lancaster County. The school board decided that it was time to close the 10 one-room schools and consolidate them into one large elementary school. An additional dilemma for the Amish of Pennsylvania occurred in July of the same year when the state legislature raised the legal age for leaving school and obtaining a work permit from 14 to 15 years of age. As a result of these two happenings, 16 Amish ministers and deacons met in September of the same year to organize peaceful resistance to laws that they felt violated their religious rights. These Amish elders started a petition drive that netted more than 3,000 signatures of protest from both Amish and non-Amish individuals. This petition was presented to the state legislature later that same fall. The petition was not successful, and things took a turn for the worse that December. Aaron King, an Amish father, was incarcerated for not sending his 14-year-old daughter to high school. Aaron was the first of numerous Amish fathers who would later face court appearances, fines, and jail time for noncompliance with Pennsylvania school laws.

The above happenings served to galvanize Amish resistance, and efforts to plan and build Amish parochial schools began in earnest. Lapp (1991) indicates that the first two Amish schools in Pennsylvania were Oak Grove School and Esh School (now Pleasant View). Both of these schools began in 1938 and are located in East Lampeter Township in Lancaster County. The twists and turns of the ensuing struggle between the local and state public school officials and Amish and Mennonite parents were chronicled in the *New York Times* in 1938. The first article ("Amish lose," 1938) reported that the Amish and Mennonite farmers lost the fight to keep eleven one-room schools. The second article ("Amish threaten," 1938) reported that the Amish were considering setting up their own schools if the one-room schools were closed. The third article ("New Amish," 1938) noted that the beginning of the school year would test the resolve of the Amish families' resistance to the consolidated school. The final article ("Amish pupils," 1938) noted that a special act of the State Legislature gave the Amish the right to operate their own

Figure 3.1. Pleasant View School, Lancaster, Pennsylvania

one-room schools. After this temporary agreement, the Amish held school in a private home and rented a former one-room school until the respective school buildings were constructed (Gordonville Print Shop, 1973). Oak Grove School was constructed on land donated by David Zook on a 99-year lease. The cost of the frame building was about $1,830, and the carpenter was John Good (Gordonville Print Shop, 1973).

Esh School, which later became Pleasant View, was built on property bought from Jacob Esh for the sum of $75 (Gordonville Print Shop, 1973). Levi Esh was the carpenter for this construction project and work began on this school in March of 1939. The cost to build this school was $156 for labor and $1,074.45 for materials.

Lapp (1991) chronicles the continued school struggle in Pennsylvania as one of considerable hardship for the Amish because of the many legal issues concerning Amish students and compulsory school attendance laws. At various points in time, Amish fathers in Lancaster County were incarcerated for not sending their children to high school. A solution to this problem was worked out in 1956 under the direction of Governor Leader (Lapp, 1991, pp. 512–513). The agreement stated that Amish children would participate in the "Vocational Plan" and thus not have to attend high school. This plan stated that Amish students would be under the supervision of their parents learning skills at home (learning by doing), and attend class for three hours per week. A more detailed account of this vocational plan in Pennsylvania will be discussed in chapter 6.

The seriousness with which the Pennsylvania Amish embraced their hard-won rights to build and operate their parochial school system is exemplified in the Standards of the Old Order Amish and Old Order Mennonite Parochial and Vocational Schools of Pennsylvania (1969). This document covers a variety of issues such as attendance, school rules, and curriculum. The document also spells out the responsibilities of the school board as well as those of the teacher.

OHIO

The world's largest Amish community is located in the Holmes/Wayne County area of Ohio, and was the scene of the first confrontation in Ohio concerning school attendance. As in Delaware part of the issue in Ohio revolved around the large number of students attending country one-room schools and the reluctance of the local public school boards to build new country schools. However, in Ohio the issue was not solved as peacefully as it was in Delaware.

Hershberger (1985) reports that in 1921 Ohio passed the Bing Law, which stated that all children between the ages of 6 and 18 must be attending school. However a 16-year-old could be excused from school attendance if he or she had employment. While some Amish parents did face legal trouble because of the Bing Law, the law did not cause major changes in the Amish community as long as the country schools remained open. Since the Amish opposed education above the eighth grade, many of their children repeated eighth grade again and again until they reached the age of 16. They then were allowed to work at home or in the community.

In 1942 the Board of Education for East Union Township in Wayne County began pressing Amish parents to send their children to high school (Hershberger, 1985). The Amish were clearly opposed to high school attendance, and Ben Raber's son John was not in compliance. Authorities gave Ben Raber the choice of going to jail or sending his son to high school. Ben chose jail and was incarcerated for 30 days. Once the sheriff found that Ben was not a threat to escape he was given different odd jobs to perform in the jail such as sweeping, window washing, and tending the furnace. After serving his time, Ben returned home and the truant officer did not monitor the family much after this incident.

In the fall of 1943 another disagreement over high school attendance surfaced in Wayne County (Hershberger, 1985). In this case Martin Hochstetler's daughter passed eighth grade in the spring but was not allowed to retake eighth grade the next fall. Authorities stated that she must attend high school. Her family refused to send her to high school, and Martin and his daughter received a summons to appear in juvenile court on December 13. By early spring of 1944 eleven fathers were involved in similar cases—all charged with child neglect since there was no penalty in Ohio law for not attending school.

The Amish in the area knew that something needed to be done, and this led to a meeting in July of 1944, where the assembled agreed to begin parochial schools. The group hoped that these schools would be an answer to the high school attendance problem. At the same meeting a six-member school board was elected, and a three-member building committee was elected. The plan was to have two schools ready to begin in the fall of 1944.

Because of the war effort, building materials were being rationed, and the building committee decided to purchase two buildings, move them, and then refurbish them as schools (Hershberger, 1985). A building inspector noted the remodeling that needed to be done and advised the committee to hire an architect. An architect was hired, and the buildings were built to those specifications. The old Eshleman store building became Maple Grove School, and the old Center School became Fountain Nook School. A former public school teacher and a retired public school teacher were hired to teach in the schools, and a trip to Columbus, Ohio, ensued to purchase textbooks for the schools.

We now return to the pending court cases, which all were in continuance from the spring of 1943 and were to proceed on September 25 (Hershberger, 1985). Parents in the community hoped that the schools would be in session by that time so that a peaceful agreement could be attained. One school, Fountain Nook, was finished and opened its doors for school the morning of September 25; the school hearing was held that afternoon. The judge ruled that attendance at this school was not valid and the parents had 30 days to send their offspring to the public school to which they were assigned. On

Figure 3.2. Fountain Nook School, Wayne County, Ohio

October 4, Maple Grove School opened its doors for the first time. It is interesting to note that both Fountain Nook School and Maple Grove School are still in existence and remain in their original locations.

Instead of trying all the pending cases, the court decided to pick out two defendants as test cases (Hershberger, 1985). The first case involved the daughter of Martin Hochstetler. In this case Judge Saunders ruled that the Amish school was not approved to teach ninth grade subjects. Martin's daughter was removed from his custody, and he was fined $20. He was also warned that if he did not comply he would be incarcerated.

The other test case commenced on November 27 and involved Abe Weaver and his son (Hershberger, 1985). Judge Culbertson presided and heard similar testimony to that in the case against Martin Hochstetler. During the trial the judge stated, "If it had been charged that the boy was not properly dressed, the court wouldn't find that claim true only because the boy was not clothed as other youths" (Hershberger, 1985, p. 6). He thus ruled that there was no evidence of neglect and the case was closed. The case against Martin Hochstetler was then revoked and the school attendance issue was closed in that area.

The next major issue for the Amish schools in Ohio was from within the community. Several parents were not sending their ninth graders to school, or were sending them late in the term (Hershberger, 1985). This caused hardships for the teachers and jeopardized the entire parochial school movement. In the fall of 1945 about 30 fathers met to discuss the issue and voted Emery Weaver as attendance officer. This did not entirely solve the problem, and the board voted that no new pupils would be admitted after October 15. This served difficult to enforce, since not allowing the child to enroll at the late date put the parents in noncompliance with the law, and thus they faced possible jail time and fines. Before the fall term of 1946 officials in Columbus informed the Amish school board that the poor attendance at the two Amish schools might cause state action. The teachers at the schools were also not pleased with attendance, and this spurred the board into further action. The board decided that pupils could be registered for school late; however, the parents would have to pay a $100 late fee. This solved the problem of nonattendance.

The next confrontation in Ohio came after a new law to upgrade education in the state went into effect in 1956 (Hershberger, 1985). The Amish could not comply and simply went on as they had for more than 10 years. In 1957 a public school official filed a complaint in the Wayne County juvenile court against the Amish who did not send their children to school between the end of eighth grade and the age of 16. Three sets of Amish parents and their sons were summoned to court in February of 1957. The parents appeared but not the sons, and the parents were each found to be in contempt of the court and fined $500. The parents refused to pay, and they were incarcerated. The newspapers spread the word of the story and of the unattended children at home; this served to galvanize public opinion in favor of the Amish. Mr. E. Guy Hammond, an attorney from Akron, Ohio, read of the case and visited the jailed parents and offered his services free of charge. The case eventually made its way to the District Court of Appeals. The case against the Amish was dismissed on technical grounds based on the previous trials. This trial prompted several Amish elders in Ohio to visit Pennsylvania to learn about the vocational program in Lancaster County. The Amish then decided to set up a similar program in the Holmes/Wayne County area.

While all of this was going on in Wayne County, court cases against Amish parents began in Harding County, Ohio. The Amish had started a parochial school in Harding County, Ohio, in 1953. By the spring of 1955 trouble arose when three Amish fathers were incarcerated for not sending their children to an approved school. The county won the case against the Amish, and the judge ordered that the Amish schools in the area be closed. By 1956 the county also refused to grant work permits to Amish children once they reached 16. The Amish then put in place a vocational program similar to that in Wayne County, Ohio. In April 1960 the District Court heard the case and ruled in favor of the Amish. Harding County appealed to the Ohio Supreme Court and lost that case as well.

Things were more peaceful in the Geauga County, Ohio, area. In 1926 the County Superintendent of Education, Mr. Schofield, met with Amish bishops to discuss school attendance. They came to an agreement, and things were fine until the 1940s when Amish children complained of being mocked at school. The Amish decided it was time to start their own schools, but the Parkman School Board attempted to block their efforts. The Amish school board then went to Columbus to meet with state officials and was granted approval to start its own school as long as it met building code regulations. The school was built, and an Amish teacher was hired. In later years the State Board of Education questioned the Amish of Geauga County about certified teachers. The Amish presented the school board with a set of standards for their schools, and state officials later visited the schools. That ended the state questioning, and the Amish proceeded to educate their children according to the stated plan.

IOWA

Iowa was the center of a local school controversy that grew to a statewide controversy that received plenty of national press in the fall of 1965. "The dispute centered on the right of the Amish to have their own schools" (G. Raffensperger, personal communication, October, 2004). And, as some note, it was "a confrontation that did not need to happen" (D. Bechtel, personal communication, October, 2004).

The story begins in 1948 when the Hazelton and Oelwein districts in Buchanan and Fayette Counties started consolidating schools. The Amish purchased two vacant schools, and two certified teachers began teaching at the schools; until 1961 the Amish provided full funding for the schools (Meyers, 1993; Rodgers, 1969; Schwieder & Schwieder, 1975). In 1961 an important vote was held to merge the Oelwein and Hazelton school districts, and English residents were clearly divided on this issue. The Amish, in conversations with then Superintendent of Schools A. Kasakadden, believed that if they voted for the merger, the new system would allow them to continue their schools with the added bonus of state funds. One influential Amish elder thought the Amish should support the merger. Some Amish did vote in the election, and the merger was approved in the Hazelton district. Some English neighbors were not happy and blamed the Amish for the outcome. These same individuals were quick to point out the perceived shortcomings of the Amish in the area. One statement uttered to Gene Raffensperger while investigating the confrontation points to the animosity of some of the English neighbors in the area. When asking one resident the name of one of the fathers in the case, the resident stated, "If you've seen one 'hookie' you've seen them all" (G. Raffensperger, personal communication, October, 2004). Since the Amish use hooks and eyes and not buttons, "hookie" is a derogatory term for the Amish used by non-Amish in Iowa as well as some other states.

Things deteriorated quickly for the Amish schools when in May of 1962 the Oelwein school board ruled that the Amish schools could exist only on a temporary basis and the curriculum must conform to the public school curriculum (Hayes, 1972; Meyers, 1993; Rodgers, 1969; Schwieder & Schwieder, 1975). Later the same month the Iowa Department of Education visited the schools, found them lacking in many ways, and ruled that seventh- and eighth-grade students must enroll in public schools at once. One can only imagine the confusion on the part of the Amish after they perceived local authorities would support their schools.

There are several key components to this controversy that made things hard for all of those involved (Meyers, 1993; Rodgers, 1969; Schwieder & Schwieder, 1975). First, the school superintendent who had been involved with the Amish before the election died unexpectedly, and the new superintendent, Arthur Sensor, had no information relative to any agreements with the Amish elders. Second, the new superintendent thought he had the backing of the state of Iowa on the issue of requiring the enrollment of Amish students in public school.

Several efforts at compromise failed to alleviate the eventual fateful actions in November of 1965 (Harlan Lemon, personal communication, October, 2004). One unsuccessful compromise was offered by nuns who offered to teach in the Amish schools for free. In another effort at compromise school officials found an Amish man in Kansas who had a teaching certificate and offered to teach. The Amish elders' response was that "he is not our kind of Amish," and they did not agree to that compromise either.

Gene Raffensperger, a *Des Moines Register* reporter assigned to the eastern portion of the state of Iowa, became aware of the ongoing dilemma in Hazleton, Iowa, early in the court proceedings against the Amish fathers (personal communication). Raffensperger's articles about the ongoing dilemma recorded many of the important details of the case as well as interesting side details about the conversations between the plaintiffs and the general atmosphere at the District Court, held at the home of the justice of the peace for the township. For example his article of November 7, 1965, stated that each defendant was found guilty of not sending his children to public school and was fined $20 plus $4 in court costs. The article also noted the friendly atmosphere: "There's Mrs. Wengert, fussing over the coffee pot and setting out some cookies" (Raffensperger, 1965a). As fines continued to mount, an anonymous donor came forward on two separate occasions to pay some of the fines of the Amish fathers since some of their bank accounts were being attached (G. Raffensperger, personal communication, October, 2004). This is interesting to note and points to the fact that not all the English in the area were steadfastly against the Amish.

As the drama continued through the fall, the court costs continued to mount in the forms of liens against the property of the Amish defendants. Later in November a series of events served to escalate the matter and draw the attention of national media. On the morning of Friday, November 20, 1965, school officials and the district attorney Harlan Lemon rode a public school bus to Amish School #1 and attempted to require students to board the bus and go to the public school in town. As the children were coming out of the Charity Flats School a female voice shouted "Run" in German and the children scurried into the surrounding fields of corn. A *Des Moines Register* photographer on the scene snapped a photo of this event. This photograph, which was printed in newspapers across the country, eventually served to help galvanize public sentiment in favor of the Amish. School officials then left the area and stated that there would be no further attempt to take the children to public school that day. However, they returned that afternoon and transported many of the Amish children to public school. "At school they took part in classes and recess. Some of the boys played basketball" (Raffensperger, 1965b, p. 1).

On the next Monday, thinking that the children would board the buses willingly, school superintendent Sensor and Snively, a principal in the school district, first went to Amish farms to pick up the children (Raffensperger, 1965c). The children were not at home except at one farm and those three children, as well as their mother, Mrs. Schwartz, boarded the bus. "Before doing so, she knelt before Sensor in prayer and asked that he not take the children. Then she embraced Snively and made the same plea" (Raffensperger, 1965c, p. 1). The three children stayed on the bus as it traveled to Charity Flats School. Amish fathers stood in the doorway of the school to prevent the children from being taken to school, and during the confrontation at the school the mother and her three children left the school bus. The Amish also had two attorneys present to articulate their beliefs about the case. The public school officials soon left the scene with an empty school bus.

Given public reaction in favor of the Amish, Governor Harold Hughes worked out a moratorium of the situation later that day. This moratorium allowed the Amish to continue to operate their schools and stopped further court proceedings against Amish parents. However, the issue was not resolved until 1967 when the governor and legislators voted to allow religious groups to seek exemptions from state education standards. In writing about this new legislation, Sherman (1967) found that most newspapers in Iowa were not in favor of the solution, especially those newspapers that were in locales close to the site of the conflict. Sherman found that newspapers far removed from the locale were generally in favor of the Amish and the resulting compromise.

INDIANA

The school situation in Indiana was never as complicated as that in Iowa, Ohio, or Pennsylvania but was not resolved as quickly or with the degree of cooperation that occurred in Delaware. As in other states, the issues revolved around school attendance until age 16, the closing of one-room schools, curriculum issues, and the busing of students to large schools in town. Farmweld's research (2004) found that Amish parents in the area of LaGrange were in trouble with school attendance issues as early as 1921. At this time students were to attend school until 16 unless they had passed eighth grade and were gainfully employed. This meant that the Amish would have to send their children to ninth grade at the high school. To get around this, some parents sent their older children to live with a relative in Michigan, some had their children repeat eighth grade, and other parents kept their 15-year-olds at home. Farmweld (2004) further notes that in October 1921, 11 Amish fathers were arrested for failure to send their children to school. This case continued until July of 1922 when the fathers were fined. This did not change the minds of the parents, and in July of 1923 the state superintendent met with nine Amish parents to discuss the issue. This did not resolve the issue, and by January of 1925 four Amish men were on trial for failure to send their children to school. This case was dismissed in February of the same year, and some speculate that this may have been due to the fact that other states were granting exemptions to religious groups from compulsory school attendance.

Several issues with the curriculum of the public schools come to the forefront in 1944 when Amish parents met with the local school board (Farmweld, 2004). The parents requested that their children be exempt from physical education classes, movies, and certain aspects of science. The board granted an exemption from the movies. As in other states, school attendance was always at issue for Amish children, and in May of 1947 the state superintendent met with 500 Amish parents and elders from across the state concerning the school attendance issue; however, no compromise was reached at that time.

One of the most troubling aspects for the Indiana Amish was the closing of the rural one-room schools, and this forced them to make a major decision (Farmweld, 2004). As school consolidation progressed, one-room schools in northern Indiana continued to be closed, and students were bused to town. The Amish tolerated this arrangement for the 1947–48 school year and part of the next term. In the summer of 1948 Amish parents of students at a recently closed school met to discuss their options. Those in attendance agreed that it was time to start their own parochial school so that their children would not be bused to school in town. Over $2,200 was pledged and the group bought the local one-room school at an auction for $3,225. Classes began October 11, 1948, and the school was renamed Plain View School.

Once the Amish began their own schools in Indiana, the next hurdle was to convince the state that their schools were a valid alternative to public schools. The validity of Amish schools in Indiana was repeatedly questioned by school officials at various locations throughout the state, with action taken in Allen and Adams counties.

It took almost 20 years until the Amish and the state of Indiana came to some agreement about whether the Amish could have their own schools, and this agreement was signed by the Amish State School Board in 1967. Among other things, the agreement stated that school must be in session for 167 days and that each school must have a 97% attendance rate. In addition, the teacher must have passed the GED test or another 12th-grade standardized test administered and graded by the state. Teachers who taught successfully for two years would receive a license from the local parochial school board. As it turned out, the state never did enforce the teacher testing component of the agreement.

A vocational plan was also part of the agreement. Students who had passed eighth grade would continue to attend school one day per week for five hours. Students would be required to work on vocational projects and must be at home or the home of a neighbor. Projects could be in any trade related to farming/construction. After the Supreme Court decision of *Wis-*

consin v. Yoder in 1972, the state of Indiana dismissed the vocational plan agreed upon in 1967 and indicated the Amish could utilize the Pennsylvania vocational plan.

MICHIGAN

In the mid-1960s the state of Michigan attempted to close an Amish school near Camden, Michigan. In a letter dated May 22, 1964, attorney Maxwell Bagley requested the help of Dr. John Hostetler in defending several Hillsdale County Amish parents who had been arrested for failure to send their children to public school (Heritage Historical Library). Bagley noted that the Amish had tremendous support from the local English residents. On June 1, 1964, Bagley wrote to the *Blackboard Bulletin* seeking assistance as well (Heritage Historical Library). Editor Joseph Stoll wrote a two-page response indicating that he personally knew most of the 125 teachers working in Amish schools at that time (Heritage Historical Library). Stoll admitted that some of them were not great teachers but stated that he had total confidence in the scholastic ability of students attending Amish schools. In fact, he felt that Amish students were higher in scholastic ability than many of the public school students he had gone to school with as a student in Hillsdale County.

In January of 1965 the Amish received the support of then Governor George Romney as well as two state legislators ("Michigan moves," 1965). Things seemed to be even brighter for the Amish in May of the same year when the Michigan Senate approved an exemption for Amish schools in a "heated" two-hour debate ("Budget," 1965). However, in October of 1965, the Amish were ordered to close their school unless they hired a certified teacher ("Amish told," 1965). Finally, in late November of the same year the State Board of Education approved a plan that would allow the Amish to retain their own teachers ("Amish win," 1966). This plan included a proviso that indicated that the local public school board would visit the Amish schools to provide oversight and suggestions on curriculum and instruction.

Discussions about Amish schools in Michigan continued at the state level for many years. One of these discussions resulted in a set of guidelines concerning the construction of new Amish schools. A memo from J. Welborn dated October 30, 1981, to the State Directors of the Old Order Amish Steering Committee outlined the school construction guideline agreement with the state of Michigan. Some of the guidelines in that memo included the following: 1) the school should have 20 square feet of space for each pupil, 2) the fire marshall must have two weeks' notice to inspect the new building prior to the school's being opened, and (3) wood-burning stoves must have shields to prevent accidental burning (Heritage Historical Library).

WISCONSIN

Hoping to leave some of the school controversy that occurred in Iowa behind them, several Amish in the Hazleton area moved to New Glarus, Wisconsin, in the first half of 1964 (Peters, 2003). Another incentive to move was that land prices were also cheaper in this area of Wisconsin than in Iowa. Little did the new residents know that they would soon be drawn into the school controversy that would eventually lead to a historic decision affirming the right of the Amish to build, maintain, and staff their own schools.

Residents to this new Amish community also arrived from Plant City, Ohio, and the new residents worked with local education officials to enroll their children in the public schools (Peters, 2003). One member of the Amish community, Jonas Yoder, cautioned his daughters not to participate in physical education classes since they required one to change into clearly non-Amish attire.

The Yoder family's appeal to have their daughter exempted from wearing a physical education uniform received broad support in the local Amish community and received support from several state legislators (Peters, 2003). Despite the efforts of several politicians, the legislature refused to grant an exemption for the Amish.

This failure served to galvanize the Amish community in New Glarus, and the community decided to start its own schools modeled after those in other states (Peters, 2003). In the summer of 1968 the Amish elders informed the local public school superintendent that the children would no longer be attending public schools and that they intended to start a parochial school. In an effort to comply with state regulations, the Amish contacted the Wisconsin Department of Public Instruction and were informed that the only requirement would be to have a 180-day school year and that the school itself would have to meet building codes. There were no requirements relative to teacher certification or curriculum.

The Amish pressed forward and planned to open two schools in the New Glarus area in September of 1968 (Peters, 2003). Superintendent Glewen realized that the exodus of Amish children from the district would significantly reduce state funding to the district. Rather than raise taxes for local residents, Superintendent Glewen approached the Amish in a scheme to enroll all Amish children in the public schools until the third Friday in September. This would allow the district to obtain state funding for all the Amish students, and at this point the Amish could send their children to their own schools. Naturally, the Amish balked at being part of the deception and went ahead with their plans to open their schools in September.

Obviously, Superintendent Glewen was not pleased with the Amish response, and once schools opened he investigated the class rolls of the Amish schools (Peters, 2003). He noted that the students who had completed eighth grade but had not yet turned 16 were not enrolled. Once he confirmed that this was indeed correct, he notified the Amish parents that they were in noncompliance with the school attendance laws and that charges would be filed if their children did not attend school.

Efforts to work out a compromise in the case were not successful, and state officials made it clear that those in noncompliance with the school attendance law would be prosecuted (Peters, 2003). At this point the Amish accepted the offer of Rev. William Lindholm, a Lutheran pastor from Michigan and leader of the National Committee for Amish Religious Freedom (NCARF). Rev. Lindholm had first heard of the plight of the Amish in Buchanan County in the 1960s and was led to form this committee. Lindholm contacted William Ball, an attorney in Pennsylvania, to represent the Amish in the pending Wisconsin case. Ball accepted the offer to help the Amish and attempted to work with the Wisconsin Superintendent of Public Instruction. This effort was not fruitful, and Ball proceeded to build a case to support the Amish.

The trial of the three Amish fathers began in the Green County Court House on the morning of April 2, 1969 (Peters, 2003; Nolt, 1992). Lawyers on both sides of the case were well-prepared with several witnesses. The key witness for the Amish was Dr. John Hostetler, noted expert on the Amish faith, and a professor at Temple University. On cross-examination the prosecuting attorneys attempted to poke holes in Dr. Hostetler's testimony. Since the prosecuting attorney's original questions were unsuccessful, he attempted to use a series of questions to corner Hostetler. Hostetler, however, did not fall into the trap. He testified,"There is a great deal of difference of what [*sic*] education means education for what" (Peters, 2003, p. 93). The prosecuting attorney then stated, "To put it bluntly, education so the child can take his place in the world [*sic*]." After a pause, which brought silence and an air of anticipation to the courtroom, Hostetler stated, "It depends on which world" (Peters, 2003, p. 93).

While other witnesses were called for the defense, the testimony of Hostetler was crucial. Peters (2003, p. 93) states, "It is difficult to overestimate the importance of Hostetler's testimony. His examination of the Amish beliefs and their bearing on the trial would serve as a backbone of the exhaustive trial record."

The Amish fathers were found guilty, and the case was then unsuccessfully appealed at the Wisconsin district court level. Undaunted, Ball appealed the case to the Wisconsin Supreme Court. This time the ruling was in favor of the Amish (Meyers, 1993; Peters, 2003). The state of Wisconsin then decided to appeal the decision to the United States Supreme Court and the case was accepted. Arguments in the case that became known as *Wisconsin v. Yoder* began in December of 1971. The Supreme Court ruled that the First and Fourteenth Amendments prevented states from compelling the Amish to attend formal high school through age 16. Chief Justice Warren Burger wrote, "Amish objection to formal education beyond eighth grade is firmly grounded in central religious beliefs. They object to high school because the values it teaches are in marked variance with Amish values" (*Wisconsin v. Yoder*, 1972). This auspicious decision validates the freedom of the Amish and Old Order Mennonites to maintain their own schools and to limit school-based formal education to eight grades. Both the Amish and interested non-Amish observers reckoned that this decision would bring an end to the strife concerning Amish education. As we shall see, that was not the case in Nebraska just six years later.

NEBRASKA

The most recent disagreement over the Amish educational system occurred near Pawnee City, Nebraska, between 1978 and 1982 ("Amish seek relief," 1982; "Amish school controversy," 1982; Luthy, 2003). Amish families from Ohio moved to this area in the southeast portion of Nebraska because of crowded conditions and the price of farmland in Ohio. As is the case in all new Amish settlements, the community made sure that its children were getting an education and home-schooled its children. A foreshadowing of future events for this tiny community was found in a newspaper article that described the settlement and its schooling. The *Sunday Journal and Star* stated, "So far at least, no one has attempted to force the children into public school" (Dean, 1978). Soon after this article was printed, two Amish fathers were fined $5 for each of their children who were not attending public school. Once other families moved to the area, the Amish established a school and to placate county officials searched for and found a certified teacher to teach at the school. This, however, did not solve the situation since it was soon found that the teacher had failed to update her teaching certificate as required. Local English residents in the area were split on the issue. Some, as Luthy (2003) notes, feared that the Amish would take over the area while others felt that the county should leave the Amish alone ("Nebraska Amish plan," 1979). Nonetheless, by 1981 fines for the Amish fathers continued to mount, and since they refused to pay those fines, county officials confiscated the buggy of one Amish father and sold it at auction for the sum of $420, which was well below the actual value of the buggy. The county also seized another $160 from the family's checking account. Despite the offer of Attorney William Ball to represent them, the Amish in the area decided to not press the case further and moved out of the state. The decision to leave Nebraska was also influenced by the fact that the Amish in the area also faced a dilemma with the way they kept milk cool.

This chapter has outlined the beginning of the Amish parochial school system in several states during the 20th century. In the next chapter we will explore Amish schools in the 21st century.

4

The Amish Parochial School in the 21st Century

> From the windows of an Indiana Amish school, children see barns, draft horses, and cows in pastures rimmed by woods.
>
> —Harroff, 2004

In the previous chapter we reviewed some of the struggles associated with the birth of Amish parochial schools in North America. We will now take a look at several aspects of those schools, including the building and grounds, the location of the schools, and the organizational structure that supports these schools. The chapter will conclude as we explore the favorite part of the day for many students at public and private schools alike—lunch and recess. Each of these topics is important, for each has a key role in building community among members of the church family.

A majority of Amish schools are one-room schools, and this is especially true in Lancaster County, Pennsylvania, and any daughter communities that have been started by emigrants from Lancaster. In other areas, such as the Holmes County, Ohio, settlement, the school will be a larger one-room structure that usually has two teachers.

Some of the schools in Indiana and Illinois will be two-room structures. In some areas, such as Indiana, schools will include an anteroom with three sets of steps. Upon entrance to the school one will see the first set of steps directly in front, which lead up to the classroom; a second set of steps located to one's left will lead to the basement; and a third set of steps to one's right will lead to a small room on the second floor. This room may serve as living quarters for the teacher or teachers. If teachers do not need lodging, this second-floor room may serve as additional classroom space and is often used as a room for special education.

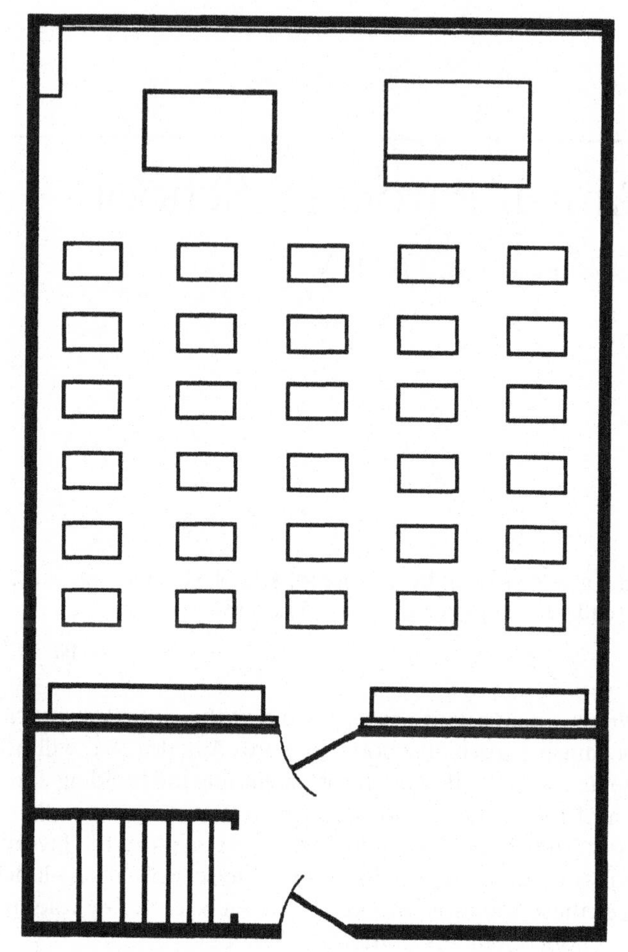

Figure 4.1. One-room, one-teacher school with anteroom and steps to basement

Schools take a variety of shapes and sizes but in most cases look like a traditional one-room school. In Pennsylvania, Ohio, and Iowa some of the Amish schools will be buildings that were originally built and utilized as public one-room schools. Most schools are of wood frame construction, but one may find an occasional stone school or a stone school that has been covered with stucco, especially in the Lancaster, Pennsylvania, area. There are also instances of red brick schools, and in the Holmes County area one will also see schools built from yellow brick or cement block. The yellow brick is about twice the size of traditional brick. Most new schools will be built using wood frame construction and have white aluminum or vinyl siding. Schools that are remodeled will usually add vinyl windows and a new roof.

Figure 4.2. One-room, two-teacher school with anteroom and steps to basement

In most cases the community and the parents of the children who will attend the school will finance the new school structure. School building costs vary by settlement and may be more than $50,000 for a new school. For example, a new two-teacher school with a full basement in the Holmes County area will cost about $60,000. Because it is often hard for the people in the community that needs a new school to pay for it themselves, the Holmes/Wayne County settlement has agreed to assess or "tax" itself for new school construction. Each family in the settlement will be taxed two times per year. One assessment is per family unit, and each pays the same amount. The second assessment is based on family wealth, and it occurs at another point in the year. These funds will be used to help each local community build a new school if and when one is needed. The local community is required to come up with several thousand dollars before money is added from the Holmes/Wayne County school fund. Most new schools are built to relieve overcrowding at area schools.

In addition to building funds, local school boards will also need to raise the funds necessary to finance the ongoing expenses of the school. This can occur in two ways. First, some locales will group several schools together and collect funds from all the church members and disburse funds from a common account. In other cases each school takes care of its own collection and disbursement of funds.

In some communities work frolics are held to earn the funds for a new school, while in others annual auctions or sales are held to provide funds for new schools and ongoing expenses. For example, one community in the southeastern United States decided that it needed to replace the two trailers that served as its school. Work frolics were held to build barns and sheds for several English residents in the area, and all the proceeds went to purchase the materials needed for the new two-room school. Once the building materials were purchased a frolic was held to construct the school.

Other communities may hold sales to fund schools. For example, the building of Whispering Pines Parochial School near Yoder, Kansas, was funded through donations and fundraisers (D. Miller, 2000). Ongoing funds are sometimes collected in the same way. Beaver Run School in central Pennsylvania has been holding a sale each April for over 25 years, with proceeds going to the school budget. In other cases an entire settlement works together to hold a fundraiser for school budgets as is the case in Dover, Delaware.

Tuition may also be a revenue source for the ongoing expenses needed to run a school. The amount of tuition required from each parent will vary by community and the amount of fundraising organized by the school. In the Holmes County, Ohio, settlement parents pay about $530 per year for each child attending school.

Planning a new school requires support from the community in terms of funding, agreement on where the school will be located, the time frame for building the school, and determining who will take leadership of various aspects of planning and building a new school.

One such planning event occurred on a June evening in 2002 near Loganville, Wisconsin (Miller, 2002b). After a meeting to discuss financing of a new school, one of the men had just loaded his three small children on the buggy and stood beside it watching the horse as he waited for his spouse. As he turned around to speak to someone the horse took off. Although the man yelled "WHOA!" the horse took off at full speed. The father ran after the buggy, and several other men jumped on bikes to race after the runaway horse and buggy. Given that this horse was considered one of the fastest in the community, one can only imagine the anguish of the bystanders, especially the mother of the children in the buggy. Most in the group figured that the horse would head for home, and this was a terrifying thought given that the way home had several sharp curves and busy roads to traverse. As the men chasing the runaway horse and buggy approached a T intersection they saw the three children (all safe) walking toward them. Further ahead the horse was found at a standstill and still hitched to the buggy. Apparently, the horse had taken the turn for home at full speed and had slipped. Fortunately for the children, the horse was stunned enough to stop after getting back to his feet. A new school was later built in this community, so the plans agreed upon that evening must have been fruitful despite the excitement that followed.

While Amish school buildings may differ from settlement to settlement, within a settlement schools will be about the same in size and structure. For example, all of the schools in the St. Mary's County, Maryland, community are similar in shape and size, as are all of the school buildings in the Romulus, New York, community. In settlements that include several different orders of Amish, such as the Big Valley of Pennsylvania, the school buildings will be different depending on the church that sponsors the school. Generally, more conservative orders prefer smaller and plainer schools.

Table 4.1. Types of Amish Schools

Type	*Settlements*
1. Small, one-room, small porch, one teacher	*Lamoni, Iowa* *Ashland, Ohio* *Nebraska Amish* *Mifflin County, Pennsylvania* *Etheridge, Tennessee*
2. Traditional size, one-room, large porch, one teacher	*Mifflin County, Pennsylvania* *Buchanan County, Iowa* *Lancaster, Pennsylvania* *Aylmer, Ontario* *Romulus, New York* *St. Mary's County, Maryland*
3. Large, one-room, porch, basement, two teachers	*Holmes/Wayne County, Ohio* *Elkhart/LaGrange, Indiana*
4. Large, two-room, porch, two teachers	*Daviess County, Indiana* *Arthur, Illinois* *Geauga County, Ohio*
5. Large, three or more rooms, basement, three or more teachers	*Allen County, Indiana*

All Amish schools are built without frills and will utilize standard windows and doors. There will be no fancy woodwork on the eaves, no fancy bell towers, no fancy colors, no fancy brickwork, no sidewalks from the road to the school, and no shrubbery. In communities where the teacher and students drive buggies to school, a horse shed will also be built. Schoolyards in the more conservative orders will not have any playground equipment or backstops for softball. Other communities may permit a set of swings, one or two seesaws, a basketball hoop, tetherball pole, a merry-go-round and/or a backstop for softball in the schoolyard. Schools located in areas that are frequented by tourists or near a main road will have a fence around the schoolyard. This fence may be a wood fence that is painted white or a chain-link fence. School buildings in areas that are prone to vandalism will have heavy wire over the windows of the school to keep out the pranksters. Amish schools are sometimes targets of vandals, which was the case at Pleasant Ridge School near Harmony, Minnesota, in the spring of 1997 (Miller, 2002b). About two weeks before the end of the term arsonists burned down the school and all its contents.

Each school board is responsible for the upkeep of its own school, and prior to the beginning of the school term each board will hold a frolic to make necessary repairs and to give the school a thorough cleaning. Students who are old enough to help with this fall cleaning will attend as well. After cleaning the school many communities will hold a picnic or cookout on the school grounds that evening. For example the Lyndonville, New York, community held its schoolhouse cleaning on the afternoon of August 29, 2005, and had a "wiener roast" that evening (*The Diary*, 2005).

During the school year it is the teacher's responsibility to help with the upkeep of the school by letting the board know when things are in need of repair. This might include things such as a leaky roof, a broken windowpane, or a damaged door knob. The school board members will make any necessary repairs and make sure the school has an adequate supply of wood or coal for heating purposes. School board members are responsible for the upkeep of the schoolyard and will keep the yard mowed during the school year. In the summer months the schoolyard will be kept mowed only if the yard is used for weekly events such as volleyball or softball. In most cases the yard will be fenced, and goats, cows, or horses will comprise the work crew that keeps the grass trimmed and fertilized until the school term begins. The school board is also responsible for calling the meeting to determine when the school term will begin, and when the fall cleaning will be held. Furthermore, as one Ohio teacher stated, "The school board must at times encourage the community to work together to have a good school term."

Schools are always located in a rural setting and away from busy roads if possible. Since the preferred mode of travel to school is walking, school board members try to locate the school in a central location for the families the school serves. Most schools are within shouting distance of an Amish home and will always have pastures, fields, or woods nearby. This is not by accident. School boards want schools to be in rural settings, as it is important for the scholars to see, hear, and smell the ongoing life of a farm setting. In addition, most schools have some level land that will serve as the playground even if the school is located in a hilly area. Schoolyards are usually grass, with no bushes or flowers of any kind planted on the property. Stone may be used as the surface for a heavily traveled entrance or driveway. Some schools also have stone around the entrance to the building. On occasion a schoolyard will contain a tree or two, while other schools will have one or more trees at the end of the schoolyard or along the road that passes the school.

Construction of new schools usually requires building permits prior to construction. For example, the Tulpehocken Township supervisors in Berks County, Pennsylvania, issued a building permit for the construction of a new Amish school in that area (Urban, 2005). The school was built in the summer of 2005 and was ready for the 2005–06 school term. On a sunny Saturday in early August of 2005 a crew of about 10 men and numerous children were busy on this construction project. The men working outside were laying the white textured brick exterior of the building while the men inside the building were completing interior trim. The youngsters present had numerous jobs related to the building project.

In some cases building codes may delay construction until permits are obtained. Delays may be due to perk tests, type of heating unit to be installed, number of entrances, or size of windows. A school in the Kingston, Wisconsin, settlement was delayed for a unique reason in 2001 (Miller, 2002b). A new school, Grand River, was planned to relieve crowding at three schools. The building was delayed, however, when English neighbors and the town board brought up issues concerning hunting rights in the area around the school and the fact that children would be walking along the road in that area. Construction of the school was delayed one year until some agreement could be reached. The school was finally built in 2002.

Once a community decides that a new school is required and building permits are approved, a master carpenter will gather the materials needed for the construction of the new school, and the community will hold a frolic to construct the building. Frolics are always fun events for the entire community, and, with numerous participants, a school can be completed in a matter of days once the foundation has been completed. There are standard plans for schools in Pennsylvania, Ohio, Michigan, and Indiana that have been approved by public officials.

Schools, especially in established settlements, are built with the knowledge that they will remain at the site where they are built. In other cases the community will build a school that can easily be moved, which is fairly easy if the school is a small building. If a community desires a larger school with some degree of mobility, it will be built so that it can be moved in pieces. For example, some schools are built so that they can be taken apart at the center and moved in two pieces. Some communities will even add a porch that serves as a coatroom with the knowledge that the school might eventually be moved. In this case the porch is built in such a way that it may be disassembled and moved at a later date.

SCHOOLS IN NEW COMMUNITIES

There are a variety of ways that a newly established community will provide schooling for the students in the area. In some cases children will be home-schooled until there are enough pupils in the area to warrant a school. In other cases a family will use parts of its home for a school until there are enough students to require the building of a school. New schools may be in a family's home, a granary, a brooder house, a trailer, a remodeled garage, or a vacant house. The building of new schools takes place in a variety of ways and serves to document the responsibility the entire community takes for establishing schools. We will now explore some of the ways schools are established in new communities.

A new settlement in Athens, Wisconsin, was begun in 1990, and in the initial year of the settlement the students were home-schooled (Miller, 2002b). As more children moved into the community, part of a trailer was utilized as a school, and the other part of the trailer served as living quarters for the teacher. The subsequent year the trailer was moved to another farm to be more centrally located for the students. In 1993 the community decided it was time to construct a new school building, and on completion it was named Shady Pine School. Most of the material for the new school was obtained from a partially burned home. The materials were free to anyone who would tear down the home. The community worked together to tear down the old house, haul the material to the school location, and build Shady Pine School.

Another example of the way a new settlement provides schooling for the children is in Bonduel, Wisconsin (Miller, 2002b). In the first year of the settlement the upstairs portion of a home was used to accommodate the school and its 11 scholars. By the next term there would be 21 students, and the community needed a school. A small house was obtained and moved to a local farm. Several interior walls of the house were then removed to provide the space for the schoolroom. By the next term there would be over 40 scholars, and more renovations were planned. The renovations included removing interior walls and adding a porch to provide storage and a coatroom. With almost 50 pupils expected for the next school term in 1990–91, the school board decided to add a basement and a large addition to double the size of the school. The new basement was built, and in the process getting ready to move the school onto the basement it was decided that it would be easier just to build a brand new school. The old school was then remodeled to serve as living quarters for the teachers.

In other cases, fledgling communities will utilize former public one-room schools or church schools to house an Amish school. The Loganville, Wisconsin, community, which began in 1988, illustrates one of these situations (Miller, 2002b). In the years prior to the building of a new school the Amish held their school in an old Lutheran church that had been built in about 1935. This school is still in use to this day. In another part of the community an old one-room school was rented from the local historical society to serve as an Amish school for several years.

SCHOOL ORGANIZATION

The main organizational structure for all Amish schools is the school board, and in most cases, each school has its own three-man school board. Some areas will have a school board that oversees three or four schools, and in this case the school board will be composed of five men. These school boards have complete oversight of all aspects of the school, including the building, the schoolyard, the teacher(s), the curriculum, and the materials. School board members consistently indicate that they appreciate the fact that they are allowed to have their own schools and thus feel a genuine responsibility to provide the best education possible within the Amish belief system. School board members are expected to visit the school on a regular basis and sometimes must serve as mediators between parents and the teacher. The only paid position in the Amish educational system is the teacher; school board members or others involved with schools serve without remuneration, just as the ministers, deacons, and bishops. It is important to emphasize here that the Amish rarely make decisions without consulting others in the immediate church community. So in the event that the school board must make a key decision, it will call a meeting of all parents or visit every home before making that decision.

Just as in public schools, school board members may find themselves in a difficult situation and struggle with ways to meet the needs of all parties involved. There are two common difficult situations that board members address. The first is the situation where the child is not doing well in school and the parents do not support the teacher in the solution to the problem. The second is the situation where the parents feel the teacher does not give their child or children equal treatment as compared to other students. If the school board members cannot resolve the issue, they will ask for additional help from another source.

Larger settlements may have a school oversight committee that works with all of the school boards as needed. In the Holmes/Wayne County, Ohio, area, the school oversight committee has been in existence for over 20 years. The settlement, which was originally divided into three sections (north, middle, and south), is now divided into four sections (north, middle, southeast, and southwest), and one person is selected from each area to serve a six-year term. This committee oversees teachers' meetings, which occur every six weeks, oversees the summer teachers' meeting, and assists local school boards as needed. The school oversight committee advises all boards on new laws or regulations as they come up. This committee has been called to other settlements in Ohio if a problem there cannot be solved locally.

In the Holmes County settlement the local school boards solve 95% of all problems. Most of the problems the school oversight committee must deal with involve problems with parents. For example, one parent felt that the teacher picked on his child. The teacher indicated that the child would not do his work and thus had low grades. This student was sent home from school on two different days for refusal to obey the teacher. As time went on the teacher was ready to resign because of the unresolved situation. After lots of meetings with the local school board and the oversight committee, the parent finally had to admit that he had to change his attitude about the school and teacher. Once this happened the student's grades improved.

The school oversight committee in Holmes County recommends that school boards meet each month, and 95% do meet monthly. Parent meetings are held once per month during the school term. The teacher meets with the board before the parent meeting and they decide what will be discussed. After this general parent meeting, the teacher will meet individually with each set of parents. Meetings usually begin at 7:30. In the rare case that parents do not come to the meeting and their children are not doing well in school, the school board will go visit them.

The school oversight committee in Holmes County holds teachers' meetings every six weeks. Four teachers are appointed to the teacher committee, and they determine topics, get speakers, and arrange the question-and-answer period. The teachers usually request that someone on the oversight committee run the meeting if there is no male on the teacher committee. The oversight committee seeks input from the community and holds a meeting each May to review rules and determine if any changes are warranted for the coming year. The delegate committee holds a communitywide meeting in early August to inform all interested persons of guidelines for the new school term. The delegate committee and the oversight committee work together. The 15-to-20-man delegate committee presents the oversight committee with what it sees as potential problems and will ask the oversight committee to look into and solve these problems.

The oversight committee is responsible for organizing and holding the summer teachers' meeting, which takes a tremendous amount of time and hard work to plan and conduct. Because of the popularity of this event the state of Ohio now holds two teachers' meetings each summer. The north meeting is usually held somewhere between Middlefield and Mt. Hope while the south meeting is held anywhere south of Mt. Hope. The south meeting is usually in Holmes County, and the meeting has an attendance of 450–500 people each year.

Another area of responsibility of the oversight committee in Holmes County, Ohio, is the instructors' class, a daylong class for all of the new teachers in the area. At this daylong event the committee gives new teachers tips on instructional strategies, discipline, and effective ways to communicate with students and parents. An oversight committee veteran stated, "One thing we suggest is that teachers should use a little humor. This relaxes people, and the students and parents enjoy this." Another topic for the 'instructors' class is to make sure everyone knows how to complete the paperwork for the mundane but necessary tasks of enrollment and attendance.

Some of the larger settlements have a specific school board to oversee the special-education program because students are coming from all over the settlement. This is the case in the Arthur, Illinois, settlement, which has a three-member school board for the special-education program. One can serve on this board only if he has previously served as a school board member in another capacity.

Another type of organizational pattern for schools is found in the Kalona, Iowa, community. Each school in the area has a school board, and in addition there is a nine-member steering committee as well as a superintendent. The steering committee and superintendent provide a degree of uniformity of curriculum and instruction to all schools in the area. The superintendent coordinates the funding, budget, and payroll for the schools, monitors attendance, and coordinates the standardized achievement test program. The superintendent also visits each school and works with parents as needed. All funds for school operations come from free-will offerings, and the budget for this area is about $75,000 per year. Since parochial schools in Kalona are supported by free-will offerings, the superintendent reminds all church members of their responsibility for the schools even if they do not have children or do not have children attending school at that time. Some communities in Ohio may have a superintendent, and as in Kalona, the superintendent will usually be one picked from the men who serve on the oversight or delegate committee.

Not all settlements have an oversight committee, and some elders indicate that this may soon pose a problem because different schools eventually have different rules and different student expectations. An oversight committee would be helpful for ensuring a common school experience on key issues for all students in the settlement.

In most states an Amish state committee will serve as the liaison between the Amish community and officials in state offices. In Pennsylvania, the Old Order Book Society was formed to "keep unity among all the Amish and Old Order Mennonite School Boards" (Kinsinger, 1997, p. 163). Kinsinger (1997) further notes that the Book Society presents the Amish perspective on school issues in Harrisburg if and when the need arises, and approves curriculum and textbooks for Old Order schools. At one time, Pennsylvania also had a Vocational Committee that was responsible for the oversight of the vocational plan that was adopted in Pennsylvania in 1956. The Vocational Committee merged with the Book Society in 1978, and the Old Order Book Society is now composed of five elected individuals. Indiana has a state school board composed of about ten members from throughout the state (J. Miller, 1995). This group serves in a similar manner to the Old Order Book Society in Pennsylvania.

The seriousness with which school boards and teachers approach their roles is exemplified by school attendance and rules regarding attendance. Interviews with teachers in all states visited indicated that all schools are aware that they must maintain an attendance rate of 97%. Attendance at Amish schools is very good. For example, one school in Daviess County, Indiana, had a 99.6% attendance rate for the 2003–04 school term. In Indiana pupil attendance data must be sent to the state board chairman who keeps records for the state. One teacher in Indiana stated, "Nonattendance is not tolerated; people know to take vacation time in the summer." My travels to Amish schools in the winter and spring of 2005 confirmed this excellent attendance record, as most schools had perfect attendance on the day of my visit.

Amish schools do not have paid superintendents, assistant superintendents, principals, assistant principals, curriculum coordinators, school counselors, school psychologists, coaches, janitors, secretaries, food-service personnel, bus drivers, business officers, athletic directors, or subject matter specialists in art, music, or physical education. They do have active parental support that is encouraged and expected. Parents and community members are expected to visit schools on a regular basis. Amish schools also have a very large percentage of the community serving on school boards. For example, a typical one-room school of 25 pupils will have students from ten to twelve families. Since all school boards are composed of at least three people, that means that about 25% of the families are serving on the school board.

LUNCH

The noon meal is a time for children and teachers to eat, relax, and converse. At the end of the second work period of the morning, the students will sing a prayer, recite a prayer, or pray silently. After this the scholars are dismissed in an orderly fashion to wash hands and retrieve their lunches. Students then come back to the room and sit at their desks to eat. It is not uncommon for two students to share a seat at this time. On nice sunny days the pupils may sit in a big group in the schoolyard to eat lunch. Most children bring their lunch in a small hard-sided cooler or other plain lunch box. A typical lunch will include bread, cheese, fruit, chips, pretzels, cookies, or some type of dessert and a drink. Instead of bread and cheese some children may bring a sandwich while others may bring yogurt. Drinks may be water or a juice box, and in a very few schools children may bring a can of pop or soda on selected days. In the winter months the teacher and students will place sandwiches in aluminum foil on a metal stand atop the wood or coal stove in the classroom. They will then have a hot lunch. In a few schools students may also bring slices of pizza, potatoes, or other foods to heat up in this manner.

When lunchtime arrives, the students' first priority is eating because it has been a long time since breakfast and most have walked to school. Another reason that the students concentrate on eating is that once everyone is finished they will be able to go out for the noon recess. During lunch, students may also engage in conversations about upcoming trips, a funny event, going to the auction, what to play at recess, or chores they have to do after school. The teacher or teachers take part in the conversations. This fellowship during lunch serves to build bonds of friendship between the students and the teachers.

Parents periodically work together to bring a hot meal. When the term begins the mothers decide which month each will bring a hot lunch. In most cases there are two families responsible for bringing a hot lunch each month. Parents often help each other depending on the size of the school. A typical meal in the Holmes/Wayne County, Ohio, community is potato casserole, corn, salad, bread, cupcakes, a snack food, and ice cream. Both the teachers and scholars appreciate the hot meal no matter the menu selected, and teachers and students enjoy these meals, for it is a nice change from the normal lunch. These days are also enjoyed because they bring visitors to the school.

When mothers are at their homes baking donuts, fried pies, cream sticks, and/or cookies, they will often make extra and take them to the schoolhouse for a treat for the scholars. In other cases mothers bake something specifically to take to the school as a surprise for the teacher and students; they will usually stay and visit the school that day as well. This happens more often in January and February and serves as a break from the winter boredom for the mothers, teachers, and pupils alike.

RECESS

Recess is an important part of the day at any Amish school, for it is a time to relax, talk with friends, and play games. Going out for recess is one time of the day when Amish pupils are likely to be loud inside the building as students to get out to the playground. This exuberance may include verbal joking with one another as well as jostling to get out the door quickly. Recess is a significant time because it is here that Amish children form bonds of friendship that will be essential for the strength of the community in the future. Children at Amish schools forge community in both work and play. Amish schools have three recess periods per day, with fifteen-minute recesses held midmorning and midafternoon. The noon break is an hour, so recess may be as long as 45 minutes depending on how quickly the students finish their lunches. At many schools, the scholars must clean the inside of the school before going out for the midafternoon recess period. This cleaning will include sweeping the floor, collecting trash, washing the blackboard, and cleaning the erasers. It should be noted that at many schools students arrive early so that they can play some of their favorite games before school begins. In the vast majority of schools the teachers are actively engaged in the games played before school and at recess.

Amish school board members are well aware of the importance of recess. Interviews revealed that school board members expect the teachers to play alongside the students. Furthermore, school board members expect students to work during class sessions and play during recess. As one stated, "When it is time to work it is time to work, when it is time to play it is time to play." Amish elders also know that recess must be closely monitored so that some students are not left out of conversations or games. Thus in many schools the class decides what game they will play before going out, and then everyone plays that game. Teachers like to play with the students at recess, and several indicated that their favorite part of the day is recess.

There are many outdoor games that are popular with Amish students. These include a wide variety of tag games, Dutch ball, volleyball, basketball, soccer, and softball. Softball is the preferred game at recess, and students in northern climates look forward to warmer weather and the chance to play their favorite game. Softball is reserved for days when it is not too cold and the schoolyard or pasture is dry. Teachers often serve as the pitcher for both teams. Some schools have elaborate backstops while others will have none. In either case, one can see the well-worn areas that indicate the location of home plate and each of the bases. Bases may be as simple as a worn patch in the grass, a board, or a disc from a farm implement. One will also see a wide variety of baseball gloves in use at these games, and many of the gloves are kept at school the entire school year. During warm weather students will often shed their coats as the game proceeds. A common schoolyard sight is black coats strewn about at the end of recess.

Softball is the game of choice for many of the end-of-year picnics at Amish schools in the United States and Canada. Parents, teachers, and children will engage in a lively game before or after the noon meal. Softball is also a popular summer pastime in Ohio. Several communities get together one evening per week for a game that involves both parents and children.

There is a wide variety of tag games played at Amish parochial schools, and similar games may have different names, depending on the locale. Some of these tag games are 22 Eskimo, prisoner's base, jail, circle base, and grade base. A popular tag game in the Arthur, Illinois, area is 21 skip to do. In this game several children serve as "taggers" or "itters" and chase the other students about the schoolyard. When children are tagged they must go to an area enclosed by a rope on the ground. They remain here until there are 21 students tagged. Once this occurs they shout "21 skip to do" and scatter about the schoolyard to start the game anew. Descriptions of other popular tag games are found in Appendix C.

A well-liked and fun game involving a ball is rabbit. In this game there is one "itter" (the hunter) who has the ball. He counts to ten, and all the rabbits scatter. The hunter attempts to hit rabbits with the ball. Once a rabbit is hit he/she becomes a dog. The dog now assists the hunter by helping chase the rabbits. The dog chases and catches them until they are touched or hit by the hunter. When all the rabbits become dogs the game is over, and the hunter picks a new person to be the hunter.

Indiana is well known as being "basketball country," and this also applies to many Amish settlements in the state. Most Amish parochial schools in Indiana will have basketball goals in the schoolyard, and some schools will even have a concrete area for full-court basketball games. Further evidence of the popularity of basketball is that some Amish in the Elkhart/LaGrange community attend basketball games at local public high schools.

Dutch ball is a game that is very similar to kickball, but the game has only two bases in addition to the home plate area. This game serves as a fun substitute for softball if the weather is not suited for that activity.

Volleyball is another popular school game as well as an evening activity in the summer. In the summer one will see many of the schoolyards in the Lancaster area with one or more volleyball nets in place. Volleyball is also a fun summer evening activity for the young people in Holmes County. In some schools in Indiana the girls play volleyball while the boys play basketball. At larger schools upper-grade students will be allowed to play basketball or volleyball, and the lower-grade students will play some type of tag.

In areas with an appropriate climate and topography, sledding and ice-skating are well-liked recess activities. At schools located in hilly areas one will often see students sledding in nearby pastures after a good snowfall. Some schools are located near ponds that freeze over, and the scholars will then engage in ice-skating as weather permits. For safety reasons, some school boards will create a man-made pond just for ice-skating. Students enjoy building snow houses and igloos after a heavy snowfall.

In addition to the above games lower-grade students may play on the playground equipment or engage in games of freeze tag, hide and seek, "duck duck goose," or follow the leader as they make paths through the snow. Lower-grade students enjoy playing "high waters," which involves jumping over a rope held by classmates. One starts this game with the rope held near the ground. The remaining students then take turns jumping over the rope. After each round the rope is held further from the ground. The game continues until only one person can successfully jump over the rope.

During heavy rain or bitter-cold temperatures students will have recess indoors. Games that are played may include checkers, Parcheesi, Candy Land, Connect 4, Scrabble, Blitz, Uno, Skip-bo, Sorry, and marbles. Some schools with basements may have one or two Ping-Pong tables, a foursquare box, or in a rare instance a foosball table. Most schools strive to have recess outdoors if at all possible, and a snowstorm will usually not result in school being closed or recess being held indoors.

Teachers, parents, and school board members view recess as an important part of the school day because they believe that working and playing together builds community. Students are expected to go out to play at recess unless they have a medical excuse. Both teachers and students enjoy recess. In many schools all students are expected to participate in one activity, while in other schools there may be two or three games going on at one time. Teachers make sure that every student is included in a game. In addition, teachers will not tolerate small groups just talking at recess, and they will not allow inappropriate behavior. Amish teachers may ask students who have not completed some work to stay in at recess, but it would be very rare for a student to miss all the recesses in the day because of incomplete work. One Ohio teacher stated, "Even though this happens at times, board members and parents disapprove. It is not fair to the child for he needs to refresh his brain, too."

SPECIAL EVENTS AND PROGRAMS

While Amish schools do not have band, chorus, clubs, dances, or sports teams, they do have a variety of special events or programs throughout the year. As in public schools these events may be connected with a holiday.

Christmas Programs

On the last day of school before Christmas some Amish schools will have a Christmas program. The schoolroom will be decorated with student produced materials such as paper stars, paper chains, and coloring related to the season. The program, which is delivered by the children from memory, will include singing, the reciting of poetry, the presentation of several short skits, and the exchange of small gifts (Fisher and Stahl, 1986).

The prevalence of Christmas programs in many Amish communities is best illustrated by the fact that over 25 different communities in the United States and Canada reported on the school Christmas programs in the December 2005 issue of the *Diary*. Most communities reported that there was a full house for the events. Other reports mentioned that residents attended one or more Christmas programs if there were several schools in their vicinity. The buzz of activity leading up to one of these events was noted in the November 2005 issue of the *Diary*, which stated that schoolchildren were busy at school with the memorization of songs and poems for the Christmas program.

At Indiana schools favorite skits at the Christmas Program include the alphabet song in German (Harroff, 2004). In this skit each scholar has one or more large cards with German letters. In turn, the scholar will step forward and say the letter and its aphorism. For example, for M the student would say, "*M, Morgen Stund hat Gold im Mund*." Scholars will also sing songs such as "*Stille Nacht*," "We Wish You a Merry Christmas," and "Amazing Grace." After the program the parents, students, and guests will enjoy refreshments of homemade cookies, candy, coffee, and soda.

End-of-Year Picnic

Numerous schools will hold an end-of-year picnic that serves to officially end the year on a positive note. It is a special occasion for all in attendance, including students, teachers, and parents alike. Parents will bring the entire family as well as plenty of food to share. Those in attendance will take part in energetic games of softball or volleyball. Soon after the picnic the school will close for the summer vacation, with books and materials placed in storage until the new school year arrives.

In some cases the end-of-year picnic may be held in conjunction with graduation for the eighth graders. Harroff (2004) has found that many schools in Indiana will provide a diploma for the graduates as a way to remind them of the importance of schooling to a disciplined life.

Other Holidays

Some schools may do something special on Valentine's Day, such as decorating the school with hearts and red/pink construction paper chains. Students will prepare valentines to share with their classmates. Parents may get together to bring the students a treat, such as cookies or cupcakes. In 2005, one school in southern Indiana had a balloon release after enjoying the baked treats.

Many schools will decorate the building for Easter season. Decorations may include colored pictures of Easter eggs and flowers. A few schools will hold an Easter program that includes singing and a visit by an elder or elders who will elaborate on the importance of Good Friday and Easter to the Amish faith.

As we have seen in this chapter, buildings, schoolyards, organization, lunch, and recess are all important components of building community among both the students who attend the school and the settlement at large. Tradition and *Ordnung* serve to regulate these aspects of Amish education, and one can expect future schools to be built, organized, and conducted in similar ways.

5

Amish Students

> The primary function of the Amish school is to teach Amish children the three R's in an environment where they can learn discipline, true values, and getting along with each other in life.
>
> —Hostetler and Huntington, 1992

Observations at numerous schools over the past year indicate that Amish scholars seem to enjoy school. Students participate in small group lessons, and they learn early in their school career to work independently on their assignments for each day. Students also learn that it is their responsibility to learn the content presented by their teacher. Students know that teachers will hold them accountable for completing all assignments in a prompt and accurate fashion. As in other types of schools, some Amish scholars excel in their school studies, and others need more time and review to master the content of their lessons.

Most Amish pupils walk to and from school, while others may ride scooters or bikes, and others may get rides in a buggy or pony cart. In any case, travel to school can at times be dangerous since some scholars must traverse busy rural roads. For example, in the Hillsboro, Wisconsin, community a horse shied away from a snow plow, and the buggy ended up in a ditch. One of the children heading home from school aboard the buggy suffered a broken arm, while the other occupants and the horse were not seriously injured (*Diary*, 2006).

Another accident in Fennimore, Wisconsin, illustrates the dangers that children may face while walking to school. In this case, a small pickup truck lost control on the slippery road and hit four students on their way to school.

The impact with the truck threw the four students into the snowbank by the road. Amazingly, all four survived the incident with no broken bones (*Diary*, 2006).

Most schools have about the same rules that students must follow. Some of the common rules are contained in the *Standards of the Old Order Amish and Old Order Mennonite Parochial and Vocational Schools of Pennsylvania* (1969, pp. 12, 27, 28). Some of the rules are:

- Tardiness will not be tolerated
- Stay off roads during school
- No nicknames
- No competitive games with other schools
- No whispering
- No throwing paper or unruliness
- Love and respect others without partiality

Hostetler and Huntington (1971, p. 95) describe the Amish as "quiet, responsible and conscientious." My observations in schools in 2005 confirm this as a very good description of Amish scholars. They like to complete their school tasks in an accurate, ordered, and quiet manner. They are encouraged by their teachers to be prompt but are not encouraged to be quick, because accuracy is more important than speed. Hostetler (1993, p. 185) provides a succinct statement of the Amish view of students and learning capabilities in this way: "Since a person's individual talents are God-given, no one should be praised if he is a fast learner, nor should he be condemned if he is a slow learner."

Amish students, like their parents, do lots of reading. One reason for this is that homes are not filled with electronic equipment such as televisions, CD players, video games, and radios. Amish homes have plenty of written material, including numerous Amish publications as well as farm and garden periodicals. Fishman's (1988) ethnographic research in Lancaster, Pennsylvania, found that the Amish community in her study engaged in lots of reading and that there was a wide interest in reading in the community. This characteristic exhibits itself in school, as students in school like to spend their free time reading. Fishman (1988) found that students at the school in her study liked to read books such as the *Sugar Creek Gang* series, the Little House on the Prairie series, and the *Bobsey Twins* series.

Haroff (2004) believes that in general students in Indiana Amish schools exhibit five characteristics. First, Amish pupils have a pronounced work ethic. They get their work done in an efficient manner. Second, the scholars utilize very quiet voices while in the classroom. In many cases visitors may not even hear the conversation between an individual student and the teacher. Third and strongly related to the second characteristic, Amish pupils develop a keen sense of hearing. This is an important characteristic in an Amish school because teachers generally do not repeat themselves. Fourth, Amish pupils want to do well in school and are disappointed when they earn a grade that is below average. However, Amish pupils are generally not boastful, nor are they overtly concerned with getting the best grade. Any exuberant expression of pride by a student will not be tolerated by parents or teachers. Lastly, Amish pupils quickly respond to nonverbal and verbal correction. A teacher will utilize clear and direct language to correct a student; yelling or lecturing will not be needed. These characteristics are very similar to those that I have observed Amish scholars exhibit in schools throughout the United States and Canada. I have generally found Amish schools to be quiet places. My only noted exception to this was a school in Ohio in which the teacher had a loud voice. In this case some students exhibited this verbal style as well.

While Amish students are quiet and conscientious in the classroom and like to complete their work, Amish scholars also enjoy recess. At recess they will engage in active play and will be as loud as any other children. Each school and community will have favorite games that they enjoy playing, with softball and various games of tag being popular recess activities. In the winter students enjoy activities in the snow such as sledding.

Smucker (1988) found that Amish scholars exhibit different personality traits than their English counterparts. For example, Amish youth use fewer personal pronouns such as I, me, or mine than non-Amish youth. Amish youth express less aggressive fantasy responses than English youth.

Hostetler and Huntington (1971) further note that about 30% of Amish youth exhibited the ISFJ personality type as compared to only 6% of non-Amish youth. This personality type is sensitive to the needs of others, is attentive to detail, and is conscientious in all activities.

Hostetler and Huntington (1971) also report striking differences between Amish youth and English youth in their drawings of a "happy time." The drawings of a happy time by Amish youth usually included some type of work such as baking, collecting eggs, or raking leaves. In contrast, the happy time drawings of English youth included a variety of sporting activities or even hostile actions such as snowball fights.

A DAY IN THE LIFE OF AN AMISH STUDENT

The following realistic fictional account is based on my numerous observations at schools in the United States. The story portrays a typical day in the life of an Amish student. The format of the day is similar to that experienced by Amish students in schools in the United States and Canada. The setting of the story will be in Holmes County, Ohio, and the student we will follow is

Ben. Ben is a third-grade student at Maple Lane School in Holmes County, Ohio. He has three siblings: Martha, who is in the first grade; Eli, who is four years old; and Mary, who is one. Ben lives on a 45-acre farm. In addition to his farming duties his father, Daniel, has a leather and harness shop in a large building near the barn. His mother Susan was a schoolteacher for three years before getting married to his father. It is a Thursday in late October of 2004. On this Thursday Ben rises at 5:45, and after getting dressed in his white shirt, black pants, and black shoes, he puts on his boots and heads to the barn to help his dad with the morning chores. His favorite part of the chores is giving fresh milk to Smokey and Bess, the cats that live in the barn. Smokey and Bess will follow Ben all morning till they get their breakfast and will brush against his legs and meow as he feeds the horses. Once the chores are finished Ben gathers an armload of firewood for the stove in the kitchen and heads to the house. Upon entrance to the house Ben smells the breakfast that his mother and sister have been preparing.

After washing up, Ben sits at his place at the kitchen table. When everyone has assembled, his father leads devotions before everyone eats breakfast. Today's breakfast is scrambled eggs, bacon, bread, butter, jelly, home-canned peaches, milk, and orange juice. While eating the family discusses the jobs that need to be done in the shop, house, and farm that day. At 7:30 Ben and his sister head off to school with their black lunch buckets. It is a mostly cloudy day in the mid-40s, and there is a heavy mist along the creek beds in the valley. Their dog, Red, walks with them to the end of their lane. After giving Red a pat on the head, they start the trek up the hill along the blacktop road toward David and Emma's house. Ben and Martha have been cautioned about the automobiles and trucks on this road, and they are extra careful while walking up this hill. After about seven minutes they have reached the top of the hill, and they see David and Emma running to greet them. David is in the fourth grade, and Emma is in the second grade. Emma says, "Guess what?"

Martha replies, "What?"

Emma is so excited the words flow in rapid succession: "We have six kittens. They are so cute and cuddly."

David adds, "I like the black kitten the best!"

Ben chimes in, "When can we see them?"

And Emma says, "Maybe this Saturday." As the four scholars continue the journey to school they continue their conversation about cats and kittens. They head down the hill and to the bridge over the creek. They stop at the creek each morning to gaze into the water to see if they can see any fish or other wildlife. Since they see no fish they continue across the bridge and up the hill to the Maple Lane School. As they walk up the hill they see some other students heading across the field to the school as well.

The students arrive at school at about 8:05 and exchange good mornings with Rachel (teacher of grades 1–4) and Elizabeth (teacher of grades 5–8).

They then put their lunch buckets on the shelf in the basement and head outside to play freeze tag with their classmates. Rachel comes out to play with the children as well. By 8:20 all of the children have arrived at school and are outside playing. At 8:30 Elizabeth rings the bell signaling the start of the school day. Ben and his fellow scholars quickly get to their seats, and Elizabeth takes attendance. As is the case on most days everyone is present. Elizabeth then reads a chapter from her *Egemeyers Bible Story Book.* Today's story is about the Apostle Paul, and Ben listens attentively since he likes to listen to the teacher read. After the teacher finishes the reading she asks several questions about the reading. Ben raised his hand to answer each time but Elizabeth did not call on him. Next the class prays the Lord's Prayer. Elizabeth then calls the students to the front of the room for the morning singing. Today the seventh graders get to pick two songs to sing. Ben is happy when his favorite song, "Lift Your Glad Voice," is picked.

After singing is finished, Ben and his classmates return to their desks and get busy on their assignments. Ben looks at the board and notices that the third graders must do pages 45 and 46 for arithmetic, write their spelling words, and complete pages 47 and 48 in the phonics workbook. He also knows that they will be reading the first part of the story, "A Fitting Name," during reading today and that he should study his multiplication facts if he has extra time during the morning. Since Ben likes arithmetic the best, he starts that assignment first, and at this time Rachel calls the fourth graders to the front for reading while Elizabeth calls the eighth graders to the front for reading. About fifteen minutes later Rachel calls the third graders to the front for reading. Ben grabs his reading book, titled *New Friends,* and takes a seat at the table near the teacher's desk. Rachel says, "Let's read your story." The students each read one paragraph at a time, and since Ben is sitting by the first student to read, he gets to read the second paragraph. After the students complete reading the first part of the story, Rachel asks them several questions. Ben gets to answer the second question, which is, "Why was Star their favorite cow?" Ben answers, "She was gentle and was not hard to milk at all." Rachel nods her agreement and moves on to the next question. Third-grade reading is over in about 15 minutes, and Ben heads back to his seat to continue with his arithmetic. First-grade reading is next. Ben likes to listen to the first graders because he likes to hear his sister read. He enjoys the stories about Peter and Rachel, the characters in the book. When the first graders start their reading, Ben's ears perk up because he hears them reading one of his favorite stories in the book—"A Doll in the Tree." Ben continues doing his math while listening to the first graders. After the first graders are finished, it is time for second-grade reading with teacher Rachel, and about the same time, teacher Elizabeth is working with the seventh graders. As Ben finishes up his math he cannot help hearing the seventh graders talking about camels during their reading lesson. Camels, he thinks. What does that have to do with reading? He soon finds out that the seventh-grade reading selection for today is about the camel experiment conducted by the U.S. government in 1865. Apparently things didn't go that well because people in the U.S. did not know how to care for them, and the camels scared most of the farm animals they came in contact with.

Elizabeth rings the bell for recess at about 10:00, and the students put on their coats, hats, and bonnets and head outdoors for a lively 15-minute game of tag. Ben likes tag but hopes that they will be able to play softball at the noon recess.

After recess Ben finishes his spelling words and has begun his phonics work when Rachel calls the third graders to the front for arithmetic. Arithmetic is Ben's favorite subject so he always looks forward to this part of the day. The class exchanges papers, and the students correct each other's work while the teacher recites the answer. After this the teacher records each student's grade in her grade book. Ben is happy that he earned a grade of 100 but is careful to not be boastful. He remembers his father saying that it is important to do well in school but that one should not demonstrate pride when earning a good grade. Rachel then teaches the students how to measure the perimeter of squares, rectangles, and triangles. Ben thinks this is fairly easy since he often has to help his father measure boards when fixing things in the barn. After arithmetic is finished, Ben finishes his phonics workbook and his new arithmetic assignment while the other grades have arithmetic. Ben also notices that the sun was shining, and he thinks, perhaps the grass will dry enough so that we can play softball at noon. Ben is finished with all his class work about fifteen minutes before the lunch break, and he studies his multiplication facts a little bit. His teacher then asks him to help one of the first graders with his reading workbook. Ben enjoys helping younger students and is happy that he was picked to help. At 11:30 Elizabeth rings the bell that indicates that it is time for the noon lunch break. All of the scholars quickly put their things away as two other students carry trash cans around the room so that the students can throw away their trash. The class then says a prayer before being dismissed, one grade at a time, to wash up and retrieve lunch buckets. Ben likes the lunch break, but he likes recess even better. While the students are eating Elizabeth asks the students what they want to play at recess. Several of the older boys and girls immediately say, "Softball."

Elizabeth says, "It looks like the grass is dry so I think we can play softball today." Ben is ecstatic when he hears the word *softball*! After a quick lunch the teachers and students go out to play. The teachers serve as pitchers for each team, and the class plays until 12:30. It is a good game, and the class is lucky today since no foul balls end up in the muddy ditch by the road. During softball games Ben likes to play in the outfield, but he likes batting the best. Today he has two hits in three tries and scores one run. Ben is also happy that recess did not have to be interrupted because of misbehavior by some students. About two weeks ago, teacher Elizabeth had to stop the ballgame to talk about sportsmanship when some of the older boys became too competitive and started arguing about whether the runner was safe.

After recess Elizabeth reads the entire school a chapter from the book *Lantern in the Window*. Ben always enjoys listening to the teachers read. It is soon time for everyone to get back to work, and the third graders know that they need to study their spelling, words, and multiplication facts and/or complete their phonics workbooks. Ben is studying his spelling words but cannot help noticing the clip-clop of a horse's hooves approaching. A few minutes later it sounds as if the buggy is pulling into the school. He can hear the horse being hitched to the rail and people approaching. He wonders, "Who will our visitors be?" A few moments later there is a knock on the door. Elizabeth goes to the door and greets David and Emma's mother and their two older sisters. They are carrying a big basket with something inside. He wonders if it might be the kittens, but then he smells the aroma of fresh-baked oatmeal raisin cookies. Maybe they will have a treat later that afternoon. The visitors sit on the benches at the back of the room and watch the students and teachers as they complete their work. Elizabeth soon asks one of the fifth graders to take the visitors' notebook back to the visitors so that they can record their presence. Rachel then calls the first graders to the front of the room and indicates that they should write each of their spelling words on the blackboard. As soon as the first graders are engaged in that task, Rachel calls the third graders for phonics, and Ben takes his workbook to the table at the front of the room. After checking their work the students practice words with short vowel sounds. Rachel then assigns ten new vocabulary words for the students to look up in the dictionary.

With David and Emma's mother and two sisters seated at the back of the room, some students find it hard not to glance at the visitors. Right before recess teacher Elizabeth asks one of the sisters to help a second grader with his reading, and she is happy to assist the student. The first graders have a quick math review of their addition facts before recess, and Ben enjoys listening to the students' quick answers as the teacher shows the flash cards.

Ben has been so busy with his work and paying attention to other classes that he does not realize that it is recess time when Elizabeth rings the bell. After ringing the bell, she says, "Our visitors have brought some cookies. You may each have one on your way out to recess after you finish your cleaning chores." Ben's job for the week is to sweep the porch, and he gets busy right away. When he is finished he gets a cookie from one of David and Emma's sisters, thanks her for the cookie, and asks about the kittens before heading out the door. To Ben the afternoon recess seems to go by too quickly since the students must clean the school before going out.

After recess the older grades have geography or history while the younger grades have vocabulary and/or math recitation. By this time in the day Ben is getting tired, and it is much harder to concentrate on his work. Since Ben has completed all his work he may read a book or color. He chooses to read a book from the library. About 15 minutes before the end of the school day, Elizabeth asks the students, "Would you like to sing for the visitors?"

Most of the scholars, including Ben and his sister, quickly respond, "Yes." Elizabeth then calls the students to the front of the room one grade at a time. Before singing, each scholar states his or her name grade and recites the memory verse or saying he or she has been studying. They then sing a song about their school and each of the students in the school. Next they sing a song in German and finally they sing a song in English. Elizabeth then rings the bell signaling the end of the school day. After cautioning the students about cars and trucks on the road, she dismisses the students one row at a time. Since Ben was dismissed first, he waits for his sister Martha before leaving the school. Ben and Martha usually walk home with David and Emma, but since David and Emma's mother and sisters were at the school today they will get a ride home in the buggy. Before leaving, Ben and Martha stick their heads back in the school to say good-bye to their teacher before heading home.

Ben and Martha then head down the hill to the bridge over the creek and talk about the funny things that happened in school that day. They also wonder whether they will see any fish or other animals in the creek. At the bridge they peer into the water and see no fish or other creatures moving about, but they do see three crows on the fence row. Ben takes a pebble and tosses it into the creek to watch the ripples. Ben and Martha then pick up two sticks and go to the other side of the bridge and toss them into the water. They then run to the other side to see whose stick had made it under the bridge first. Martha's is first, and Ben says, "Your stick always seems to be first!" Martha laughs and says, "Let's get home. I am hungry!"

The children walk quickly up the hill and pass the lane for David and Emma's house and wonder about those new kittens. They then walk briskly down the hill and get home by 3:45. Mother is in the kitchen finishing some baking and asks them how things went at school. Ben says, "It was a good day and we had visitors."

Before Ben finishes his sentence Martha chimes in, "It was David and Emma's mother and sister and they brought cookies!"

Mother then says with a smile, "I guess you do not need a snack then do you!"

Ben quickly says, "That was a long time ago, and we just walked home—we are hungry and thirsty!"

Mother then says, "I will get you some cool milk, and each of you may have one and only one of those fried schnitz pies. Then each of you may play with your sisters before it is time to help with the chores."

After finishing their snack Ben, Martha, and Eli head to the barn to look for their cats. Perhaps they have kittens in their barn too. No kittens, but they do find the cats sleeping in the sunshine on the south side of the barn. After petting Smokey and Bess they head back inside to play with their baby sister. At about 4:15 Ben and Eli head back to the barn to do some of their chores while Martha helps her mother with dinner. The roast beef mother has in the wood stove oven sure smells good to Ben, who is already hungry again. Each afternoon Ben and Eli must sweep the barn floor and assist with the cleaning of the stalls for the horses and cows. Smokey and Bess follow the boys around, hoping for a treat. After the cows have been milked and all the animals fed, it is time for dinner. If Ben was hungry earlier he is even hungrier now. Upon entrance to the house to wash up he is treated to the smell of roast beef, mashed potatoes, noodles, green beans, and cabbage. After everyone is seated the family bows their heads for silent prayer, and then it is time to eat. While eating, the family shares the events of the day. Father talks about the auction at a farm near Charm two weeks from Saturday and wonders aloud if anyone would like to go along. All the children respond that they would like to go. After dessert of yellow cake with chocolate frosting and some rhubarb sauce, Father and the boys head back to the barn to finish the chores while Mother and Martha clean up in the kitchen.

When Ben and Eli are finished in the barn they pat each of the horses on the snout, hug each of the cats, and head inside. When Ben gets to the door he realizes he forgot the armload of firewood he is to bring in each evening and heads to the woodpile. With a possible trip to the auction near Charm in two weeks he wants to make sure he does all his chores properly. To miss out on that trip because of not doing one's chores would not be good. After cleaning up, Ben heads to the living room where everyone is seated reading a book, *The Budget* or *Young Companion*, or playing with their baby sister. At 8:45 Mother says, "Time for bed." It has been a long day but a good day: kittens at the neighbors that he might get to see this weekend, a grade of 100 in arithmetic, and a chance to go to the sale near Charm in two weeks. Ben has lots to be thankful for as he says his evening prayers before going to sleep. Since it will be cold tonight, that quilt made by his grandmother will keep him warm throughout the night.

6

Curriculum, Textbooks, and Academic Achievement

> Adolescents learn faster by actual participation than by talking about participation. Working at real jobs outside the school walls helps students to envision their adult roles and their place in society.
>
> —Hostetler and Huntington (1992), describing the advantage of the Amish educational system

In this chapter we will take a detailed look at components of Amish education that further enhance the sense of community, the importance of literacy in reading, writing, and arithmetic, and community responsibility. We will look at curriculum, textbooks, aphorisms, pleasure reading material, and the vocational school plan, and finish the chapter with a review of academic achievement of Amish parochial school students.

The most important subjects in Amish schools are reading, writing (penmanship), and arithmetic. Or, as one Ohio teacher wrote, "We call them the 3 R's: Reading, wRiting, aRithmetic." Students also receive instruction in English/language arts, history, geography, health, vocabulary, phonics, German, art, and singing. As we explore each subject area we will also study some of the textbooks and workbooks used to teach each subject. In the beginning of the Amish parochial school movement the schools used textbooks that were common to most rural country schools at that time. In fact, in many cases the Amish were able to buy not only the school building but all of the furniture and educational supplies in the school as well. As noted previously, the closing of small rural schools was one of the main reasons the Amish started their own schools. Thus for many years there were plenty of books and materials they could buy to supply their schools, and usually these materials could be purchased for a very reasonable price.

READING

Reading is clearly the most important subject in any Amish school, and teachers make sure that every student has a chance to master this skill. Reading instruction usually takes place each morning. A typical reading lesson in first and second grade will include direct instruction in using phonics to decode words, learning sight words, building vocabulary, and reading comprehension. In grades three and above the general reading lesson will include oral reading of a story, some review questions about that story, and the study of new vocabulary in the next story. In the early years of the Amish parochial school movement the schools used the same textbooks as those in use at most rural public schools at that time. Today, the majority of Amish and Old Order Mennonite schools in the United States and Canada use the *Pathway Readers* as the textbooks for reading instruction. These readers were designed and written by former Amish teachers and follow the organizational style and teaching methods utilized in public school readers at that time. Other readers in use at Amish schools may include the *McGuffey Eclectic Reader* (Avenatti, 1991), which was first used in the 19th century, as well as the "Dick and Jane" readers, which were utilized in many public schools.

Pathway Readers

Pathway Publishers first printed a set of reading textbooks, the *Pathway Reading Series*, for grades 5–8 in 1968. These books, edited by Joseph Stoll, David Luthy, and Elmo Stoll, include many stories written by the editors. The *Pathway Readers* also contain some excerpts, stories, and poems from other sources, and many of these stories and poems will be familiar to teachers and students in public schools. Some examples of the material from other sources include excerpts from *Amos Fortune, Free Man*, the 1951 Newberry Medal Winner as the best new novel in children's literature for that year, *Rikki-Tikki-Tavi* by Rudyard Kipling, and poems by Walt Whitman, John Greenleaf Whittier, Louisa M. Alcott, and Henry Longfellow. The upper-grade readers contain many stories specifically written for an Amish audience. For example, the eighth-grade reader in the *Pathway Readers* contains eight units of study. The third unit, or chapter, is on Amish heritage and includes stories about Menno Simons, Christopher Dock, William Penn, and Martin Luther. Unit five includes readings about the wonders of nature, and unit six has stories and poems based on events chronicled in the Bible.

In contrast to the reading textbooks currently used in most public and private schools, the *Pathway Readers* in grade 5–8 are printed without the use of color and contain no photographs and virtually no illustrations. By 1977 the Pathway series was expanded to grades 1–8. Like the readers for grades 5–8, the readers in grades 1–4 are printed without the use of color and con-

Figure 6.1. Pathway Publishers, Aylmer, Ontario

tain no photographs. The readers for younger children do, however, contain more illustrations.

The *Pathway Readers* contain stories and illustrations that relate to the Amish culture. For instance, the first grade reader, *Busy Times*, contains stories titled "A Pet Goat," "A Good Dog," "The New Farm," and "We Want a Pony." In the story "A Good Dog," the two characters, Peter and Levi, compare their dogs. As the story continues Peter makes some statements about Levi's dog that hurt his feelings. Levi then decides to go home to play with his own dog. Peter eventually realizes that his statements may have hurt Levi's feelings and apologizes; the story ends with the boys happily playing together with Peter's dog. The third-grade reader contains an interesting story titled "Report Cards." In this story Noah learns that getting good grades on his report card does not make him better than his siblings. In fact, one has to "learn that getting along with people, making friends, and being kind and thoughtful are just as important as good grades" (*New Friends*, 1977, p. 249).

Origin and History of the Pathway Readers

Because the *Pathway Readers* play such a crucial role in Amish education, we will explore their origin and some of the difficulties the early writers had in producing a new series of readers. Three of the writers involved in the process of starting and completing the reading series were interviewed in the spring of 2005.

Joseph Stoll, editor of the *Blackboard Bulletin*, had the idea of producing a set of readers especially for the Plain People in the spring of 1966. He then wrote letters and sent samples of some possible stories for the series to elders and teachers in other communities, seeking their input about such an undertaking. These early reviews were favorable, and Joseph proceeded with the project in earnest. Joseph's original idea was to use selected materials from out-of-print readers such as the *McGuffey's Readers*, but this changed later that year. David Luthy, a teacher from LaGrange, Indiana, visited the Alymer, Ontario, community in July of 1966 and convinced Joseph that Amish children deserved better stories. David volunteered to help write some of the stories. On the train back home later that month, David, 24 years of age at the time, wrote the first draft of the story "The Jokers," which is now part of the eighth-grade reader, *Our Heritage*. David moved to Aylmer in May of 1967 and teamed with his future brother-in-law Elmo Stoll to do much of the writing of the readers for grades 5–8. These three men spent the summer of 1967 on the readers, and by September of that same year one remarked that the job was "more formidable than I had realized." By December, the eighth-grade reader had been finished and sent to the printers to be typeset. The writers needed about $3,000 for typesetting and solicited donations from the Old Order community. Donations started to trickle in but in total were nowhere near the goal. Fortunately, the month of December 1967 brought a surprise in the mail, a check in the amount of $1,000 for the project.

By March of 1968 the seventh-grade reader was getting close to completion but a lot of work was still to be done. Much of that work was accomplished by May, with the fifth- and sixth-grade readers also nearing completion. The readers for grades 5–8 were finally ready for production later that year.

In 1970 another former teacher was asked to take on the arduous task of writing readers for students in grades one through four. She took the challenge and began this immense project by carefully studying readers in use in public schools at that time. This research helped her design and write the first-grade readers, which she indicated were the most difficult to write given the limit on vocabulary. One decision that she made at the beginning of the project was that she would try to limit proper nouns to those that could be easily decoded using phonics. For example, she used the name Bess for a horse.

Her goal in designing the first- and second-grade readers was to use a combination of sight vocabulary and phonics to teach reading. Another objective she set for herself was to complete one reader and accompanying workbook each year, and she completed the writing on the first- and second-grade readers by herself.

She had assistance from another former teacher for the third- and fourth-grade readers, and for these readers they did adapt some writing from other

Amish periodicals, such as *Family Life.* It is important to note that as she progressed through the writing she was always seeking input on her writing from teachers in various Amish communities in the United States and Canada.

These early writers of the *Pathway Readers* could not have imagined the huge success that the *Pathway Readers* and accompanying workbooks have enjoyed. In fact, records at Pathway Publishers indicate that there have been 389 press runs of the series with a total of 2.8 million copies printed since 1968! *Pathway Readers* are used in most Amish and Old Order Mennonite schools in North America, and in the mid-1980s the books became quite popular with many parents in the United States who home-schooled their children. In addition to the *Pathway Readers,* Pathway Publishers produces a variety of materials, including books for children and adults, workbooks, German books, and the *Blackboard Bulletin,* the education journal for Amish and Mennonite teachers, parents, and students.

Additional Readers in Use at Amish Parochial Schools

While the *Pathway Readers* are the primary reading textbooks in use at Amish schools, there are other reading textbooks available and in use at a variety of schools. For example, some Amish schools still utilize old readers such as *The New Basic Readers* series (Gray, 1956) by Scott Foresman and Company. These readers are most often known as the "Dick and Jane Readers" and are available from the Gordonville Print Shop. The Gordonville Print Shop is an important supplier of textbooks and reading material for the Plain People. The shop, which is located in Gordonville, Pennsylvania, is in the heart of the Amish community in Lancaster County. The company prints textbooks, workbooks, and teachers' guides for numerous subjects, including phonics (workbooks for grades 1–6), spelling (grades 1–8), health (grades 1–8), geography (grades 3–8), history (grades 4–8), English (workbooks for grades 1–8), and the Strayer-Upton arithmetic series (grades 1–8). In addition, the company produces end-of-term final tests, coloring books, poem books, song books, immunization cards, enrollment sheets, report cards, teacher-records books, and vocational reports intended for use in Old Order schools.

In addition to Pathway Publishers and the Gordonville Print Shop, there are other Old Order businesses that produce reading texts and workbooks. Echo Printers of Arthur, Illinois, is one example and prints reading workbooks for the upper grades that may be utilized with the *Pathway Readers.* In typical Amish fashion a group of teachers worked together to write these workbooks. Echo Printers also produces workbooks for teaching German in the upper grades.

ARITHMETIC

Arithmetic is an important subject in all Amish schools and, like reading, is a subject that is usually taught in the morning hours. The routine teaching procedure is for the teacher to explain the new concept or algorithm, show the students how to do the problems, make sure all pupils know how to solve the problems, and then have them practice the skill individually at their desks using problems from the text or a workbook. Amish students are generally very good in arithmetic and, as we will verify later in this chapter, on or even above grade level as compared to their counterparts in other schools in the United States. Haroff (2004) has also noticed this fact and has found that in Indiana Amish schools the eighth-grade students are routinely exposed to applied mathematical problems indicative of the mathematics presented in public high schools in the 1950s. Students are usually quite successful at solving these complex problems and do so without the use of a calculator.

Most Amish schools utilize one of five textbooks for instruction in arithmetic. One of the most popular textbooks for arithmetic is the *Practical Arithmetic Series* by Strayer-Upton, published in 1934 and reprinted by the Gordonville Print Shop in 1989. Some schools may also use the arithmetic series by Silver Burdett Company (Morton, 1958) titled *Making Sure of Arithmetic*, the arithmetic series by Schoolaid (East Earl, Pennsylvania), commonly called the Spunky series by Amish teachers, the arithmetic series by Study Time Publishers (Topeka, Indiana), or the arithmetic textbooks produced by Rod and Staff Publishers. In some cases schools may use a combination of these textbooks. For example, a school may use the Schoolaid textbooks for the younger grades and either Strayer-Upton or Study Time textbooks for the upper grades.

In the Holmes/Wayne County, Ohio, community, schools have been asked to utilize the Spunky arithmetic series for first and second grades and Rod and Staff Arithmetic for grades three through eight. Many schools have already moved to the use of these books. There were two reasons for this decision. First, some thought the former arithmetic series was out of date. Second, the community is trying to use a similar curriculum across all of the schools.

Rod and Staff Publishers

Given the fact that Holmes/Wayne County, Ohio, settlement is the largest Amish community in the world, it is important to note this move to the use of Rod and Staff arithmetic textbooks for the upper grades and to know something about Rod and Staff Publishers.

Rod and Staff Publishers is based in Crockett, Kentucky, and was founded "to meet the print needs of conservative Mennonite schools" (J. Ball, personal communication, January 13, 2005). It produces arithmetic workbooks for first and second grade, and arithmetic textbooks for grades three and up. In the early years of the company textbooks were mainly the vision of the writers. Since then, a textbook committee has envisioned the textbook and the professional writers and practicing teachers have written the revised or new text utilizing this vision. Because most conservative Mennonite schools go only to the tenth grade, Rod and Staff produces textbooks from preschool to 10th grade. Besides selling textbooks to Amish and Mennonite schools, the company sells many of its products to those who home-school their children. Rod and Staff Publishers prints textbooks, workbooks, curriculum guides, and teacher editions in the following subject areas: Bible, mathematics, reading, science, English, health, spelling, history, geography, penmanship, music, and art (Rod and Staff, 2005). The Rod and Staff fourth-grade textbook, *Progressing with Arithmetic*, has 17 chapters. The textbook has several chapters on multiplication and division as well as a chapter on fractions, decimals, and metric measurement. The text provides concrete examples for new operations and gives students plenty of practice on important algorithms. The text will on occasion incorporate word problems using people or events from the Bible, or church-related events.

Study Time Arithmetic Series

The Study Time arithmetic series was produced by Amish teachers in Indiana. The series has workbooks for grades 3 and 4 and textbooks for grades 5 though 8. Study Time Publishers also produces tests, timed drills, and flashcards to be used with these arithmetic workbooks and textbooks. To add interest to the subject, the books are built around themes. For example, the sixth-grade arithmetic book has six units of study, including Farm, About the House, Insects, Bible Facts, The Greenhouse, and Asia. In an effort to make the arithmetic series more relevant to Amish pupils the authors build content around the lives of four students: Steve Raber, James Fry, Ida Yoder, and Becky Byler. Word problems in the story use these students within the unit topics. Math concepts covered include multiplication, division, linear measurement, liquid measurement, fractions, decimals, and mixed numbers. This arithmetic series was prepared in traditional Amish fashion with teachers working on one grade per year and giving each book a trial run with Amish teachers before going into full-scale production.

SPELLING

Amish students study spelling in grades 1–8. Teachers assign new words each week, and students are tested on those words each week as well. Lower-grade students can often be seen writing their spelling words on blackboards as a way to practice both writing and spelling. Schools use a variety of used textbooks for spelling, such as the Zaner Bloser series, which is obtained from book companies such as Follett Educational Services, a company that stocks used textbooks. Some schools may use other old spelling books, such as *Learning to Spell* by Ginn and Company, published in 1956 and now reprinted by the Gordonville Print Shop. Amish teachers have designed a series of workbooks that may be utilized in conjunction with these *Learning to Spell* textbooks. The workbooks are also available from the Gordonville Print Shop. Even though Amish schools do not stress competition between students, spelling bees or spelldowns may take place in some schools. For example, in the Geauga County, Ohio, settlement, schools have spelling bees on a regular basis and will even have spelling bees that comprise students from several schools. In the Dover, Delaware, settlement some schools may permit spelling bees between scholars from different schools while others do not participate in this type of academic competition.

Spelling bees also occur in some schools in Indiana, and Haroff's (2004) research found that Amish scholars are good spellers, enjoy the subject, and like to take part in spelldowns. Spelldowns will be held by grade level and may take numerous rounds to determine the winner. In some cases teachers will have stickers, stars, candy, or some other small prize for the two or three best spellers in each grade.

ENGLISH

Amish students learn the fundamentals of English grammar and usage and will utilize most of those skills as adults since many Amish are involved with writing on a weekly or even daily basis. For example, many Amish adults write for periodicals such as *The Budget, The Diary, Family Life,* and the *Blackboard Bulletin.* Others are actively engaged in writing family histories, community histories, or school histories, or in serving on a variety of committees that require written communication between parties. Furthermore, since Amish homes do not have telephones, letters are a main form of communication between friends and relatives who live in other communities.

Harroff (2004) notes that most Amish schools in Indiana utilize the *Climbing to Good English* series produced by Schoolaid, an Old Order Mennonite Publishing House in Pennsylvania. Harroff (2004, p. 111) has found this English series to be rigorous since it is based on "American Public school standards at a time when many, if not most citizens had 'only' an eighth grade education." The last section of the eighth-grade text is a guide to writing for adult life and commerce.

Amish students do not study literature as students in public schools do. For example, Richardson's study (2005) in the Holmes County settlement found that besides reading textbooks there is little in the way of literature reading, discussion of literature, or writing about literature. Students are more likely to write about a history or geography lesson than literature. Discussions of reading selections are about the moral of the story, and individual opinions are not given or sought.

PHONICS

Teaching students to decode words using a phonetic approach is part of the curriculum at most Amish schools. Teachers will spend time in reading class as well as other points in the day helping the younger-grade students get a firm foundation with this skill. It is not unusual to see younger students practicing phonics at the chalkboard as time permits during the school day. The workbooks written to accompany the *Pathway Readers* have workbook pages titled *Learning Through Sounds.* On these pages students develop phonics skills necessary for independent reading. The importance of phonics to Amish teachers is best illustrated by the fact that several years ago the editors of Pathway Publishers removed many of the phonics pages from the workbooks in a revised edition. The Pathway editors received numerous letters wanting to know what had happened to the phonics pages. As a result, they added the phonics lessons back into the workbook (personal communication from Amish elder, May 2005).

VOCABULARY

Because the primary language of the Amish is Pennsylvania Dutch, Amish school leaders understand that additional instruction in English vocabulary is often necessary. Thus, Amish schools often have specific instruction in English vocabulary. The vocabulary workbook, *Working with Words,* produced and published by Pathway Publishers, is designed to accompany the *Pathway Readers* as well as to introduce additional vocabulary.

WRITING/PENMANSHIP

Most Amish teachers have excellent writing skills. For example, my observations in Amish classrooms found that teachers demonstrated these skills while writing information on the board or in written comments on student work. My written communications with Amish teachers also revealed the excellent penmanship skills of these individuals. Amish schools stress the importance of good penmanship, and teachers make sure that the first graders get a good start on the essentials of writing. As in other subjects, teachers stress accuracy rather than speed and encourage their students to practice proper letter formation. All Amish classrooms have the printed alphabet and the cursive alphabet posted in the classroom, usually located above the chalkboard. Some schools will also have the German script alphabet as well. Younger students practice penmanship on a daily basis and have a notebook or workbook for practicing their skills. Teachers may check these workbooks each day or some will check them on a weekly basis.

Pentime Publishers of Arthur, Illinois, produces handwriting workbooks for grades 1–8. There are two workbooks for first grade, with the first workbook prepared especially for use in conjunction with the *Learning through Sounds* workbook produced by Pathway Publishers. Students learn the basics of manuscript writing in grades 1–2, with cursive writing being introduced at the midpoint of second grade. The Pentime writing workbooks also cover a variety of topics as the students practice their writing. These topics include health, safety, and courtesy in third grade; state birds, flowers, and facts in fourth grade; and wildlife, Bible verses, songs, and poems in fifth through eighth grades.

Another penmanship workbook series is produced by Mrs. J. J. Yoder of Marion, Kentucky, and features a variety of topics in each grade. For example, the sixth-grade workbook covers topics including Bible verses, famous Americans, types of minerals, and animals. The workbook has two writing assignments per week, with the first assignment a Bible verse in German or English. The author notes that this Bible verse may also serve as the memory verse for the week. The last page of the workbook outlines common mistakes in handwriting and how to avoid each of these mistakes.

HISTORY

Amish schools may begin lessons in history as early as fourth grade. The curriculum will include topics about great Americans, the history of their respective state, and United States or Canadian history. Schools will utilize old public school textbooks or old textbooks reprinted by the Gordonville Print Shop. Used public school textbooks in use in Amish schools include books such as *The United States and other Americas* by Macmillan (1982), *Ohio: Geography, History and Government* by Macmillan (1990), and *The United States and its Neighbors* by Macmillan (1993). Some schools in northern Indiana will use A Beka textbooks for history and geography instruction. A Beka textbooks are produced in Pensacola, Florida, and the company writes its textbooks with a Christian perspective. The textbooks include full-color maps, drawings, and photographs to enhance the text.

In addition to their history textbook, Amish students learn about historical events and people, as well as the history of the Anabaptist people, in the seventh- and eighth-grade *Pathway Readers.* For example, in the seventh-grade textbook the students will read stories and poems on a variety of topics in nine units. Unit topics include the animal world, history, helping others, appreciating our past, and broadening our horizons. The unit on broadening our horizons includes stories about the great plague of London, the Johnstown flood, and tornadoes on Palm Sunday.

GEOGRAPHY

Instruction in geography may begin as early as third grade, and students are expected to be able to identify states, important cities, nations, mountain ranges, and bodies of water by the eighth grade. Instruction in geography will begin with the local environment, and move to the state, national, and then international level as the grades progress. Teachers will also teach students how to use maps to plan trips. Teachers will introduce topics during class time, and then students will read further about that topic during individual study. During study time, students will also work on memorizing the locations required for that grade level. In some Indiana schools drill in geography will be accomplished using a map that does not have labels for states, cities, bodies of water, and nations. The teacher will then point to different features on the map, and the class must quickly identify the state, nation, or body of water. In many cases seventh- and eighth-grade classes are combined for geography and history instruction. A school might have instruction in geography for the combined seventh- and eighth-grade class for half the school year and then instruction in history for the same group in the second half of the year. In addition to having students memorize locations, some schools will require students to memorize each state and its capital in alphabetical order by state.

The Gordonville Print Shop has geography textbooks for use in grades 3–8. These textbooks are reprints of books produced by the General Learning Corporation in 1968. *The American Continents,* which is a fifth/sixth-grade book, contains 248 pages on the United States and 100 pages on Canada. In the Holmes/Wayne County, Ohio, area *The American Continents* textbook series is in the process of being replaced by Rod and Staff geography textbooks or the *Eastern Hemisphere* textbooks printed by Pathway Publishers.

The Rod and Staff history/geography textbook for grade six is composed of eight chapters on the geography of Central and South America and four chapters on the history of these areas. In addition to teaching about Central and South America, the text has numerous activities where students hone their ability to read and interpret several types of maps, charts, and graphs.

HEALTH

Amish students will learn the basics of human health and may utilize textbooks such as the *Road to Health* series published in 1957 by Laidlaw Brothers and now reprinted by the Gordonville Print Shop. Amish students usually have a small amount of time each week from second through eighth grades devoted to this subject. Some of the chapters in the sixth-grade text include "Why You Eat," "Food Nutrition," "Bacteria," "Preventing Disease," and "Protecting Your Health." Some schools will use the health workbooks that have been designed and produced by Schoolaid. These workbooks are designed by Old Order teachers for use in Old Order schools and cover a variety of topics. For example, the fourth-grade workbook, *Good Growth Guide* (2004), includes topics on safety, first aid, digestion, sportsmanship, skin, eyes, ears, and nose. The curriculum of Amish schools will not include information or discussion about reproduction since that topic is reserved for the home.

GERMAN

Part of the curriculum at many Amish schools is to teach students to read in German. The first task is to teach children the German script alphabet. Teaching students the German alphabet will usually not occur until the scholars have mastered English and in most cases will not occur until third or fourth grade. Most schools will have the German script alphabet posted under the English script and cursive alphabets. When teaching the German alphabet, teachers will utilize flash cards during recitation and drill. Once students have mastered the alphabet, instruction in German reading will begin. Pathway Publishers has produced six workbooks that can be used as the basis for the German curriculum. In the first workbook, *Let's Learn German* (Pathway Publishers, 1974), students practice the German alphabet before moving on to German words, phonics, and short sentences. Another source for German textbooks for upper-grade students has been written by David Zehr. David is an Amish teacher in Indiana and has written and published four workbooks that teach the German language. Each book focuses on one of the Gospels of Mathew, Mark, Luke, and John. David is thinking about writing four workbooks for German-language instruction that that would focus on the Old Testament.

In addition to textbooks in German, schools may utilize bilingual editions of the Bible that have German text on one page and English text on the facing page. This enables students to read the same text in both languages. Amish schools in southern Indiana will have two or three sets of parents come to the school each Friday afternoon to assist with German instruction.

ART

Amish students do not receive specific in-depth instruction in drawing, painting, or pottery. However, they do complete projects that allow them to color, draw, or make materials that may be used to decorate the room. Art is usually reserved for Friday afternoons, and the projects will not be frilly or elaborate and will not encourage individual expression. For example, an art activity might be a coloring sheet of a farm scene that each child colors. All of the student work will then be displayed. In other cases students might draw Easter eggs on paper and then color the eggs for room decorations in the spring. Paper chains of construction paper are another decoration one might see in an Amish school. As with all subjects, students who have special skills in the area of art will not be singled out for individual recognition.

COLORING BOOKS

Many of the lower-grade Amish scholars bring coloring books to school. Students will be allowed to color in these books if they have completed all their work, know their memory work, and have studied for the upcoming lesson. Coloring books are available at most Amish-owned bookstores. Most of these books are drawn, produced, and printed by adults in the Amish community. Some examples of the type of coloring books available are those drawn by Mrs. Fisher, a resident of an Amish community in central Pennsylvania. She got involved in this project because she loves horses, and there were not many good coloring books related to horses in the market at that time (personal communication, April, 2005). She currently has three sizes of coloring books available and has sold thousands since starting this venture. As with many Amish publications, the coloring books are printed at the Gordonville Print Shop.

One of the most interesting examples of community providence among the Amish is the *Aunt Sarah's* coloring book series sponsored by an Amish printer in Ontario, Canada. Sarah was stricken with rheumatoid arthritis at a young age, and the printer solicited drawings from the Old Order community on her behalf. Sarah used many of the drawings sent to her to produce five coloring books. One of these coloring books, *Aunt Sarah's Country Cousins*, has been printed at least seven times since 1987. The coloring book has numerous farm-related scenes for children to color. Coloring books in the *Aunt Sarah's* series will not portray adults but will portray children on occasion.

Hoosier School Master Supply, LLC, of Milford, Indiana, sells eight coloring books that it has created and printed. The 2005 catalog has coloring books on the following topics: birds, flowers, the zoo, and farm animals. In keeping with Amish tradition concerning photos or images of people, these coloring books do not portray adults.

SINGING

Students sing each day but do not receive musical instruction. Amish singing is always in unison, and song books will include the lyrics but no musical notation. Musical instruments are never used by the Amish in school, church, or home. Since Amish schools do not have electricity, students will not sing along to a CD, tape, or record. Schools will sing songs in English and German, and all songs will be on topics related to the Amish religious heritage. Amish students enjoy singing for visitors from other settlements.

APHORISMS

Aphorisms, maxims, or mottoes are a key component of the Amish school curriculum and play an important role in the building of responsible behavior. Amish teachers incorporate the use of aphorisms in several ways. First, a school will always have at least one or more aphorisms posted on a teacher-made bulletin board or poster. Second, most teachers require memory work, and sayings are often part of the memory work. For example, at one school in Indiana all of the scholars introduced themselves to visitors by giving their first names and grade levels and reciting their memory verses or aphorisms. Finally, a majority of schools will post the Golden Rule as one of the aphorisms presented in the school.

Teachers like to display an aphorism on bulletin boards or posters in the classroom. A sampling of the maxims displayed in classrooms in the winter and spring of 2005 is described below. One school in Delaware had the following saying posted: "If you want to feel rich just count the things you have that money can't buy." A school in Geauga County, Ohio, had the following aphorism posted: "The secret of happiness is in helping others find it." A school near the LaGrange community in Indiana had two very nice teacher-drawn bulletin boards with winter scenes. The first bulletin board included this saying: "The future lies before us like a sheet of fallen snow Be careful how you tread it for every step will show." The winter scene that accompanied this maxim depicted a child traipsing through the snow with his footprints clearly visible in the new-fallen snow. Another school in the LaGrange community had this aphorism posted on the bulletin board: "Character—It's how you live your life when no one is watching."

A school in Illinois had this maxim posted: "If you aren't big enough for criticism, you are too small for praise." Another Illinois school had this aphorism posted: "A thing done right today means less trouble tomorrow." And finally, a school in Iowa had this saying posted in a prominent place: "The best way to cheer yourself up, is to find someone else to cheer up." These sayings reinforce the Amish life of simplicity, servanthood, humility, and community. Students will remember these sayings for a lifetime. These and other aphorisms posted in Amish schools can be found in Appendix E.

Hostetler (1989) writes that the interiors of Amish classrooms contain mottoes that teach ideals and character and records over 20 different mottoes that were displayed in Amish schools in Pennsylvania. One such motto was "You can be pleasant without talking a lot. Think twice before you speak once" (p. 221). Another interesting motto was "The longer you put off doing a job, the harder it becomes" (p. 221).

MEMORY WORK

In addition to the maxims posted in the schoolroom, the memorization of aphorisms is a small but important component of the school week. For example, in the Holmes County settlement of Ohio, students will usually be given a new saying to memorize each Monday with the goal of having the saying memorized by Friday. Students will write the saying in their notebooks and will spend about five minutes of quiet time each morning memorizing the aphorism. If the aphorism is longer, the scholar may have two weeks to learn to recite it from memory. In most cases students do not receive grades for memory work, but report cards do usually have a section where the teacher can record good, fair, or poor on this aspect of a student's work. Memory work may also include poems, Bible verses, presidents, states and capitals, and counties in the state. On Friday morning the scholars will recite their memory work individually while standing beside their desks. At this time other students will be working quietly on their written work or studying until it is their turn to recite. In addition to memory work, most schools will have a Christmas program that will require the students to memorize their parts of the program.

REPORT CARDS AND GRADING

Students receive a percentage-correct grade on their class assignments and tests; teachers do not grade students on a curve. For example, teachers do not add points so that some students in the class will receive an A grade even though no one in the class earned higher than an 88 on the test. In addition, teachers do not adjust academic grades up or down for effort or class participation. Grades are given in the key academic subjects of arithmetic, reading, and spelling and are based on class assignments and tests. If a child receives a 95 in arithmetic then the parents know that the child has mastered 95% of the material for that grading period.

Students receive report cards six times per year. Students receive a percentage correct grade for each academic subject, such as reading, arithmetic, health, and spelling. Students will also receive such grades as "satisfactory" or "needs improvement" for various dispositions and habits. For example, Hoosier Schoolmaster Supply, LLC, of Milford, Indiana, prints report cards for use in Old Order Schools. Some of the dispositions and habits listed for grading on this card include courteous, honest, respects authority, listens attentively, work is neat, and accepts constructive criticism. The front of the report card includes a message for parents that encourages them to discuss the report card with their children, support good attendance, and visit the school. Report cards are also produced by the Gordonville Print Shop and Rod and Staff Publishers.

HOMEWORK

Because Amish children have plenty of chores to do each morning and evening, teachers do not generally give extensive amounts of written homework. Amish teachers and parents know that the younger students benefit from parent assistance in learning to read and mastering the basics of arithmetic. In my observations in schools and visits to Amish communities I have never noticed pupils carrying lots of books to or from school, and in fact most children I have observed carry, at most, one book or workbook home each evening.

LIBRARY BOOKS

All Amish schools have a three- or four-shelf bookshelf that contains library books for use by the scholars. In addition, most schools will have a set of dictionaries and at least one set of encyclopedias. Library books available to students are carefully screened, and the shelves will usually contain old books from public school libraries as well as books available from companies such as Pathway Publishers. Richardson's (2005) research in Holmes County, Ohio, is illustrative of the library holdings in most Amish schools. Richardson found that classroom libraries had one or two shelves of books. Most schools had the *Character Sketches*, a book series that teaches lessons about character through nature or Bible teachings. Some books in the series are titled *Character First* and *The Power of True Success*. Most schools also had books in the *Hardy Boys* series, *Little House on the Prairie* series, and the *Boxcar Children* series. Some teachers brought in magazines such as *Farm and Ranch*, *Ranger Rick*, and *TIME for Kids* for the students.

The school board is usually involved in the review of reading material for the school. In cases where the school serves children from different Amish affiliations, the review of books for the library may be more difficult because each church affiliation will have a different *Ordnung*. In some cases school boards may give the teacher lots of leeway, but most school boards usually want to be involved in all decisions. If teachers are unsure about a book's use in the classroom, they will usually ask the school board for advice prior to placing the book in the library.

Richardson (2005) found that the Holmes County Public Library has one of the largest bookmobile services in the United States, with two units that can carry about 5,000 titles. The bookmobiles mainly serve the Amish and Mennonite Community. The bookmobiles visit Amish schools about every two to three weeks, and some teachers set limits on the number of books children may check out as well as place limits on the type of book they may check out. For example, at one school the teacher will let students check out four books. The children then put the books on her desk, and she reviews them that evening. Objectionable books are not allowed and would include books with topics of fictional violence, romance, comics, westerns, fantasy, witches, evolution, and plays, except those about Jesus. Other teachers do not monitor bookmobile books at all. For example, one teacher arranged for the bookmobile to come after school was out, and thus she did not have to worry about the type of books students were checking out and reading at home.

Richardson (2005) found that the most popular bookmobile books for Amish students in grades 4–8 were the books in the following series: *Hardy Boys, Little House on the Prairie, American Girl, Boxcar Children, Caddie Woodlawn, Sugarcreek Gang,* and the *Bobsey Twins.* Popular magazines on the bookmobile were *Ranger Rick* and *Country Women.* Less popular books for the upper graders were in the *Heartland* and *Focus on Family* series, as well those that involve animals. How-to books on typical Amish pastimes were also popular. A similar bookmobile service is available through the Wayne County, Ohio, public library for Amish schools in that county.

In some Amish schools in Geauga County, Ohio, the teachers will rotate a group of 30–50 books on their bookshelf from the public library for use by the students. A similar pattern is employed by teachers in many schools in northern Indiana who will augment their library holdings with books from the local bookmobile service. Popular books for younger Amish children in northern Indiana include books in the *Berenstain Bears* series and the *Amelia Bedelia* series.

VOCATIONAL SCHOOL PLAN—LEARNING BY DOING

A crucial component of the Amish educational system is the vocational school plan. Once Amish students complete the eighth grade, the curriculum will focus on learning vocational skills at home from their parents. Skills learned are gender specific with girls learning to become proficient at home-making skills and vegetable gardening. Girls also assist in the barn and may often be seen helping to disk a field in the spring, hoe weeds in the summer, and help with the harvest in the fall. Boys will become adept at farming as well as any small business that is owned by the father. In addition to farming skills, most males will also learn carpenter skills and mechanical skills for the maintenance of farm machinery. Amish children have always learned at home in this manner, but the process became more formalized in Pennsylvania in 1956.

The key component of the vocational school plans is that students learn by doing. This component of Amish education serves not only to teach skills but also to build community. This community building occurs during the formative adolescent years. The Supreme Court decision of *Wisconsin v. Yoder* (1972) noted that requiring students to attend high school during adolescence would take them out of the community during these formative years and that this would have a detrimental effect on the community.

The Vocational School System in Pennsylvania

As noted in chapter 4, numerous fathers in Pennsylvania were jailed for failure to send their children to high school. A solution to this problem was worked out in 1956 under the direction of Governor Leader (Lapp, 1991, pp. 512–513). The agreement stated that Amish children would be under the supervision of their parents, learn skills at home (learning by doing), attend class for three hours per week, and complete a journal outlining the skills that they were learning each day. Amish elders are grateful for the resolution of this dilemma and have been careful to make sure that all schools in Pennsylvania follow the system. Kinsinger (1997) states that students are required to attend the vocational class until age 15 and are required to complete journal entries until age 17. Subjects in the vocational class include spelling, arithmetic, German, singing, and penmanship. A partial listing of the rules for the vocational class is listed below (Kinsinger, 1997, p. 158):

1. Children should not be absent from Vocational Class even for ½ day, as the ½ day represents one week.
2. Children enrolled in the Vocational Class should be doing farm or domestic work from 8 a.m. to 3 p.m., Monday through Friday.

3. Diary should be wrote up [*sic*] in a form that can readily be seen that they are doing something worth-while, when enrolled in the Vocational class.
4. German lessons should be read and studied at home.

THE VOCATIONAL CLASS IS A PRIVILEGE; LET US STOP AND THINK! AND LET US NOT MISUSE THIS PRIVILEGE.

Over the years, two periodicals, *Die Botschaft* and *The Diary*, have contained numerous references by community scribes to the vocational system. These writings serve to illustrate the importance of the vocational school program to the Amish and verify various aspects of the program. For example, the August 18, 1993, edition of *Die Botschaft* indicated that the vocational program has prospered and that two vanloads of Nebraska Amish from Big Valley, Pennsylvania, had attended the vocational school meeting in Lebanon, Pennsylvania, earlier that month. The August 25, 1993, edition of the *Die Botschaft* further noted that over 400 individuals from all over Pennsylvania attended the same meeting. Three years later in the December 25, 1996, edition of the *Die Botschaft* (p. 32), a scribe from Lancaster, Pennsylvania, wrote that the board visited four vocational schools in session earlier in the month and further stated that it was "nice to see the vocational plan being implemented so well." In 1999 a Lancaster scribe wrote in the March 17 edition of *Die Botschaft* that he had visited a local vocational class in session at a local residence and noted that the "scholars were well mannered." He further stated that "we (the Plain People) should remember our hard-won right to have this system."

In the August 25, 1999, and the September 26, 2001, editions of *Die Botschaft* a writer shared a letter from the Commonwealth of Pennsylvania dated July 31, 1997, which stated that an Old Order school was not following the vocational plan as the agreement with the state stipulated. The writer urged members of the Old Order Book Society and the Vocational Steering Committee to remind all churches of the regulations agreed upon in the 1956 agreement with the state of Pennsylvania. Since these letters appeared at the beginning of the school year, one can surmise that the writer was using this forum to remind everyone of the importance of keeping the agreement so as not to jeopardize the Amish parochial school plan.

ACADEMIC ACHIEVEMENT

A common question asked by the general public is how Amish parochial school students compare to their public school counterparts on achievement tests. The academic achievement of Amish-educated students has been the topic of several studies during the last 50 years. Hostetler and Huntington (1992) documented the achievement of Amish scholars compared to a rural sample of non-Amish students as measured by the Iowa Tests of Basic Skills. The Amish students scored significantly lower on vocabulary as compared to the public school sample but scored significantly higher in spelling, word usage, and arithmetic problem solving. In all other subtests the groups were not significantly different.

In another study, Hostetler and Huntington (1992) investigated Amish students' academic achievement using the Canadian Tests of Basic Skills. This study, conducted in 1989, found that Amish parochial students scored above grade level in word usage, spelling, and arithmetic computation and below grade level on mathematical concepts and interpreting visual materials such as maps and graphs.

In a 1987 study utilizing the Iowa Tests of Basic Skills, Hostetler and Huntington (1992) reported that the 197 Amish parochial school (grades 3–8) students were above grade level in reading, language skills, work skills, and mathematical skills. The Amish students scored at the average on vocabulary, and they were not tested in the subjects of science or social studies. At every grade level the total composite scores for Amish students were above grade level, and the eighth graders scored almost a full grade higher. A later study involving 117 students in 1988 found that the Amish students scored at or above grade level for each grade tested (Hostetler & Huntington, 1992).

Additional achievement test data were collected during the winter of 2005 from the school superintendent for Amish parochial schools in the Kalona, Iowa, settlement. The Iowa Tests of Basic Skills are given each January, and students complete tests in the core subjects of reading, language arts, and arithmetic. An average score would be at the fifth month for each grade level. For example, students scoring at grade level for fifth grade would be at 5.5. The composite grade-equivalent scores for students in grades 3–8 are found in Table 6.1, and the data are based on about 30 scholars per grade level. The table indicates that in general Amish students in these schools are below grade level in third and fourth grade, at grade level in fifth grade, and

Table 6.1. Iowa Tests of Basic Skills for Kalona, Iowa, Amish Students

Grade	*01–02*	*02–03*	*03–04*	*04–05*
3	3.3	3.2	3.5	3.3
4	4.1	4.5	4.2	4.6
5	5.4	5.7	5.6	5.1
6	6.8	6.7	7.0	6.4
7	7.2	7.9	7.5	8.2
8	9.1	8.7	8.6	8.9

above grade level in grades six through eight as compared to a national sample of students in the United States.

Taken together, these four studies of academic achievement indicate that upper grade Amish parochial students score at or above grade level in key subjects such as reading and arithmetic.

AMISH CHILDREN IN PUBLIC SCHOOLS

Chapter 1 documented the rapid rise of the Amish parochial school movement. However, as of 2005, there were still some Amish children who attended public schools. There are three general patterns associated with Amish pupils attending public schools. The first pattern is exhibited in Geauga County, Ohio, where many Amish children attend public school kindergarten prior to enrolling in an Amish parochial school in first grade. The second prevalent pattern is the enrollment of Amish children in public school special-education programs, and this occurs in many different states and communities. The third common pattern is for public school officials to work closely with Amish parents to operate public schools for Amish pupils. This third pattern is in evidence in Illinois, Indiana, Iowa, Maryland, and Ohio.

In the large Amish community near Arthur, Illinois, about 33% of its youth are still attending public school until the eighth grade (The Illinois Amish Interpretive Center, 2005). Currently, public school staff work in conjunction with Amish elders and parents to provide an appropriate curriculum for the pupils. This pattern of cooperation began in the 1960s, when small one-room schools were being closed in the area (Miller, 1980). Because of school consolidation in the area three Amish parochial schools were opened in the area between 1966 and 1968. Because of the long-standing history of cooperation between the Amish and their English neighbors, the local public school district worked with the Amish to create two public schools for Amish pupils in 1968. The two schools were named North Center and Otto Center.

A slightly different pattern is evident in Iowa, where the Wapsie Valley and Jesup school districts operate seven one-room schools for Amish pupils. Again, the public school officials work with Amish elders on curriculum issues. An interview with one of the teachers at these schools indicated that the thing she liked best about working with the Amish pupils was "watching my children grow." She stated that she had "complete support by the parents." She further noted that "All of the students that graduated from this school have employment. Some of my children have become teachers in Amish schools."

Honeyville Elementary School in LaGrange County, Indiana, is a public elementary school that serves primarily Amish students (Haroff, 2004). As of

1997 only 1 of the 120 students in attendance at the school was not Amish. Amish parents actively support the school through a variety of community events and fundraisers throughout the year.

Swann Meadow School in Garrett County in western Maryland is a four-room public school that serves the Amish students in the area. The current Swan Meadow School was built using public funds and labor donated by the Amish parents. The school has a spacious playground, and one will often see two softball games being played by the pupils at recess.

The largest Amish settlement in the world is centered in Holmes County, Ohio, and some students in this community attend public school until the eighth grade. In the East Holmes School District there are seven public schools that are composed of mostly Amish students. Mykrantz (1994) reported on the detailed vocational program for seventh- and eighth-grade pupils at one of these schools. The program takes place in a remodeled brick one-room school. The eighth-grade course of study includes the study of welding, woodworking, and small-engine repair.

Amish pupils attending public school on occasion receive state and national recognition. For example, in 1999 Chestnut Ridge School, one of the seven schools in the East Holmes School District that serves primarily Amish children, received state recognition as the highest-ranking high-poverty school in Ohio (Troy, 2000). The school attained a 100% pass rate on the mathematics exam and a 97% pass rate on the reading exam. The June 21 edition of the *Budget* reported that Katie Hochstetler, an eighth grader at the same school, was a finalist in the National Spelling Bee held in Washington, D.C., that month.

7

Teaching Strategies and Styles

> If education is judged by its achievements, the Amish may have one of the most effective instructional systems in the world today.
>
> —Wittmer, 2001

In this chapter we will discuss the typical teaching strategies employed in an Amish parochial school. The teaching methods utilized are key components in the building and nurturing of literacy, responsibility, and community. In the beginning of the chapter we will explore typical classroom instruction. After this, several sample vignettes of classroom instruction in schools in several states will be presented. These vignettes are noted because they are very characteristic of the teaching that occurs each day at an Amish school in the United States and Canada. In addition, these vignettes have been picked because they are illustrative of the many types of schools.

Amish teachers and parents view school not only as a place to learn basic academic skills but also as a place to learn to value work. Thus, teachers and parents view school as the work of children. This is best exemplified in the words of Hostetler and Huntington (1992, p. 198), who stated, "Learning is not disguised as a game. The children are taught that it is work." While games that focus on the learning of academic skills may be prevalent in other schools, the Amish usually reserve games for recess time. In addition, academic competition between students is not encouraged. Research by Ammon (1994) and Hostetler and Huntington (1992) found little or no academic competition between individual students at Amish schools. Competition that does occur is used to facilitate the learning of the entire school community. For example, teachers may encourage a school to improve the class average in spelling rather than having a contest to see who can earn the highest grade to receive some special reward. Amish teachers do use positive reinforcement, but this is usually limited to small stickers, stars, pencils, or candy that all students receive in a matter-of-fact way for improved performance.

In many Amish schools older pupils assist younger students at various points throughout the day. *The Standards of the Old Order Amish and Old Order Mennonite Parochial and Vocational Schools of Pennsylvania* state, "Pupils of the eighth and seventh grades who have good marks can be of great help to the teacher by assisting with the lower grades or other work which they are capable of doing. . . . It may also serve as experience for future teachers" (1969, pp. 25–26).

Amish schools are quiet places and in some cases one gets the sense that they are a retreat from the industrialized world. During instructional times Amish schools are quiet places for several reasons; first, in general, teachers and students use quiet voices. If one is seated at the back of the classroom it is often very difficult to hear the discussion at the front of the classroom. In fact, if visitors are present the teacher will usually ask children to speak louder. Second, there are short periods throughout the day when all students will be studying and a teacher may be assisting individual pupils with class work. At these times the classroom almost seems like a library at a monastery. Another reason that Amish schools are quiet is because they do not have any electronic devices. Thus there will be no noise from fans, heating or cooling systems, computers, or even fluorescent light fixtures. Finally, Amish schools are quiet places because they are located in rural areas. One thus does not have all of the noises associated with car and truck traffic, large factories, or large farm machinery in the fields.

The quietness of an Amish school in the Lancaster, Pennsylvania, area prompted Fishman (1988, p. 75) to write, "The most noticeable feature on first entering Meadow Brook, however, was none of the above for me, nor was it the twenty-some children usually present. Even when a lesson was in progress and even after months of observation, the feature most invariably striking was the silence."

The quiet in schools is also associated with the fact that Amish teachers speak less and more softly than their counterparts in other types of schools. Later in this chapter, as we explore the teaching strategies and styles employed in Amish schools, we will note that there are many lessons in which the teacher is not speaking a great deal. This is exemplified by other research in Pennsylvania. In a study of classroom verbal interaction in an Amish school as compared to public schools in central Pennsylvania, Payne (1970) found significant differences on several verbal-interaction variables. In terms of percentage of teacher talk in the classroom only about 35% of the verbal interaction in an Amish classroom was by the teacher, whereas public school teachers in the sample talked about 60% of the time. In addition, there was little or no praise by the teacher in Amish schools, while the public schools had significantly more teacher praise.

AN OVERVIEW OF TEACHING

The school day at most Amish schools begins on the playground, as many children arrive early to engage in variety of games of tag or softball if the weather permits, and teachers can often been seen playing with the students. Teachers make it a point to greet each and every student by name each morning, and the students will greet the teacher as well. In keeping with Amish tradition the students refer to the teacher by her first name. In Amish society adults are never referred to as Mr. Miller or Mrs. Yoder, but by their first names. The school day usually begins at 8:00 or 8:30, and the teacher will ring the bell to announce that school is about to start. Students get to their assigned seats quickly and in an orderly manner. School begins with the taking of attendance. The students and teacher will then say the Lord's Prayer in English or German. Next, the teacher will read either a chapter from the Bible or a Bible story from a book such as *Egermeyer's Bible Story Book*. The teacher may ask a few comprehension questions about the story; however, the teacher will not do any religious teaching. In Amish society religious teaching is strictly the responsibility of the church and the home. The children will then sing religious songs in English or German, and most schools will have song books or notebooks for the students. Students are usually allowed to pick the songs they want to sing. Once singing concludes, the students will quickly get to their seats and start their work for the day without any direction from the teacher. Work for each grade will be written on the chalkboard. Scholars know what is expected of them, and they know each is responsible for getting his or her own work done completely and accurately. The teacher expects accuracy and promptness, but completing assignments quickly is not encouraged.

Arithmetic and reading are usually the subjects taught in the morning, with the teacher usually spending about 10–15 minutes with each grade. Teachers will usually take more time with first graders, especially at the beginning of the school term. Most schools will have about 90 minutes of instructional time before the first recess. If the teacher has students in eight grades, this will allow her about 10 minutes for each grade. Teachers in two-teacher schools will have more time to spend with each group; however, these schools usually have more students, so each grade will have more students. Classes are held in the front of the room, and in most cases students will be seated around a table with the teacher while they are engaged in their lesson. In other cases scholars will stand at the front of the room for their lessons. Teachers will utilize the chalkboard as needed. While the teacher is conducting the lesson, students in other grades are engaged in their daily written work and in preparation for their next class with the teacher. After a break for recess the students will come back to class for another 75–90 minutes of class and continue work on arithmetic, reading, vocabulary, or language. After an hour break for lunch and recess, the scholars return for the afternoon session. The first afternoon session is about 90 minutes in length, and the second afternoon session is about 45 minutes in length. Teachers will usually begin the first afternoon session by reading a chapter or two from a book to the students. Then it is back to their lessons. The afternoon will be used to catch up on any unfinished class lessons from the morning. The teacher will then delve into new topics with each grade level. Social studies (geography and history), health, vocabulary, spelling, English, and German are common subjects for the two afternoon sessions. At many schools the first part of the afternoon recess is reserved for cleaning the school, and once this is accomplished pupils will be allowed to go out and play.

During the day students are doing a variety of written work that will usually coincide with their studies in each subject. Teachers use a variety of methods to correct all this work, including checking the work in class and checking the work after school. Most teachers use a little of both of these methods, depending on the lesson, the length of the assignment, and the ability of the students. Students are graded on a percentage-correct basis and receive report cards every six weeks. The report card grade is based on student daily work and any tests given during the marking period. In some areas the report card has a place to indicate how often the parents have visited the school during that grading period. Students receive grades in most classes each day, and the grades reflect the knowledge demonstrated and are not modified for effort. Students' grades on report cards are a percentage correct, not letter grades such as A, B, or C. Report cards are taken home and shared with the parents. The cards are then signed by the parents and returned to the school the next day.

There is little time for class discussions at an Amish school. Teachers teach a new concept, the students practice the skill, the work is corrected, and the students move to a new topic. A sense of community is established because competition between students does not occur and because older students help younger students. Responsibility for one's own learning is modeled by the older students for the younger students. Because literacy in reading and arithmetic is essential to Amish life as an adult, teachers give students plenty of instruction and practice in these core subjects.

To accomplish everything an Amish teacher does each day requires one to be very organized. An Amish teacher at a one-teacher school must be able to juggle lessons for eight grades across at least six subjects each day. This requires clear focus and attention to the time spent with each grade and class.

When asked about how she stays so organized, a teacher in northern Indiana stated, "Well I went to a one-room school, so that helps, careful planning, and you also get better over time." A teacher in Illinois stated, "You must plan your year carefully in August (before school starts) so that you plan the correct amount of time for each subject each week."

TYPICAL CLASS SESSIONS

A similar pattern of instruction is followed for each subject, and the first graders soon learn this pattern of instruction. Because of this teachers spend very little time in giving directions to the class. For example, a typical reading lesson will be the oral reading of a story, with students taking turns reading one paragraph at a time (sometimes referred to by public school teachers as "round robin reading"). After one student finishes reading a paragraph the next student begins with no prompting from the teacher. The teacher will speak if a child needs assistance or if he or she makes a mistake while reading. Teachers do take a turn reading a paragraph of the story. After the story the teacher may have several comprehension questions and then will quickly assign a follow-up activity in the workbook or review new vocabulary for the next lesson.

A typical lesson in arithmetic usually involves checking the assignment and then moving to the next topic. The teacher will give an example of how to do the problem. Students will then practice the problem on the board or on a sheet of paper. The teacher will utilize objects and drawings so that students can see the arithmetic principle for new concepts. Students are dismissed once the teacher has a good idea that each child knows how to successfully work the problems.

While lessons are being conducted, students in other grades are busy on their assigned work. Students who have questions will raise their hands and wait patiently until the teacher has time to address their question. Sometimes the teacher will have the students bring their work to her, and other times the teacher will go to the student's desk. In other cases the teacher will ask an older student to assist the younger student. In some instances the students will lower their hand and try to figure out the information or problem themselves.

In the remaining pages of this chapter the reader will be taken on a tour of several classrooms across the United States. This tour will focus on the teaching strategies that are employed by the teachers and will focus on the verbal interaction in the classroom and the assignments students are completing. In keeping with my agreements with Amish teachers and elders, the actual names of the schools, students, or teachers will not be used. Instead, I will use typical Amish names. Types of schools visited, state, and subject observed are outlined in table 7.1.

Table 7.1. Types of School Visited, State, and Subjects Observed

One-room, three-teacher school with one teacher assigned to special education	Indiana	Opening exercises,* reading, & arithmetic
Two-room, two-teacher school	North Carolina	English, reading, recess & lunch
One-room, one-teacher school	Delaware	English, spelling, & reading
Two-room, two-teacher school	Illinois	Opening exercises, reading, & arithmetic
Two-room, two-teacher school with special-education annex	Illinois	Reading & arithmetic
One-room, two-teacher school	Indiana	English, German, & geography
One-room, two-teacher school	Ohio	Arithmetic & spelling
One-room, one-teacher school	Pennsylvania	Phonics, geography, & singing

*Opening exercises include attendance, Lord's Prayer, Bible reading, and singing.

A COLD AND SNOWY DAY IN INDIANA

Our first stop on the tour will be in a school in the Elkhart/LaGrange community of Indiana in February of 2005. It was a Monday morning, very cold with a driving snow. The school has white siding and white windows and doors. The school sits just north of a county road and has a fence around the schoolyard. The schoolyard has a set of swings, a softball backstop, a shed for horses, and a large rail for hitching horses. This school is a classic example of a one-room school with three teachers. Two teachers teach in the large main room, and the special-education teacher instructs students in the basement.

Although public schools in the area were closed due to the heavy snowfall, the Amish schools were open. I arrived at the school at about 7:00 a.m. and found that the three teachers had been there at least 45 minutes preparing their lessons for the day. The school was nice and warm, despite the cold conditions outside. The school was clean, with desks aligned in rows facing the front of the class. The teachers' desks were placed in the front of the room, and a table with chairs was beside each desk. Banks of windows on the west and east sides of the school provided plenty of light, even on cloudy days. A large chalkboard ran across the length of the front room.

Students are allowed to arrive no earlier than 8:00 and may go out to play once they put their lunch boxes and school materials in the shelves provided in the basement. Names used in the following scene are not the real names of either the teachers or the students.

By 8:00 it was still snowing pretty hard, and the first scholar arrived for the day. Before entering the anteroom of the school he shook the snow from his black hat and coat. Each teacher said, "Good morning, Henry," and Henry replied, "Good morning." He put his things away and went out to the playground. By 8:10, Lydia, Mary, Joe, and Sam had arrived, and again the teachers greeted all of them by name. The students put their things away and then proceeded outside to play. At this point one of the teachers put on her wrap and went out to play as well. They were playing a tag game. In short order, all of the remaining 30 students at the school arrived, and every child was greeted in the manner stated previously. Most of the scholars walked to school, while some rode in covered horse-drawn buggies.

The lead teacher rang the bell at 8:30, and scholars moved to their seats quickly even though they each had to remove boots, coats/shawls, and hats or bonnets. The lead teacher took attendance for the day and all were present. They then recited the Lord's Prayer in German. Next, the students rearranged themselves and sat two to a seat to sing morning songs. The teacher lets students select the songs from the songbook. The first selected was "I'll Be Listening," and the second selected was "Between Here and Sunset."

A school board member who stopped by the school for a water sample stayed for the opening of the day and provided a short message for the students. The message for the students was how one builds a "character résumé." He emphasized that how one conducts his or her life is noticed by others and is more important than the résumé on paper. This lesson was conducted in Pennsylvania Dutch.

Once this message was completed everyone got to work immediately without a word of direction from any of the teachers present. Two students returned corrected notebooks and workbooks to their classmates. Rebecca (teacher of grades 3, 5, 7, and 8) has a desk and a teaching table at the right front of the classroom, and Anna (teacher of grades 1, 2, and 4) has a desk and teaching table at the left front of the classroom. This year the school has no sixth-grade students. It should be noted that both students and teachers used very soft voices while speaking, so if visitors were seated in the back of the room they needed to listen very attentively.

The morning academic teaching began when Anna asked the fourth graders to come up for reading while Rebecca asked the third graders to come up for reading. The fourth graders answered comprehension questions related to their assigned story. The children then proceeded to read the story out loud, with each child reading a paragraph at a time. They did this until they had finished the story. Anna provided no directions during this time. Anna then reviewed vocabulary for the next story in their book and the workbook assignment; the students returned to their desks at 9:06. During this time some first graders went to upper-grade students for assistance if they had a question or needed help. At 9:08 Anna began the first-grade arithmetic class. The students recited the answers on their workbook pages—for example, "8 minus 8 is 0." Each child had at least four chances to recite. Then the teacher taught the students the ones, tens, and hundreds places and how to correctly pronounce the numbers—for example, "two hundred sixty-one." Then each child had a chance to read one of the numbers in the book. The students then counted by tens as a group. Next the teacher had this problem on the board: 25 _____ ______ 100. Students raised their hands if they knew the number that fills in one of the blanks. One student stated 60 and the teacher said, "No, not quite." She then picked another student, who provided the correct answer. This group was finished at 9:16, and then it was time for second-grade arithmetic. During this time Anna reviewed liquid measurement (cups, pints, quarts, and gallons) with the students. She then reviewed the assignment for the day and after stating, "Any questions on this page?" sent the students back to their desks. At 9:23 the teacher worked with the first graders, who remained in their desks as a group. She reviewed the words "prince," "wish," "pull," and "they." Anna then gave the first graders individual help at their desks while they completed their workbook page. At 9:30 the teacher wrote the following on the blackboard: "Long vowel words" and "Short vowel words." Anna asked the first graders to come to the front of the room, and she stated, "Can anyone read what this says?" The students then raised their hands to respond, and she picked one student to answer. After this she put the word "mop" on the board and asked, "What vowel sound does this word have?"

One scholar stated, "Short o."

"Correct," said Anna. "What do I do before adding 'ing'?"

"One student stated, "Double the p."

"Correct," said Anna. She then wrote "mopping" on the board and had the students recite it together. She continued in this manner, reviewing about ten words and adding "er," "ed," or "ing." "OK, go get your reading books," directed Anna. The students quickly retrieved their books and sat at the teaching table. They then read the story in round robin fashion, and she interspersed a few comprehension questions after some paragraphs. After each answer she said, "Good, very good." All of the children were able to answer her questions. After finishing the story she said, "Open your workbooks. Let's say these words." At one point the children said, "kitty," and the teacher said, "Not kitty."

The children immediately replied, "Kitten." Later, when they got to the word "hear," she stated, "Do you see the difference between the words 'her' and 'hear'?"

The students nodded yes.

"Good, let's stop here," said a smiling Anna. Students then went back to their seats and circled the words in their workbook page, as the teacher stated the word and a sentence to illustrate the word. For example, the teacher stated, "Number 1, 'ready': He has to be ready." After a pause to allow the students to work Anna stated, "Number 2, 'your': Your coat is on the floor." At 10:00 she stated, "Put your books in your desk. We will finish after recess."

During the time that Anna has been teaching, Rebecca has been teaching as well. After the conclusion of third-grade reading and a break to assist one student, she began fifth-grade vocabulary at the teaching table at about 9:00. She reviewed the answers with the children as they corrected each other's workbooks. At 9:04 the teacher asked for the number wrong, and she gave the percentage correct and recorded this in her grade book for each child. The teacher recorded the grades without making any statements about the grades. At 9:05 she reviewed new words with the students. She stated the word, and the scholars then repeated the new word. At 9:07 it was time for seventh- and eighth-grade reading. They came to the teaching table and proceeded to read the story out loud, with each student in turn reading a paragraph. The students did this with no direction from the teacher. They finished reading the story by 9:18, and she showed them what to do on the next workbook page. This group was soon finished, and the teacher then did some work at her desk before assisting students in the schoolroom with questions.

At 9:35 it was time for third-grade arithmetic. The students sat at the teaching table, exchanged workbooks, and then corrected the notebooks as the teacher stated the answers to each question. (Each teaching table had a small can with a supply of red pens for correcting work.) By 9:41 the arithmetic class was finished, and students went back to their desks. At 9:45 students in eighth grade came to the teaching table with their arithmetic notebooks and textbooks. Students exchanged notebooks to be graded. Next, Rebecca stated the answer to each question. Students then tallied the number wrong, and the teacher recorded grades for each student after determining the percentage correct. Rebecca then read the directions for the next topic—parallel lines and parallelograms. By 9:50 all of the eighth graders had returned to their seats. The teacher then reminded the third graders to complete their work. Just before 10:00 one student took the trash can around so that the scholars could throw away any trash. Rebecca then dismissed rows for recess one at a time. Students proceeded in a swift, orderly manner to the basement to put on their winter garments and boots before heading for the snow-covered playground. All of the teachers in the school soon joined them for a game of prisoner's base.

It should be noted that during this 90 minutes of class time all the students were engaged with their assignments. These assignments included workbook pages, penmanship exercises, reading the next story in their reader, or assisting younger students as needed. On occasion it would be noted that a student at his or her seat might take a break to listen to the reading or recitation of the students at the teaching tables in the front of the classroom. The schoolroom was in fact very quiet, and since it was very snowy there were few automobiles or trucks driving past the school. On occasion a gust of wind or the clip-clop of horses' hooves hitting the pavement as a buggy proceeded past the school would interrupt the quiet.

DELAWARE

We will now travel to the East Coast and the community of Dover, Delaware. This school is a classic example of a one-room, one-teacher school, and the lessons recounted here occurred in February of 2005. The school had white clapboard siding, white doors, and windows trimmed in white. It was a cold, cloudy day, and the ground was covered with five inches of snow. The school sits atop a slight rise and is located near an intersection of two blacktop roads. The classroom had a large chalkboard across the front of the room, and student desks were arranged in rows facing the front.

All of the children who attend the school were present on the day of the observation, which began just before first recess. The second graders were standing around a table in the front of the room opposite the teacher's desk. They were reviewing contractions at the same time that Elam, the teacher, was giving spelling words to the first graders to write on their papers. He would state a spelling word to the first graders and then teach the second graders and so forth. Two classes were thus going on at one time. All of the other students were engaged in individual work at their desks. Right before recess, Elam chose a student to carry around the trash can to collect unwanted paper from the students. Since it was snowy outside, Elam allowed students to play inside or go out for recess. The students who stayed inside talked and partook of a morning snack. Recess was about 15 minutes, and Elam rang the bell to signal the end of recess. Once the bell rang, the students quickly reassembled and began their schoolwork anew.

The teacher moved to the third-grade seating area and stated, "Nouns are a person, place, or thing, while verbs are doing words." He then began to ask questions related to the lesson on nouns and verbs; he asked a question, and they would answer without raising hands. Sometimes he would address a question to a single student. After about ten minutes the lesson was over, and fourth-grade English began. Elam read the textbook and explained what the children were to learn and do. This lesson was about six minutes in length. Fifth-grade English was next, and he reviewed how to divide words into syllables, place the accent mark, and arrange words in alphabetical order. The students found this lesson humorous because he would mispronounce some of the well-known words by accenting the incorrect syllable. The students immediately picked up on this and would raise their hands to say the word correctly.

Next was second-grade reading, and the children picked up their books, walked to the front of the room, and stood facing the class. First Elam asked comprehension questions related to the story. The students found this lesson humorous as well. For example, he would say, "Why did Rachel put the flowers on the kitchen table? Were they going to eat them?"

The scholars laughed and said, "No, they are to look at." The children then read the story one paragraph at a time. At the same time that he was listening to the second graders read, Elam helped some seventh and eighth graders with their geography work. One of the geography assignments for the day was to find selected towns or cities along interstate highways. Towns they had to find included Stuarts Draft, Va., and Elkin, N.C. As the second graders were reading he asked them to read louder one time, and they immediately responded to this request. At the end of second-grade reading he asked questions that assessed their comprehension of the story, and he did this until all children had a chance to answer at least one question.

First-grade reading was next, and the scholars took their *Pathway Readers* and went to the front of the room and stood. After answering several comprehension questions, the scholars read the story out loud in typical Amish-school fashion. Several students struggled with some of the more difficult words, and Elam helped them in a kind manner. Elam took much more time with first graders than with any other grade. He also posted new vocabulary on the blackboard. During the entire time of the observation at this school the scholars were actively engaged in their work, and those that had finished would color, read, or listen to other lessons.

NORTH CAROLINA

We will now visit a typical example of a two-room, two-teacher school. The school is located in North Carolina and was visited in January of 2005. The school was recently built and has white vinyl siding, white doors, and windows with white trim. The windows are on the east and west sides of the school. Each classroom had desks placed in rows facing the front of the classroom. On the day of the observation it was a sunny, cold, and windy day with temperatures in the low 30s most of the day. There were eleven students in each class at this school, and all were present on this date. This school has lots of visitors, as evidenced by the guest register that I signed for both teachers. I arrived at the school at 11:00 and went to the class of the teacher for grades 3–7 (the school had no eighth graders). The third-grade English class had just commenced, and the three scholars were seated at the teaching table at the front of the room. The topic for the day was nouns, and Ada, the teacher, read the content of the lesson to the students. When she finished the reading, Ada had the students identify nouns in sentences in their books. After giving them their assignment, she fielded questions from the students before sending them back to their desks at 11:13. For the next five minutes Ada gave individual help to each student as needed. During this time she remarked to one student, "Oh, that is good." At about 11:20 Ada stated, "Fifth-grade reading," and the four scholars immediately gathered their books and sat at the teaching table. Ada asked, "Did you study your story?"

They all stated, "Yes."

Ada then said, "Let's read the story," and looked at the first child to her left. The students read the story, with each child in succession reading one paragraph at a time until they had completed the story. Ada only interrupted the reading if a child mispronounced a word, which was rare. Reading class was completed at 11:30.

The students sang their blessing and then were dismissed to retrieve their lunches. After washing up they came back to the room to eat. The children talked together as they ate, with the main topics of conversation being bears in the mountains and an upcoming train trip for two of the children. After the fifteen-minute lunch the children went out for recess. All the children and the teachers played grade base (a tag game) for about 45 minutes. The children really enjoyed this game and by the end of recess were nice and warm from all the running, despite the cold temperatures.

After recess I visited the first–fourth grade classroom. There were eleven students in this class as well. It should be noted that this school had six third graders, and these students were divided between the two classes. Emma, the teacher, read one chapter from a nature storybook to the class after recess, and the children were very attentive. After completing the chapter, Emma stated, "Second-grade spelling." The second graders got out their spelling books and proceeded to the front of the room. They then practiced reciting the spelling words with the teacher while seated at the teaching table. While this was going on the other students were engaged in their work for the day, reading a book, or coloring. Spelling class was finished in ten minutes, and then Emma stated, "Third-grade reading." The scholars swiftly gathered their books and headed to the teaching table. The students and teacher took turns reading out loud one paragraph at a time. At the same time students at their desks who needed help would raise their hands and wait for the teacher. Emma would help them as the reading continued, but only during the reading of a long paragraph. The third-grade reading class lasted about 15 minutes, and then it was time for first-grade reading. This short class was an extension of the morning class. The three children in the class were learning to identify nouns and proper nouns. If the children did not know a word they used phonics to sound it out, and most would eventually decode the word in this manner. If they got stuck with the word, the teacher would help them pronounce the word phonetically. Fourth-grade reading was the last class of the day, and the students read the story out loud, with each child reading a paragraph. During this lesson, the teacher gave the first graders flash cards so that they could practice the addition facts. While the lesson was going on at the teaching table, students who had finished an assignment would place their completed workbook or paper on the appropriate pile. Students who had finished their work for the day would then read a book, color, study their reading lesson, or listen to the other class in session at the front of the room. Students at this school like to color, and they use small packs of crayons and colored pencils. While I was observing, one of the first graders was really enjoying coloring a picture of a robin in her coloring book.

An interesting note about this visit was that one of the teachers observed was in fact a substitute teacher for the day. If she had not told me this at the end of the day I would not have known because the class was so well organized, she worked well with the students, and she knew all of the students.

ILLINOIS

School One

The next stop on our tour will be at a school near Arthur, Illinois, in the winter of 2005. It was a cool morning, but by the afternoon it was a balmy 60 degrees and mostly sunny. The school visited is a typical example of a two-room school with two teachers and with an annex to the school specifically designed and built for special education. The annex was connected to the school building by a rather large hallway that served as a place to store materials and supplies. Interestingly, the room also housed a very small copy machine that was operated by electricity from an automobile battery.

Before school the students and teachers were outside playing tag games. At 8:15 the teacher rang the bell, and the students quickly came in and sat in their assigned seats. At this school each child is greeted by name upon entrance into the building. For example, the teacher says, "Good morning, Titus," and Titus will reply, "Good morning, Miriam." I first visited the fifth–eighth grade classroom. After the teacher took attendance the students filed to the front of the class for singing. The students picked the songs they would sing from a booklet titled "*Ninety-eight Selected Songs.*" They sang "Lift Your Glad Voice," "Kneel Down by the Side," and "Sailing On." The students then said the Lord's Prayer. Rachel, the teacher, read the verse for the day from a German Bible. After this she read two Bible stories in English to the students. After each story she had one or two comprehension questions about the story. The students raised their hands to answer the questions. After the Bible stories were completed the students immediately began their work for the day, with no direction given by the teacher. As in all Amish schools, the assignments for each grade were posted on the blackboard. At 8:40 Rachel stated, "Seventh-grade vocabulary," and the seventh-grade pupils immediately brought their materials to the teaching table at the front of the room. The students then checked their vocabulary assignment while Rachel stated the answers. The pupils checked their work with red pens. After this Rachel recorded the percentage correct for each student in her grade book. Rachel then explained the next assignment. I left the room at 8:50 and went to the first–fourth grade classroom, which was on the east side of the building.

When I arrived, Miriam, the teacher, was working with the first-grade students at the teaching table. Miriam was explaining the concept to be learned and practiced in the reading workbook. The concept for today was correct word order. The students had to read a series of words and decide if they were in correct order to make a sensible sentence. Miriam picked a student to read the top portion of the page. After he successfully read the directions she stated, "Let's read number one together." After they read the words she asked, "Is this correct?"

Most of the students raised their hands to answer. Miriam picked Sam and he said, "No, the correct order is . . ." After this, each first grader had a chance to do one of the questions on the page. After this portion of the lesson was completed, Miriam stated, "Let's read about a farm dog." The scholars then opened their reading books to the story, and each read a paragraph out loud in turn. Miriam only interrupted the reading if a student made a mistake, which was rare during this lesson. This entire reading lesson was about 15 minutes in length, and at 9:05 the students returned to their desks. Miriam then stated, "Third-grade arithmetic." The third graders stood by their desks. Miriam then said, "Pass," and the students walked to the teaching table. Without any prompting by Miriam the scholars opened their workbooks. Miriam then stated the answers to the workbook pages, and the students corrected their work using red pens. After the teacher addressed any questions by the students, each student stated the number wrong, and the teacher then told them the percentage correct. These grades were then recorded by the teacher. Next, the teacher retrieved the multiplication fact cards and presented them one at a time to each pupil. If a pupil did not know the answer immediately or if he or she stated the wrong answer, the teacher had him or her recite the entire fact three times before moving to the next student. After each child had several chances, Miriam put the cards away and reminded the students to continue studying the multiplication facts. She then pulled out another pack of flash cards that were teacher made. These cards practiced key arithmetic concepts the students needed to memorize. For example, one card stated, " _____ hours in a day," another read, "____ days in a year," another read, "____ minutes in an hour," and finally one card read, "____ pounds in a ton." Miriam used the same recitation strategy with these facts as with the multiplication cards. Miriam then dismissed the third graders. This entire lesson was about 11 minutes in length.

Some further notes about this room are in order. Miriam had written the names of eight students on the board, and behind each name was a reminder of the work to be completed or redone, for example, "Jonah—phonics." Because of the plentiful windows, the room was very bright. Like most Amish schools the classroom was very quiet, with all of the scholars at their seats engaged in their work while the teacher was working with the students at the teaching table. Assignments for each subject and grade were posted on the chalkboard in the fashion indicated below.

Reading	Phonics
1 26–27	1 100–102
	2 116–117
German	3 105–106
2 46–48	
	SS*
Arith*	4 37–40
3 test	
4 L 120	
1 108–110	
2 81–83	
Reading	
3 38–39	
4 67–68	

*Arith is an abbreviation the teacher uses for arithmetic
*SS is an abbreviation the teacher uses for social studies

School Two

Upon arrival at this school on a cool day in winter of 2005, I first visited the special-education classroom that was held in the annex connected by a short hall to the main school building. The annex was a small-scale version of a one-room school and was well furnished. A short description of the teaching in this annex is found in chapter 9.

The upper-grades classroom for this school was visited the same day. The teacher for this class, Susan, had about 10 years of teaching experience, and the classroom was warm and inviting. I arrived in the classroom just after the pupils had returned from recess, and all of them were busy with their assignments. For the next five minutes the teacher was checking workbooks while the students continued their individual work. Susan then stated, "Eighth-grade reading." The students stood. After Susan nodded, the scholars filed to the teaching table in an orderly fashion. The teacher then stated the answers to the math problems as the students checked their work. A student with a question would occasionally raise his or her hand about a certain answer, and the teacher would explain the problem as needed. This lesson continued for about 15 minutes. Susan then recorded the grades earned by each scholar. All the grades were above 90 on this lesson. Susan then explained the next set of word problems, which required the students to compute the area of several types of figures. After sending the eighth graders back to their seats, Susan helped several students in the class who had their hands raised. As in most Amish schools, when a teacher is helping an individual student it is very difficult to hear the conversation from the back of the room since both the teacher and students use soft voices. In one conversation that occurred not too far from me, the student had a question about changing a fraction into a decimal. After quickly helping each student, Susan recorded some information at her desk and then stated, "Seventh-grade arithmetic." The students stood at their desks with their material before walking to the front of the room for class. Before leaving the room I noted that all students were busily engaged in their morning work and that no students were reading library books or just listening to the lessons going on at the front of the classroom. Below are the assignments that were posted on the chalkboard in this classroom.

Arithmetic	Social Studies	English	German
L 118		L 75 & 76	Quiz 11
L 125	Quiz 15	L 82 & 83	
L 120	Chapter 20		
L 104	Chapter 16		

INDIANA

We will continue our tour of Amish schools as we return to northern Indiana on a cold day in the winter of 2005. We will take an afternoon visit to a one-room school that had two classroom teachers. The school had a full basement and a room above the entrance that was used for special-education instruction. Esther taught grades 1 through 4, and Amanda taught grades 5 through 8. All students were in attendance on the date of the observation. There were 13 students in the upper grades and 12 students in the lower grades.

At 12:30 the scholars returned to the classroom from recess, and the head teacher stated, "We have a visitor from North Carolina." She then had each student stand beside his or her desk and state his or her name, grade, and memory verse. After each student had a chance the students assembled at the front of the classroom and sang one song in English.

At 12:50 the students returned to their desks, and the head teacher moved the curtain to separate the front quarter of the classroom. Esther called the first graders to the front table for reading class, and Amanda called the seventh and eighth graders to the front for history.

We will focus on the lower grades first and then describe the instructional events of the upper-grade students. The first graders took turns reading their story for the day, and after a few questions about the story the teacher sent the students back to their desks at 12:50. Esther then stated, "Second-grade English." The students assembled at the front table, and the teacher asked, "What is a noun?" "After listening to several answers, Esther taught the students about nouns in sentences. The three second graders then went to the blackboard and practiced writing complete sentences under the watchful direction of the teacher. During second-grade English, the third and fourth graders who had completed their work quizzed the first graders on their addition facts. At 1:10 the third graders had a typical reading lesson, which was followed by a typical reading lesson for the fourth grade. At 1:30 Esther stated the spelling words for the week, and the first graders wrote them on the chalkboard.

We will now return to the upper-grade students, who had history and geography lessons prior to the afternoon recess. At 12:50 Amanda discussed the geography assignment for the seventh- and eighth-grade students. She then walked around the class and assisted the students as needed with their arithmetic problems. At 1:10 Amanda stated, "Seventh and eighth grade history," and the seven students took their books and notebooks to the table at the front of the room. Students exchanged notebooks and checked the answers as the teacher recited the answers. All students received a grade of 100 on this assignment on the American Revolution. Amanda then quizzed the students on geography related to this point in history by using a laser pointer to illuminate points on a blank map of North America. Students were permitted to state the answer as quickly as possible and did not have to raise their hands to respond. Amanda smiled and nodded affirmatively when the students quickly knew the answer and would state "Good" once in a while as well.

At 1:30 Amanda stated, "Fifth- and sixth-grade geography. Please bring your textbooks and completed work." The students stood by their desks with their material and proceeded to the table when the teacher said, "Pass." Once the students were assembled at the table they exchanged papers, and the teacher stated the answers to each question while each student checked the paper of a fellow student. Amanda then recorded the grades of each student. The teacher would state the student's name, and he or she would respond with the percentage correct. All students scored above 90 on this assignment. Amanda then gave a review of the required reading and asked two discussion questions. She then quizzed the group on states in the United States by pointing to the state on a large blank map hanging in the room. She would point to the state with a laser pointer, and students would call out the state's name. Next, Amanda used flash cards to quiz the students on state capitals.

At 1:45 Amanda rang the bell, indicating it was time for recess. Two students carried around trash cans so that the scholars could deposit their accumulated trash from the first afternoon session. The scholars were then dismissed to do their afternoon cleaning of the school before heading out to play in the fresh snow. Cleanup tasks included washing the board, sweeping the classroom, sweeping the basement, sweeping the entranceway, cleaning the erasers, watering the plants, and emptying the pencil sharpeners.

Amanda rang the bell indicating the end of recess at 2:00, and the students got back to their seats promptly. After recess the upper grade students had German classes. The fifth and sixth graders were first, and the students took turns reading out loud from the German textbook. Amanda would correct them on pronunciation as needed and stop the reading every once in a while to quiz the students on the passage just read. After about 20 minutes she used German flash cards to quiz the students on common German words and vocabulary for this lesson. At 2:30 the seventh and eighth graders were called to the front for their German lessons, and this class followed the pattern of the fifth- and sixth-grade German lesson.

We now return to the other side of the classroom, where Esther had been teaching the younger graders. Immediately after recess the teacher stated, "First graders, please get out your readers, and stand by a fourth grader to practice your reading. Second graders, get the German flash cards, and practice your alphabet and words." Esther then called the third graders to the front for German instruction. Using the German workbook, each child would pronounce a word and then spell it. At 2:15 Esther called the second graders to the table for German instruction, and the third graders used flash cards to practice their German words in pairs at their desks. At 2:30 the fourth graders had German instruction, and each child had a chance to read several sentences. At 2:40 Esther stated, "Fourth graders, you may get the multiplication and division flash cards to practice your facts."

After recording some information at her desk, Esther stated, "First and second graders, come to the front. The second graders will read words from your reading lesson, and you will write them on the board." At this point, each first grader was paired with a second grader. The second grader would read a word with a long or short vowel sound, and the first grader would write it on the board. After making sure the first grader was correct, the second grader would state the next word. Esther kept an eye on the students at the board while recording information at her desk.

At 2:57 Amanda rang the bell signaling the end of the day. Two students took trash cans around the room to gather any unwanted materials. Prior to dismissing the students the teachers cautioned the children about the slippery road and the fact that cars and trucks would have a hard time stopping on the snow-covered road. Students were then dismissed for the day. Most of the students at this school rode their bikes to school and brushed the snow off them before heading home. Esther was stationed at the side of the road watching for motorized vehicular traffic as the students left the school grounds. After about ten minutes all students had headed home. After we talked a bit, Esther and Amanda started their grading for the day.

OHIO

Our tour will continue with a visit to a one-room, two-teacher school in the Holmes County settlement in Ohio. The school had been a public one-room school for many years. The school had white siding and doors and windows with white trim. This school had about 45 scholars, and all were in attendance on this cold day in February, with snow falling off and on throughout the day. When I arrived the first graders were in arithmetic class at the front table with the teacher. The teacher would show a child a flash card, and he or she would respond as quickly as possible. If a student responded incorrectly the teacher required him or her to restate the problem correctly as she showed the answer. This flash card was put back in the deck of cards so that it would come up again during the lesson. The class spent about 10 minutes on this activity, and each child had numerous chances to participate because the teacher went around the group in a clockwise direction. When the flash card 4 – 3 was presented, one first-grade boy stated 4 – 1 = 3. At this misstatement, everyone had a good laugh. However, it was not a laugh at, but with, the child. The students really enjoyed this, and everyone, including the teacher, had big smiles on their faces. After the laugh, the teacher explained the similarities between each of the subtraction problems, and the class then quickly got back to the addition facts recitation.

At the same time as this arithmetic lesson was conducted on the right side of the classroom, the teacher on the left side of the room was working with the third graders, who were busy writing spelling words on the board as she stated each word. The teacher would check each word, and if everyone was correct they would move to the next word. As the arithmetic and spelling lessons were going on, the other children in the room were busy on a variety of school-related work. These lessons were completed in about 15 minutes. The next lesson for the right side of the room was fifth-grade arithmetic, and on the left side it was time for second-grade reading. During the fifth-grade arithmetic lesson the students checked their work using red pens under the direction of the teacher. Once the checking was completed, the teacher recorded the percentage correct for each student. On the left side of the room the second graders were busy writing word families on the board under the watchful eye of their teacher. The word families included oe, oa, and ow, with words such as hoe, toe, soap, goat, and grow. The teacher would give a sample word, and then the students would write that word and as many other words in the family as they could think of in the allotted time. The students would then read their words to their teacher. Because the practice spelling quiz was to be held after last recess, the other scholars in the room were busying studying their spelling words if they were finished with all other work.

PENNSYLVANIA

Our tour will finish on a partly sunny, cool day in April in a scenic valley in central Pennsylvania. There were 35 students in this one-teacher school, and all were in attendance. This was a small one-room school, typical of most schools in Pennsylvania. The school had white siding, white doors, and windows with white trim. When I arrived the students were just heading out to the playground for afternoon recess for a lively game of tag. At 1:45 the teacher rang the hand bell near an open window to indicate it was time to begin class. Once all the scholars were seated, Hannah, the teacher, stated, "Fifth graders, you should be studying the state capitals. Sixth graders you should study the map of Pennsylvania. First-grade phonics please bring your workbooks." All of the students in the class got busy on their work except one upper-grade boy who seemed to not be engaged in any study at all. The first grade was composed of three children, with one being a special-needs child, and they sat at the teaching table. Hannah taught them the difference between the short-i sound and the long-i sound. She then drilled the students on differentiating the sounds in several words she pronounced for them. Next, Hannah used the board to illustrate the silent e at the end of a word. She then wrote words on the board, and the students had to pick which of the two words had the long-i sound. Once all the scholars mastered the concept Hannah showed them which workbook page they needed to complete, and the class read the words on the page together before going back to their desks to complete their work. This lesson was finished in ten minutes, and Hannah then stated, "Second-grade phonics." The nine second-grade students proceeded to the teaching table, where they were engaged in a lesson about vowel sounds. After five minutes of drill the teacher explained the workbook assignment, previewed any difficult vocabulary on the page, and dismissed the class. Hannah walked around the classroom to address any individual student questions. She then wrote five review questions on the chalkboard relative to the geography assignment for the seventh and eighth graders. Hannah then called a sixth grader to the teaching table. The student proceeded to recite from memory each of the fifty states and capitals in alphabetical order by state. There were three instances where a student was unsure, and Hannah gave her a hint to help her think of the state and/or capital. After this lesson was completed Hannah asked one of the second-grade students to collect the completed workbooks from the second graders. At 2:15 the teacher stated, "Fourth-grade geography." The scholars then assembled at the teaching table, and Hannah asked comprehension questions about the assigned reading. The teacher directed questions to each student, and everyone had an opportunity to answer two questions. About halfway through this lesson, the teacher asked an eighth grader to help one of the first-grade students with his work. The eighth grader went to the first grader's desk and knelt down beside him. The fourth-grade geography lesson was about seven minutes in length, and then it was time for fifth-grade arithmetic. The fifth graders assembled at the front of the room, and the teacher drilled them on the arithmetic problems in their book. This lesson was about ten minutes in length. Hannah then asked the students, "Would you like to sing for our visitor?"

The students responded, "Yes." They then proceeded to put all their work away for the day, picked up any trash on the floor, and assembled at the front of the room. At this school the boys stood on the left side and the girls on the right side. Younger students stood by older students and shared a songbook. The students picked the songs to sing. After the singing, the students prepared to go home. They gathered their belongings, and the older girls helped the younger girls tie their black bonnets before walking home.

REVIEW

As stated at the beginning of this chapter, Amish teaching strategies are similar from school to school. These strategies serve to reinforce the importance of community, humility, responsibility, work, and literacy. Community is reinforced because students are not pitted in competition against one another; it is further reinforced when older students help younger students. This sense of community also reinforces the notion of humility because students are not recognized for excellent achievement. All are expected to learn, but no one in the class is recognized publicly by the teacher as the best reader or the best speller. As one will recall, there were several instances where students graded their papers or those of their classmates, and the teacher then recorded the percentage correct. These percentages are stated, and each child in that grade knows the percentage correct for the other students. At no time did a teacher single out individual students for good work or poor work. In some cases the teacher would remind all of the students to be more careful on their lessons or indicate to the group that they had learned the required information.

Responsibility is reinforced throughout the day. The teacher expects the work to be done in an accurate manner and without wasting time. Teachers do not do work for the students, and students learn early in their school career that the teacher is rarely able to answer questions when she is teaching other grades. Students thus learn to figure things out for themselves—to be responsible for their own learning. School is work, and in Amish society work is to be enjoyed, not avoided. Teachers may have fun activities on special occasions, but such activities are clearly not the norm. As demonstrated in the schools visited in this chapter, there were no games being played, and students were not promised stickers, stars, candy, or other rewards for completing work. However, this is not to say that rewards are never used. Some schools visited did have small charts for spelling or reading to which students would affix small stickers or stars for improved work. These charts were not, however, the center of attention in any of the schools visited. Key wall locations or bulletin boards were usually reserved for aphorisms related to good study habits or a humble spirit.

Finally, literacy in reading and arithmetic is stressed in all Amish schools, for these skills are essential for life in their community as adults. In fact, the Amish know that scholars who master these skills can learn almost anything for themselves.

8

Teacher Education, Preparation, Renewal, and Daily Life

Teachers in Amish schools are expected to teach with their whole life"

—Huntington, 1994

In the previous chapter we discussed in detail the curriculum and teaching strategies utilized by Amish teachers. In this chapter we will extend that discussion to describe various aspects of teacher selection and renewal and examine how these work in tandem to build community, literacy, and responsibility. In the first section of the chapter, we will discuss teaching as a calling and then examine the ways in which individuals prepare themselves for the role of teacher. We will also explore the important role of the summer teachers' meetings for the Amish and Old Order Mennonite communities in North America. We will then investigate the various ways that teachers stay abreast of current discussions about schools and teaching. We will thus discover the importance of the six-week teacher meetings, circle letters, and the Amish publication about teaching, the *Blackboard Bulletin*. After a brief discussion about helpers, substitute teachers, and transportation issues faced by teachers, we will spend a day from the perspective of an Amish teacher.

We will begin with the concept of teaching as a calling as opposed to preparation. As we have discussed previously, the Amish view education after the eighth grade as the process of "learning by doing." Thus, adolescents learn skills while helping their parents with a variety of tasks in the home, on the farm, or in the family business. By the time adolescents reach adulthood, they should have the skills necessary to run a household, farm, or small business. Within the community, school board members are continually aware of young people who seem to have the characteristics of good teachers.

Teachers are chosen on the basis of their Christian character, willingness to teach, and ability to work with students and parents. Hostetler (1993, p. 184) records the role of the teacher in this way: "Amish teachers teach with their whole lives. They must be people who have integrated their lives with that of the community, for every aspect of behavior and personality is related to teaching." Lapp (1991) cites the writings of three parents who reflect the general consensus of what the Amish community believes are qualifications for becoming a good Amish teacher. A good teacher will be educated, modest in dress and speech, able to discipline in a fair and equitable manner, courteous to students and visitors, and Christian in word and deed. *The Standards of the Old Order Amish and Old Order Mennonite Parochial and Vocational Schools of Pennsylvania* (1969) states that the teacher should be of good Christian character, have a good education, be willing to improve one's education, be able to get along with children, be willing to work with parents and the school board, and be able to maintain strict discipline. Fisher and Stahl (1986) further emphasize that the Amish stress "practical learning" rather than book learning, and this applies to teachers as well. The Amish believe that formal education for teachers beyond eighth grade is neither necessary nor appropriate for a successful teacher.

School board members call or select individuals to fill the role of teacher based on the characteristics just mentioned. Those interested in teaching do not obtain formal training in the strict sense of the word, and they do not necessarily actively seek teaching positions. Since the Amish value the community more than the self, a person does not overtly advertise to the school board or the community that he/she would make a great teacher for a particular school. Furthermore, an individual does not market himself by writing a résumé detailing his accomplishments. Harroff (2004) further illustrates the notion of "teaching as a calling" in his study of Amish schools in Indiana. Harroff states that a person does not seek a teaching position; the school board finds the teacher. Before the board makes this call it has a good idea of the prospective teacher's behavior, beliefs, and regard within the community.

While the Amish do not have any formal training requirements for teachers, they do value and understand the importance of having a capable teacher. When discussing this topic, Amish elders invariably state that their community is indeed thankful to have the opportunity to have its own schools. Consequently, they want the scholars to do well, and this leads to the importance of the school board's being careful in its deliberations in selecting a new teacher. They are diligent in choosing individuals who will be able to nurture the young minds they will work with during the next school term. While young people may not have a formal way to become a teacher, they can prepare themselves for this important position in the community by being of good character, being an active member in the local church, obeying all the rules of the local Amish community, and demonstrating some ability as a caregiver for younger children. This last-named skill is usually well developed in most Amish adolescents because the Amish have large families, and older children generally get plenty of experience caring for younger siblings. It should also be noted here that in some cases a potential teacher will serve as a helper for a year before being asked to teach in a subsequent year. In other instances a new teacher will be paired with a veteran teacher in a two-teacher school. In each instance, novice teachers receive assistance from a dedicated teacher. Finally, *The Standards of the Old Order Amish and Old Order Mennonite Parochial and Vocational Schools of Pennsylvania* (1969) encourages the use of capable seventh- and eighth-grade students as assistants to the teacher for two reasons. First, older students are very capable of helping younger students learn the required material. Second, helping the teacher in this manner serves as experience for future teachers.

Amish teachers usually give a school board several months' notice when they decide to give up their positions as teachers. At this point school boards that are thinking ahead will have a general idea of whom they might approach to be the next teacher. The local school board then approaches suitable candidates in the local community. If no candidate accepts the position, the board will search in neighboring communities to find a teacher. It is a very rare instance for a person not of the Amish faith to teach in an Amish school. However, currently there is at least one such teacher in a school in Pennsylvania. She was selected because of her sound moral character, her experiences teaching in a rural school setting, and her ability to communicate in German and English. Historically speaking, Harroff (2004) notes, at least one school in the Elkhart-LaGrange area of Indiana hired a non-Amish teacher for the 1996–97 school term. Another instance of an English teacher in an Amish school is chronicled in the autobiography *Teacher Daisy,* which is about an English woman who was a teacher for several years in an Amish school in Lancaster County, Pennsylvania.

In general, a significant number of teachers come from the ranks of young unmarried Amish females. Harroff's (2004) research in Indiana found that Amish teachers range in age from 18 to 60 with most being single females in their twenites. A common practice in most communities is for unmarried females to teach three to five years prior to marriage. This pattern is similar in some ways to public education, where many new teachers are young females. A key difference is that in public schools more women continue their careers as professional educators.

In newly founded small communities, one of the mothers may take the role of teacher and teach students in her home. This will be done until there are enough scholars in the area to warrant the building of a school. It should be noted that Amish schools have always had some male teachers, as well as individuals with many years of teaching experience. Harroff (2004) found that in Indiana more men are now becoming teachers than in previous years.

TEACHER PREPARATION

Once a teacher is "called," there are numerous things to do to self-prepare for the upcoming school term. These preparations include informal discussion with relatives who are or have been teachers, attending the summer teachers' meeting, attending local teachers' meetings, and reviewing textbooks in one's school, as well as reading books and periodicals about teaching produced by Pathway Publishers.

Amish teachers use methods of teaching that they learned while being in school themselves; anyone who has attended a one- or two-room Amish school will have a very good idea of the instructional patterns, daily schedules, student engagement, and curriculum utilized in most Amish schools. Therefore new teachers use many of the methods that were modeled for them while they were in school themselves, and thus they teach in the same way they were taught. In fact, one who has not had this type of education might be at a distinct disadvantage, as was the case with one such teacher in Illinois. One particular school board member noted that a teacher in his area had attended local public schools for her entire school career and really struggled during her first year of teaching. He was happy to note that through the help of other teachers and the school board members she has now been teaching successfully for several years. School boards usually like to find a new teacher early in the summer so that the teacher can prepare for the school term during the summer months. This is further exemplified by the fact that the 1967 agreement between the Indiana School Committee (Amish) and the Indiana State Department of Public Instruction indicates that school boards should hire teachers who are willing to spend a fair amount of time studying during their summer vacations. Hiring a new teacher early in the summer will also give the new teacher a chance to attend the statewide teachers' meetings that are held for one or more days in the summer at various locations. These meetings cover a broad range of topics and feature speakers from a variety of states. These meetings always draw large crowds because education is important to the community, and anyone from the local Amish community may attend. The teachers' meetings play a very important role in the education of new teachers as well as provide continuing education for experienced teachers.

In addition to the teachers' meetings, some communities will provide several days of training for new teachers. For example in the Kalona, Iowa, settlement there will be several days of meetings for all teachers in the area just before the opening of school as well as several days of additional training for new teachers.

There are also several print resources available to new teachers from Pathway Publishers. Pathway is an Amish publishing company that is based in LaGrange, Indiana, and Aylmer, Ontario. The first publication is *School Bells*

Ringing: A Manual for Amish Teachers and Parents (Byler, 1969). Some of the topics covered in this 81-page book include reading, arithmetic, the first day of school, discipline, first grade, grading, and attendance. The second book is *Tips for Teachers: A Handbook for Amish Teachers.* This book is a compilation of ideas from over 75 Amish teachers and gives very specific examples of how to teach certain skills, gives suggestions for indoor and outdoor games, and provides ideas for successful discipline. The third book, *Handbook for Creative Teaching,* covers a broad range of topics, including lesson plans, helpful tips, study guides, and inspiration. *Games for Everyone* is a compilation of indoor and outdoor games and also provides other educational activities for the school, while another book, *School Teachers Signposts,* offers helpful hints regarding teaching methods, discipline, and advice from current teachers. Teachers who would like to review or improve their content skills may utilize the arithmetic, spelling, and/or English books published by Pathway. Another written resource with some information for teachers and school board members is *Pennsylvania School History 1690–1990* (Lapp, 1991). It contains over 40 pages of articles covering a wide range of topics concerning the parochial school.

SUMMER TEACHERS' MEETINGS

As mentioned previously, one of the important ways that Amish teachers receive continuing education is through the summer teachers' meetings. The meetings are not just for teachers. School board members, writers, community leaders, and interested parents also attend and do so in great numbers. Thus all of the stakeholders involved in Amish education attend the same meetings. This is a very good way for everyone to learn about the roles of all involved and to build the concept of community responsibility for the school. A brief history of these important meetings will be shared because it is illustrative of the community involvement in and the shared responsibility for education.

Summer meetings for teachers were first held in 1955 and in those early years were international meetings. For example, a meeting was held in Alymer, Ontario, in 1958 with about 50 people in attendance. In 1966 the teachers' meeting was held in Lancaster County, Pennsylvania, with over 200 people in attendance, including about 80 teachers. These individuals came from seven different states, as well as Ontario, Canada. The minutes of the meeting (recorded by A. S. Kinsinger) included six pages of questions and answers, with key issues being discipline and advice on teaching ideas.

As the number of Amish schools increased and summer meetings became more popular, it soon became necessary to subdivide the teachers' meeting into regional affairs. Thus, by the summer of 1996 there were several regional teachers' meetings held, with the midwestern one being held August 8 and 9 in Middlebury, Indiana. Topics discussed at the meeting included receiving criticism graciously, supervision on the playground, duties of school board members, working with your co-teacher, and working with special-education students. This meeting also included demonstration classes for teachers at several local schoolhouses. These Midwest regional meetings soon became too large, and Indiana decided to have its own meeting. By 2004 the Indiana meeting was too large, and the Indiana teachers' meeting was further divided into two regions.

Topics covered in the teachers' meetings are very similar in each state or region. One example of the range of topics for these meetings is illustrated by the Illinois School Meeting that was held in August 2004. This meeting included the following topics: the duties and responsibilities of the teacher, tips for teaching the upper grades, tips for beginners, tips for teaching special-needs students, our Amish heritage, how to stimulate a genuine desire to learn, and tips for school board members. At the 2004 Michigan/Ontario teachers' meeting held in Milverton, Ontario, 200 people attended, including approximately 110 teachers. Topics at this meeting included effective discipline, accepting children as they are, renewing our Amish vision, and how to organize a parent/teacher meeting. The summer teachers' meeting in Holmes County, Ohio, in August of 2005 had more than 400 attendees, with a major topic being faith in action. Again, these meetings serve several purposes. They provide a lot of important information about teaching and schools for new and experienced teachers, school board members, and interested adults. The meetings also serve to build the community because they allow all in attendance to learn the needs of each group.

Many Amish teachers will have other jobs for the summer, but most know that the summer vacation period is a good time to learn new things by reading books, traveling, and writing. *The Standards of the Old Order Amish and Old Order Mennonite Parochial and Vocational Schools of Pennsylvania* (1969) note that teachers should devote some of their vacation time to study of the subjects that they teach. The standards further state that the best way to do this is through personal reading since formal education beyond eighth grade is not permitted. Some Amish teachers are well traveled and may use the summer vacation time to take a trip to visit different parts of the United States and Canada. Several teachers with whom I talked mentioned the fact that they spend about two weeks each August in concentrated preparation for the new school term. During this preparation time, teachers often organize their lessons for the entire year. This way they know in advance how much time to allocate for each subject per week. They also determine how far they need to get in each book for each grade level to maintain adequate weekly progress.

TEACHER RENEWAL AND STUDY DURING THE SCHOOL YEAR

Teacher renewal takes many forms once the school year begins. One interesting way that this occurs is through circle letters that go from teacher to teacher in a group of perhaps ten teachers. In the circle letter a person may indicate an interesting activity just completed at her school and then pose a question for the group to consider. The letter is then mailed to the next teacher, who reads the letter and adds information about her school and addresses the question. Teachers may even add a new question as the circle letter makes its rounds. Eventually the letter gets back to the originator, who then is able to read all 10 parts of the circle letter. Circle letters may include teachers from other settlements or states, and they have been a common form of teacher communication and support since the beginning of the Amish school movement. These letters serve to build community and responsibility among the teachers.

Types of Teacher Education and Renewal

- Summer teachers' meetings
- Circle letters
- Six-week teachers' meetings
- *Blackboard Bulletin*
- Books about teaching from Pathway Publishers
- Beginning-of-the-year workshops for new teachers
- Beginning-of-the-year workshops for teachers

Another form of feedback available for the teacher is from the school board. The school board and the teacher meet as often as once per month or sometimes as little as once per term, depending on the community. During this meeting the board and teacher(s) will discuss problems and determine what needs to be discussed (if anything) with all the parents. In many cases, the school board and teacher(s) will then meet with parents later that same evening. Once this general parent meeting finishes, the teacher has time to privately discuss the growth of children with their respective parents. These meetings are generally well attended by both fathers and mothers. Again, the parent meetings build community support for the school, the teacher, and the curriculum.

Teachers from different schools also meet about once every six weeks to discuss issues they are facing. In some communities, like Holmes County, Ohio, any of the members of the school community from the entire settlement may attend. Teachers thus have a forum where they can discuss curriculum, teaching strategies, textbooks, and parent issues in a supportive setting. Teachers find this type of meeting renewing because everyone gets a chance to voice joys and concerns. These meetings serve several purposes, but one major component is that the meetings usually validate the performance of the teacher and the work that he/she is doing with the scholars. These meetings also inspire the teachers because they know that they have a group of interested individuals who can help them with problems. More experienced teachers in the community usually lead these meetings. Fisher and Stahl (1986) note that teachers from all over Lancaster County get together several times a year for meetings designed to encourage and renew younger teachers. As in Ohio, these meetings are coordinated and led by the more experienced teachers.

Harroff (2004) notes that teachers in Indiana meet every six weeks during the school year. These meetings (which usually begin at 7:00 p.m.) are held at school, and the parents from the host school attend the meeting and provide refreshments. In larger communities, hired vans may bring groups of teachers to the meetings. Meetings may include a discussion of important issues and a panel presentation. The meetings end with a time for refreshments when those in attendance renew friendships and ask specific questions of supportive colleagues. Harroff indicates that these meetings are well attended by teachers in the settlement.

Peer observations are also utilized by some Amish teachers as a form of teacher renewal. For example, in the Dover, Delaware, settlement, the teacher may take the upper graders on a field trip to another school for the day. The teacher can observe the teaching methodology of other teachers, and students get a chance to view teaching in a different setting. Many communities in Ohio also utilize peer observations. Sometimes teachers will visit other schools in their home community, and at other times vanloads of teachers from a settlement will visit schools in another settlement. Teachers enjoy the chance to observe their peers and they return to their classroom with a renewed spirit. It is also not uncommon for vanloads of teachers from one state to visit schools in another state. For example, in April of 2005, teachers from Ohio visited several schools that were still in session in central Pennsylvania.

THE *BLACKBOARD BULLETIN*

Print publications such as the *Blackboard Bulletin,* developed and edited by Pathway Publishers, play a major role in the continuing education of teachers. The periodical provides the community with a forum to discuss issues, exchange teaching ideas, share poetry, discuss the role of parents, and provide stories for young readers. Articles are written by members of the Plain community throughout the United States and Canada and often mention the role Christian principles play in the well-run school. While the original audience for the publication was teachers, the periodical's audience has grown to include teachers, school board members, parents, and pupils. Because the periodical plays such an important role in the Plain communities, information about its history will be explored. The *Blackboard Bulletin* illustrates how the community takes the responsibility for providing a written exchange of ideas between teachers, parents, and interested citizens.

The 40th anniversary of the *Blackboard Bulletin* was celebrated in the October 1997 issue. At that time it was the second-oldest Amish publication still in print, with the *Herold der Wahrheit*, founded in 1912, being the oldest. In the 40th-anniversary issue, David Luthy (1997) documents the beginning of this important educational periodical. The idea of an educational periodical similar to the *Budget* (a weekly newspaper containing letters from scribes in numerous Amish settlements throughout the United States and Canada) first occurred to Lydia Beiler, a teacher in Pennsylvania, who felt that the periodical could be a forum for printing news, discussing classroom situations, and exchanging teaching ideas. The idea was further discussed at the teachers' meeting that was held in Geauga County, Ohio, in 1956, and included teachers from Delaware, Indiana, Pennsylvania, Ohio, and Ontario; and all present believed it to be a good idea. In the fall of 1956 Joseph Stoll mentioned the idea again in a circle letter and reaffirmed his agreement to the concept. Later that year, he again mentioned the idea in a circle letter and this time offered to submit material. At the teachers' meeting held in Snyder County, Pennsylvania, in July of 1957, the idea of a periodical for teachers was again discussed. In a circle letter in August of 1957, Joseph volunteered to get an announcement ready in a few weeks if others would submit material and if someone would volunteer to take charge of duplication. At about the same time a teacher in Ohio volunteered to do the duplication if someone would take care of putting together the materials.

Joseph, who eventually became the first editor of the periodical, mailed an announcement to potential readers stating the intent of the periodical and setting subscription rates (60 cents per year or $1.00 for two years) and announced a contest to name the new periodical, which offered a free subscription to the winning entry. Some of the names for the periodical that were submitted and not selected included *Schoolroom Echoes*, *The Lamplighter*, and *Amish Mennonite School News*. A teacher in Middelfield, Ohio, submitted the winning entry, *Blackboard Bulletin*. The first issue was eight printed pages. In December of 1957 the editor stated in a circle letter that the periodical had about 100 subscribers and the same number of headaches, but also indicated that things were improving each week.

From this humble beginning the *Blackboard Bulletin* grew to 17,000 subscribers by its 40th anniversary. Luthy (1997) quotes an early reader who was commenting on the potential of the new periodical and stated, "We hope it may encourage more young readers, sustain the older ones, and create a bond of friendship among school directors, parents and teachers of our plain schools." Luthy (1997) further stated, "Forty years later that is still our goal." As of 2005 the *Blackboard Bulletin* had 23,000 subscribers. The journal is published 10 months per year and has a yearly subscription rate of $6.00. Each issue is about 28 pages in length and includes articles, school news, activities for students, and letters to the editor. The *Blackboard Bulletin* is an integral part of teacher preparation and renewal in North America because it discusses important educational and community issues in an open forum.

TEACHER OBSERVATION

Outside the realm of Amish education, public school teachers receive formal written observations that document their strengths and weaknesses as a teacher. This is not the case within Amish education since the community is such a close-knit group. If problems arise they will be known and addressed immediately. This is the case for several reasons. First, most schools have several siblings and cousins attending the same school. As most people would agree, stories about the teacher's strengths or foibles are more credible when two or more students convey the same information to their parents. In addition, schools are open to visitors from the community at any time. In most cases the visitors are parents or school board members. They can thus get firsthand information on the success of the teacher by visiting or from students who attend the school. Finally, as noted previously, the school board and teacher meet on a regular basis, and for the teacher this forum usually provides time for feedback. Several school board members from a variety of communities have stated that their goal is to prevent as many problems as possible. Frequent meetings with the parents and the teacher tend to make this an easier goal to achieve.

TEACHING AS A CAREER

Most Amish teachers are young, unmarried females who relinquish their teaching position once they marry. Since this is the case, there is consistent teacher turnover in each settlement. There are, however, a small number of men and women who have made teaching a career choice and have served their communities for over 20 years. This can present difficulties for some because the salary for a teacher is not usually sufficient to support a home (Harroff, 2004).

Interviews with school board members, former teachers, and former school board members during the winter of 2005 indicated several factors that are considered by a school board when determining a teacher's salary. The first one is whether the person supports himself/herself, or if he/she still lives with his/her parents. The second consideration is whether the teacher is supporting a family. A third component is the number of pupils in the school and the number of homes that send children to the school. Other factors taken into consideration will be teacher experience and cost of living in the area. The school board will consider each of these factors when determining a teacher's salary. In larger settlements there may be more formality to this process, with salaries determined by a more structured and uniform manner to ensure some consistency across the community.

In 1980 teacher salaries for Amish teachers in the Arthur, Illinois, area ranged from $10 to $14 per day (Miller, 1980). Research by Dewalt and Troxell in 1986 noted that the salary for an Old Order Mennonite teacher at a school in central Pennsylvania was $16 per day. Since that time salaries for Amish teachers have increased. Harroff (2004) notes that a salary for a beginning teacher in Indiana in the early 1990s was about $5,000 per year. This salary was often supplemented with a place to live during the school week and an abundant supply of canned goods provided by the parents. More recently, Kraybill and Bowman (2001) found that teachers' salaries ranged from $25 to $35 per day, which would be about $4,500–$6,500 per school year. Many individuals in the Amish community can earn more than this at many other types of employment, so those who remain teachers do so because they view it as a calling and because they very much enjoy working with the students. Most Amish teachers engage in some type of summer work to supplement their teaching salary. For example, a male teacher in central Pennsylvania works with a carpenter crew during the summer months.

Obviously, salaries are not the only consideration for potential teachers. Some may, in fact, be interested in teaching but may decline an offer because of problems in the local church community or perceived difficulties with one family associated with the school. There are instances where older individuals feel called to teaching and will switch careers. Interviews in the winter of 2005 with two male teachers revealed that they had decided to become teachers after many years of work in farming and construction because of the needs of the community. One man felt that German instruction in the schools should be improved and he set about meeting that need by becoming a teacher and by authoring a series of workbooks that augment the German curriculum in use at that time.

TEACHER JOYS AND PROBLEMS

In my school visits I noticed that the vast majority of teachers really seem to enjoy what they are doing and take seriously the responsibilities of educating the scholars at their school. This responsibility extends beyond the academic subjects and includes the moral training to live the Golden Rule. The teachers also enjoy having visitors, and all will have a visitor register his/her name and the date of the visit. Some teachers even use a special bulletin board to celebrate visitors. For example, one school in Indiana has each visitor write his/her name on a raindrop-shaped piece of construction paper. These papers are then placed on a bulletin board with the caption "Thanks for dropping by."

When asked what they like best about teaching, teachers usually indicate the positive interactions and associations that they build with the scholars. For example, one teacher in southern Indiana responded in this manner to the question, What do you like best about teaching?: "The relationships that I build with the students." A young teacher in Illinois responded to the same question with a big smile on her face and said, "I like recess the best. It is a good time to get to know the students." A teacher with many years of experience in Ohio stated, "I like working with the students. I like watching them grow and learn."

Fisher and Stahl (1986, p. 84) cite similar responses by teachers to the question, what do you like best about teaching? "Meeting former pupils is always a pleasure. In this teacher's opinion, the smiles, firm handshakes and friendly visits are indeed the greatest and most rewarding and lasting joys teaching has to offer." Another teacher stated, "The children are my greatest joy . . . seeing them open up with mastery of new understandings is like blossoms opening in the spring. What could be more rewarding?" (Fisher and Stahl 1986, pp. 84–85).

While teaching does have its joys, Amish teachers do face some problems and will most often mention discipline as a problem area. Discipline problems faced by Amish teachers may include whispering, reading a library book when one should be studying, and misbehavior on the playground. These problems are usually easy to solve and are dealt with in a simple and direct manner. As one teacher in Indiana stated, "With misbehavior—I look at them. They usually get back to work, or sometimes I just say their name and they get back to work. If the behavior does not improve right away or if it involves something more serious, I will have them write a letter to Mom and Dad explaining what they did at school. This usually solves the problem."

Fisher and Stahl (1986) state that sometimes a new teacher at a school will face the problem of students wanting to do things as they did them the year before. Amish teachers try to address this problem quickly but carefully. It is important to choose one's words carefully so as not to imply that the way things were done last year was wrong in any way. Another problem faced by teachers may be the formation of cliques among the pupils. The teacher will need the support of parents to solve this situation and will usually receive their support. On some occasions teachers may have poor support from one or two sets of parents. In this case the teacher will need assistance from the school board to rectify the situation. More about school-related problems will be shared in chapter 13.

Teaching eight grades in a one-room school or teaching four grades in a two-room school requires plenty of organizational skills. This poses problems for some beginning teachers, but most seem to adjust rather quickly. When asked how she stayed organized one teacher in Indiana stated, "Well, I went to a one-room school, so that helps; careful planning, and you also get better over time."

TEACHING DIPLOMA

Amish teachers are not required to nor do they seek certification as a teacher by state public school standards. A person may attain "certification" to teach in an Old Order school in the state of Pennsylvania. In Pennsylvania a person who has taught for three years will be considered "qualified" by Amish standards and will be issued a diploma (*Standards of the Old Order Amish and Old Order Mennonite Parochial and Vocational Schools of Pennsylvania*, 1969, p. 31). This diploma is signed by the school board members and is issued immediately upon successful completion of three years of teaching in an Amish or Old Order Mennonite school. No matter the state, Amish elders uniformly state that a person with a public school teaching certificate is not qualified to teach in an Old Order parochial school.

TEACHER DISMISSAL

Dismissing a teacher before the end of the school year is a rare occurrence but does happen on occasion. The most likely scenario is that the school board will hear about problems at the school and work with the teacher to improve the identified problem areas. If this does not improve the situation the school board will confront the teacher in a kind way and try to help him or her as best possible. The school board will dismiss teachers only after they have been given a reasonable chance to improve their performance. If a teacher is dismissed, the school board will have someone in mind to take over the school for the rest of that term. As one veteran Amish teacher stated, "they (the school board) try to hang in there until the end of the term."

HELPERS

Some Amish schools employ "helpers" who assist the students with their work while the teacher is working with other groups of students. Depending on the needs of the teacher, helpers may be in the school any number of days per week. At two-teacher schools the helper may work with one teacher two days per week and the other teacher two days per week. Some communities (such as the Arthur, Illinois, settlement) will not allow anyone to be a helper unless he or she is a member of the church. Helpers can be an important asset, especially in schools that have a large number of scholars.

SUBSTITUTE TEACHERS

Substitute teachers are needed when the teacher becomes sick, goes on a short trip, or is away observing in other schools. During my observations, I visited several schools that were being led by substitute teachers. In one school where the regular teachers were away observing in another school, the substitute teachers for the day were young women from the community. When observing these teachers, I could not tell that they in fact were not the regular teachers because classes continued in the usual fashion. I also noticed the same scenario in a school in another state with the same positive results.

In two instances in separate communities in the Midwest the teacher had resigned or was unable to complete the term due to illness; in both cases older men from the community completed the term for the teacher. On some occasions, a mother of some of the pupils in the school may take on the role of teacher for the remainder of a term if a teacher needs to resign a position. This was the case in a school in central Pennsylvania during the winter of 2005.

Harroff's (2004) research in Indiana found that substitute teachers in schools in that state are often former teachers. One problem they face is that they may live a considerable distance from the school, and a driver may need to be arranged to transport them to and from school each day.

TEACHER AWARDS

The Amish community does not make awards to students for academic achievement, nor does it provide awards for teaching excellence. While such awards may be common in other public and private schools in the United States and Canada, they have no place in the Amish community, where recognizing a person for his or her accomplishments would be contrary to a life of humility. This is not to say that the Amish do not value their teachers. In fact, all members of the community are important, and no one individual is given special awards of any kind. For example, written histories of settlements across the United States and Canada will often mention the names of the teachers for the local schools as well as numerous other individuals in the settlement in a matter-of-fact way.

TRAVEL

Travel to and from school is a dangerous venture for some teachers. In Holmes County, Ohio, for example, one teacher must walk about a mile up the hill to her school. Her route to school requires walking along a very busy rural road. The narrow blacktop road has about a two-foot shoulder on each side of the road before one gets to the drainage ditches and then the embankment up to the fields on each side of the road. In winter, her travel to the school will be before sunrise. Since she usually wears a black dress, cape, and bonnet, this makes it difficult for motorists to see her. Having walked this road myself on several occasions, I can attest to the fact that there is not much room for walkers on this road. In addition, oncoming traffic must come up over a hill, and this makes it more dangerous because the driver has no idea what is on the other side of the hill. Because of the dangers involved on this trek to school, this teacher wears a bright yellow/green belt around her outer garments to make herself more visible to traffic.

Many Amish teachers travel to school via bicycle or horse and buggy. Many of these teachers must ride along or across roads with heavy traffic that includes large trucks. The Amish in the settlements in Lancaster County, Pennsylvania, Elkhart/LaGrange Counties in Indiana, and Holmes County, Ohio, are especially prone to travel on roads with extensive and dangerous traffic. In some instances cars or trucks do not reduce their speed when passing a buggy, while others will weave around the buggy with no idea what is on the road ahead. Crossing a major intersection is another danger point for two reasons. First, intersections are dangerous for cars and even more so for bicycles or buggies. Those going through an intersection must assume that traffic will heed the red light or stop signs. Second, one must hope that the horse will stay still until it is time to cross the intersection. Travel is even more treacherous in the winter. Conditions are slippery, and large trucks spray slush and snow on everything in their path, which is a dangerous condition for a car and even more dangerous for a horse and buggy.

Buggy accidents are a common occurrence, and most editions of *The Diary* carry several accident reports each month. For example, in the January 2006 edition, eight accidents were described on pages 21–23. In some instances the occupants of the buggy were killed, in others the horse was killed, and in some cases a buggy was ruined but the passengers escaped serious injury (*Diary*, 2006).

TEACHER PRACTICE: A TYPICAL TEACHER DAY

The following account portrays a typical day from the teacher's perspective in most Amish and Old Order Mennonite schools in the United States and Canada. This realistic fictional account takes place in Holmes County, Ohio, and is based on numerous Amish teacher interviews and observations in schools across the United States and Canada. The story will focus on a teacher named Anna who teaches at Spring Meadow School. Anna is 20 years old and lives at home with her parents and four younger siblings. Her older brother is married and lives in another settlement. The family farm is composed of about 50 acres. In addition to tending to the fields, the family has a large greenhouse in which they grow numerous plants for sale to the public. Spring Meadow School has 45 pupils with 23 in grades 1–4. It is a Wednesday in November of 2005.

At 5:30 a.m. Anna rises and helps her mother prepare breakfast for the family. She prepares lunches for herself and her siblings and then gets her things ready for school. At 6:45 the family meets for devotions in the large kitchen and then eats breakfast. Anna leaves at 7:15 for the 15-minute walk to school. She carries all of her books and papers as well as her black lunch-bucket. Her walk to school is along a gravel road, so she usually does not have to worry about cars. In dry weather the road is very dusty, but in rainy weather the road can get muddy in spots. The walk to school includes one long hill, but other than that it is a nice walk past several fields and one stand of woods. Anna enjoys watching the fields change over the course of the year and listening to the sounds of nature. The songs of the birds and the sounds of the cows or horses in the fields grazing are comforting and remind her of God's wonderful creation. As she walks to school, Anna is already busy thinking about the lessons she will teach that day.

Anna's thoughts also turn to her scholars. One of her first graders, Mary, is having a hard time with her reading. She also thinks of Titus, one of her fourth graders, who is slow to complete his work on most days. Anna makes a mental note to help Mary as best as she can today and keep a close eye on Titus.

On this November morning the weather is quite blustery, so the walk to school is cold. Anna is thankful that she has only a 15-minute walk and arrives at school at 7:30. She greets her fellow teacher, Miriam, who has been at school for about 10 minutes. Miriam has been teaching for six years and is the head teacher for the school. She has a longer commute each morning and thus uses a horse and buggy for travel each day. The school is heated by propane gas and feels nice and warm after the walk in the brisk morning air. Anna and Miriam talk a bit about happenings in the community, including any new courtships in the area, wonder if any visitors might surprise them today, and discuss Reuben and Emma, whose mother has been sick for over a week. After this they talk about the upcoming day and then prepare to teach their lessons. Anna teaches grades 1–4, and Miriam works with grades 5–8. They both place the written assignments for each grade level on the blackboard.

The first scholar arrives at 8:10 and says, "Good morning, Miriam. Good morning, Anna."

Both teachers reply, "Good morning, Henry." This greeting continues with all the other students as they arrive. After putting his lunch-bucket in its place in the cellar, Henry goes out to play. After several more students arrive, Anna goes outside to play with the children while Miriam stays inside. Students have many stories to tell the teacher each morning, and most of these stories deal with happenings with animals on their respective farms, an upcoming auction, or something interesting they saw on the way to school.

Miriam rings the bell at 8:30, signifying the start of the school day. The students quickly come to their seats, and Miriam takes attendance. She reads a chapter from the Bible, leads the children in the Lord's Prayer, and then calls the students to the front for singing. After singing two songs, the children return to their seats and begin the day's work without a word of direction required from Miriam or Anna. Anna likes to sing and wishes all of the students in the school would take a similar interest, but some older students on occasion seem less interested.

At 8:45 Anna states, "Fourth-grade arithmetic," and the scholars come to the table by her desk, where all are seated for the lesson. Anna likes arithmetic, and it is her favorite subject to teach. In her mind, an arithmetic class always seems to go faster than other subjects, and today is no exception. Anna returns the students' papers from yesterday and goes over two problems that seemed to be difficult for the students. Anna then shows the children how to do the next set of problems and gives one guided example on the board. Next she calls on children to come to the board two at a time, and she gives them a problem to work on the board. If students get the problem correct, they may return to their desks to begin the arithmetic assignment. If students' answers are not correct, Anna helps them understand the algorithm. This process continues until all students have had a chance to demonstrate their knowledge.

Around 9:10 Anna goes about the room assisting students who had their hands raised while she was teaching fourth grade. At 9:15 Anna states,"Second-grade arithmetic." Anna works with the second graders as she did with the fourth-grade arithmetic class. As she works with the students, she is always mindful of the other students in the class in case they need assistance.

About 9:30 Anna states, "First-grade arithmetic." The first graders are working on addition and subtraction facts, and Anna uses flash cards to quiz them individually. Facts that are answered incorrectly go back in the pile so that the fact will come up again during the lesson. After doing this she reads the next page in the arithmetic workbook to them and makes sure all students know what to do before sending them back to their desks. After a quick scan of the room to see if anyone has questions, Anna goes back to her desk, where she records information from the arithmetic lesson and catches her breath, and then it is back to lessons.

At 9:50 Anna states, "Third-grade arithmetic." Students come to the table and exchange workbooks. Students use red pens to correct each other's work while Anna gives the correct answers. Before third-grade arithmetic is finished Miriam rings the bell for recess, and Anna thinks, "Wow, the morning lessons went quickly. What happened to the time?" After the class decides that they will play freeze tag, Miriam and Anna dismiss the scholars one grade at a time. Miriam and Anna then go outside to play with the students. The fresh air feels good on the skin, and the fragrance of the nearby meadow is a welcome smell to the nose.

At 10:15 Miriam rings the bell, indicating that recess is over, and all students return to their seats and begin their work anew. Scholars begin their work without direction from the teachers, for all know what needs to be accomplished. Shortly thereafter, Anna states, "Third-grade arithmetic." After the students assemble at the table Anna completes the lesson and gives the students their new assignments. Anna is very pleased with the third graders, for many of them already know their multiplication tables up to the sixes.

At 10:25 Anna reviews her notes, and she realizes that she is already a little bit behind on her work for the day. Anna states, "Second-grade reading," and the students come to the table with their *Pathway Readers*. She then says, "Let's read the story about Peter, Rachel, and the new pony!" The students read the story out loud in clockwise order, starting with the scholar seated next to the teacher; each student reads a paragraph, and when one finishes the next student begins. Anna will also take a turn reading, and this process will continue until the story has been completed. The students like to listen to Anna read, especially when she reads with lots of expression. Anna will not make any statements during this process relative to directions for the group or comment about good reading. She will stop the reading only if a child is stuck on a word or mispronounces a word. Anna likes the *Pathway Readers* because children get to read about their own culture and each story has a lesson about leading a disciplined life. During reading instruction Anna will call students in other grades to the front if they have had their hands raised for a long time. After the reading is completed, Anna will ask several comprehension questions of the children before going over the assigned pages in the workbook. During this time Anna notices that Sam, one of her first graders, is not doing his work. She catches his eye and points to his desk. Sam knows what this means and gets busy. In a similar manner Anna will have reading with each of the other grades until 11:30. During third-grade reading, Mary, one of her first graders, has knocked all her papers off her desk and broken her new pencil in the process. Mary tries not to cry, but the tears come anyway. Anna does her best to console Mary and shows her that while the pencil is shorter it can still be used for its intended purpose.

By 11:15 the children are getting hungry. Many have finished their morning work; most study their memory work, get out a book to read, color a picture, or study their lessons for the next day. Anna watches for off-task students while she is with the reading groups and addresses any off-task behavior. By this time of the day, Anna is hungry as well and is a bit tired, given her many duties as the teacher. Lunch and recess are a welcome break for students and teachers alike.

At 11:30 Miriam rings the bell signaling the lunch break. After reciting a prayer, students are dismissed by grade to wash their hands and retrieve their lunches. Teachers and students sit at their desks to eat. Students enjoy a friendly conversation about upcoming trips, visitors in the community, new pets, and the sale next week at Amos Hoover's place. Since the grass is no longer wet the students decide to play softball at recess. Both teachers go outside to play with the students, and each takes a 10-minute break sometime during recess to prepare for afternoon lessons.

Immediately after the hour-long lunch and recess break, Miriam reads a chapter from the *Applecreek* book series. Students really like this part of the school day, and Anna enjoys the time as well. After the reading is over, Anna has each of her four grades take a practice spelling test. The first graders practice writing their words on the blackboard while she pronounces the spelling words to the other grades. First graders really like to work at the chalkboard, but Anna knows that it sure does make a lot of dust. Once all practice spelling tests are graded it is time for English for grades 3 and 4. She will have short lessons for each class at the table in the front of the room. In the afternoon, Anna must be vigilant to watch for off-task behavior because students are generally more talkative and restless after lunch. Whispering or getting out of one's seat is not tolerated and must be addressed before things get out of hand. Students are permitted to listen to recitations and discussions going on in other classes if their work is complete for the day and they know their memory work for the week.

At 2:00 Miriam rings the bell for the last recess of the day. Scholars must clean the room before going out to play ball. Students know their assignments and get them accomplished quickly. Anna is getting really tired at this point of the day and enjoys the fresh air and break as much as the students. After the 15-minute recess, Anna conducts phonics lessons with the first and second graders. After these two lessons are completed, students have workbook pages to complete. She then conducts a quick lesson using multiplication fact flash cards with the third graders. The fourth graders then have a lesson on vocabulary. During the afternoon session Anna will give students sets of flash cards if they have completed their work for the day. If time permits, Anna will have recitation lessons in arithmetic with the first and second graders. At this time of the day, eighth-grade students may be asked to work with a younger student who is having difficulty with a concept in math or is behind in reading. The younger students like it when older students help them, and the older students like to be helpful to the teacher. Students in the younger grades like to color if they have extra time. The students like to show their complete pictures to the teacher, and Anna really enjoys seeing their work.

At 3:00 school is dismissed for the day, and Anna takes a deep breath and relaxes a moment. It takes about ten minutes to get all the scholars on their way home. Once this occurs, Anna and Miriam talk about the day and have a light snack before correcting the mountain of papers and workbooks by each of their respective desks. While Anna corrects the papers her thoughts turn to the day's events. Today the school day seemed to go much more quickly than Tuesday. Perhaps it was due to the fact that the students were able to grasp their lessons today.

Anna usually stays at the school until most of her grading and preparation for the next day are complete. Anna and Miriam will probably spend some time talking about upcoming weddings, sales, and visitors in the community. She will leave in time to get home between 4:45 and 5:00. The walk home is downhill, so it is faster than the walk to school. Anna often thinks about her day and the success or failures of her lessons. Anna's heart is especially troubled when a student's attitude shows signs of pride, boastfulness, or disrespect. As she gets closer to home Anna's stomach reminds her that she is famished, and the thought of a hearty meal of chicken, mashed potatoes, noodles, and corn makes her pace quicken. After dinner she will assist with washing the dishes and then spend some time with her siblings and parents before correcting any additional papers and preparing lessons for the next day. Anna cherishes the time with her family each evening and enjoys her younger siblings. About 9:30 it is time for bed, given that 5:30 a.m. is not too far away.

REVIEW

This chapter has articulated the concepts of community, literacy, and responsibility. School board members have clear responsibilities to the community to keep the school running smoothly, and a major component in accomplishing this is to find a good teacher. Amish elders realize that schools build the community and that the accountability for schools rests with everyone, including the students, the teachers, the school board, the parents, and the church. In the next chapter we will explore special education in Amish schools.

9

Special Education

A smile adds a great deal to your face value.

—Aphorism posted in an Illinois Amish school in 2005

In chapter 7 we took a lengthy look at the teaching styles employed in Amish schools in the 21st century. In this chapter will take a more in-depth look at special education, and the chapter will be divided into four sections. We will first explore several ways that Amish communities have decided to address the needs of special needs students. We will then review some of the history of the special-education movement in Amish schools. The third section of the chapter will focus on observations of three special-education teaching sessions—one in Indiana, one in Illinois, and one in Ohio. We will conclude the chapter as we discover some of the ways the Amish community supports special needs adults.

Like public schools in the United States, the Amish have tried to determine the best way to meet the requirements of students with special needs. Over the course of the last 50 years, they have used a variety of approaches in different communities. Whatever the approach they utilize, they create the school or setting with the goal of building community, teaching personal responsibility for learning, and building literacy. Since Amish schools do not stress individual accomplishment, it is often easier for them to build a community that supports and includes special needs students in the ongoing activities of the school.

It is important to note here that Amish parents usually value and support teachers, and this is especially true for the teachers who are entrusted with the care of special needs students. One example of community support was the surprise birthday dinner held for the teacher at one of the special-education schools in Wisconsin in November of 2005 (*Diary*, Nov. 2005). The reporter stated that the students were happy to see the surprised teacher.

FORMATS OF SPECIAL EDUCATION

A review of the January 2005 *Blackboard Bulletin* listing of Old Order Amish and Mennonite Schools reveals that many communities now offer specific classrooms, schools, school annexes, or teachers for special needs students. One example of the way schools are meeting the needs of special education is found in Indiana. In the Elkhart/LaGrange area the school board will hire an additional teacher to work with special needs students. In some cases, the teacher and students will have a room of their own in the basement or on the second floor of the building. In other areas, such as Kalona, Iowa, the school board may build an additional building connected to or within walking distance of the original school structure.

In the Arthur, Illinois, community the school board will build an annex connected to the original school structure. This annex will house the special needs students and the teacher. In the Holmes County community of Ohio, it is not uncommon for a drape suspended from a pipe running along the ceiling to be used to separate the scholars during instructional time. For example, the one-room school will be divided in half if the school has two teachers. If there is a special-education teacher, a corner may be subdivided by a drape as well. In other communities, as is the case in central Pennsylvania, special-education students are part of the general school population and receive extra help as all students do from time to time.

Buildings or annexes for special-education students may include equipment especially designed to meet the physical needs of these students. For example, a school in western Pennsylvania has two indoor swings, a large play area with mats, and several walkers for the students. This school provides all visitors with a pamphlet about the school that contains a poem especially designed for the students attending the school during that term.

First Amish Special Education Schools

1975	Clearview Special Education School	Lancaster, Pennsylvania
1978	Bart Special Education School	Lancaster, Pennsylvania
1979	Reistville Special Education School	Lebanon, Pennsylvania
1983	Hawpatch School	Elkhart/LaGrange, Indiana
1983	Bagdad Annex	Arthur, Illinois
1990	Belmont Special Education School	Lancaster, Pennsylvania
1995	HOPE School	Kalona, Iowa

It should be noted that many Amish students with severe disabilities might attend public schools, while in other locales public school special-education teachers will visit the Amish school to provide services. Interviews with public school superintendents revealed that most believed that all Amish children with special needs were attending public school. While it is true that large numbers of Amish parents utilize public school services for special needs students in grades one through eight, others will only use the services prior to the student's enrollment in an Amish parochial school in first grade. In either case, Amish parents are usually very appreciative of the services provided for their children.

HISTORY OF SPECIAL EDUCATION

Both Esh (1986) and Kinsinger (1997) have chronicled the beginning and development of special education in Amish parochial schools. Prior to 1975 the well-being of special needs students was a topic of school leaders and elders in the Lancaster community. There were two key questions to address: Should the parochial schools be more involved in special education? Should there be established a parochial school just for special needs pupils? Eventually the idea was brought before the bishops in the Lancaster area, and it was agreed that the Old Order Book Society should take leadership in this new venture for the parochial schools. The Old Order Book Society would thus oversee the founding of a school for special needs students as well as provide funding. In July of 1975 a statewide school directors' meeting was held, and a three-man committee was elected to take the leadership roles for special schools. As part of the information-gathering process, the committee visited a public school special-education class at Garden Spot Elementary School. At the same time they began looking for a school location and a teacher. The group found that the basement of Clearview School on Old Leacock Road might be a good spot and held a frolic (work session) to clean out the space and get it painted. After a busy summer, Clearview Special School opened its doors at 8:00 a.m. on September 15, 1975, with two students and Ruth Fisher as their teacher. The success of the program became known throughout the community, and by the start of the second term in August of 1976 there were 10 pupils. In addition to all of this work, the group decided it needed to better meet the needs of deaf children, and as a result several teachers and interested persons began learning sign language in June of 1976. The group met every Tuesday evening during the summer. A hearing-impaired child was enrolled at Clearview School in the fall of 1978.

Because of the success associated with this first special-education school, Esh (1986) reports, a second school in the Lancaster settlement for special needs students was opened the fourth day of September in 1978 with three pupils. The school began in a room at the Engle planing mill. When this site was no longer viable, the school program was moved to a portion of a warehouse in Georgetown, and this was the beginning of Bart Special School.

The committee that worked to establish both of these schools had many issues to address, such as transportation, funding, deciding who could attend, textbooks, and appropriate teaching techniques. Throughout all of this they succeeded in establishing the first schools for special-education students in Lancaster County.

Esh (1986) notes that not long after these events in the Lancaster area, the Amish community in Lebanon County, Pennsylvania, built a new school. At this time it was determined that the school would include a basement that would house the Reistville Special School. This school was begun in Lebanon County in 1979. Pennsylvania had at least three schools specifically designed for special needs students by 1980.

Kinsinger (1997) observed that the Amish in Lancaster County continued to seek ways to better meet the needs of all students, and in 1990 Belmont Parochial School was purchased by the Old Order Book Society. The school was renovated by the Society to accommodate special needs students. During the first year of operation the school had five teachers and 21 pupils. One room was designed for slow learners, and the other was designed for students with more severe disabilities.

Through a variety of means, the Amish community in the Elkhart/LaGrange, Indiana, settlement heard about the success of the schools for special needs students in Lancaster and decided to start a class for special needs students in the basement of Hawpatch School in September of 1983. Esh (1986) further states that there were two students who spent three days a week in the special school and two days a week in the regular school upstairs. By January of 1984 it was decided to have the special school in session five days per week. This community started another special school at Sunnyside School northeast of Topeka in the fall of 1984. As all of this was happening in Indiana, planning for a special school in Arthur, Illinois, began in the fall of 1982, and the school opened in 1983. A 14 × 22–foot building was donated and moved to the Bagdad School grounds and named the Bagdad Annex. On a visit to this school complex in the winter of 2005 it was noted that the schools are connected and that they share restrooms, a propane fuel tank, a horse shed, and a playground.

Because of the fact that there was a hearing-impaired scholar attending Shady Grove School in Allensville, Pennsylvania (Big Valley), the school board believed that it would be appropriate to teach sign language to all the children in the school (Esh, 1986). This event further elaborates how the Amish value community. Because every scholar at the school learned sign language, everyone could communicate in the classroom and on the playground. By 1986 there were three hearing-impaired children attending this school.

An interview with an Amish elder in Kalona, Iowa, in the winter of 2005 revealed that a similar pattern emerged when a hearing-impaired student began attending school in that area. The school board, teachers, and parents believed that the best thing to do would be to have all the scholars and teachers learn sign language. Again, this is another indicator that clearly shows that the Amish value all students and strive to include everyone in the community.

As in Pennsylvania and Illinois, the Kalona, Iowa, community decided that it needed a specific school to meet the needs of special needs students. Thus they moved a small schoolhouse (Pleasant Valley School, built in 1973) to the grounds of Friendship School (Iowa Amish Directory, 2004). This building was now called Hope School (Handicapped Oriented Parochial Education) and opened with three scholars in the fall of 1995. As of 2004 this school was serving the needs of four students.

INDIANA

Amish teachers in the Nappanee and Elkhart-LaGrange communities have the most experience working with special needs students, since schools in these areas began special programs as early as 1991 (Harroff, 2004). Teachers with

Figure 9.1. Friendship School and HOPE School in Kalona, Iowa. HOPE School is the smaller building to the right, which houses the special-education program.

expertise in teaching special needs students are often invited to other Amish communities in the state to share their experiences working with this student population.

In Indiana, special-education programs are supported by parents and donations from churches (Farmweld, 2004). The Nappanee settlement began special-education classes in 1991. Funding for special education became more formalized in the area in July of 1993 when a letter went to all churches asking for donations. The response was very good. A special-education school board was elected to oversee the program. By 2001 the area had 10 schools that had special education classes. Currently, all funds for these schools come from donations.

CURRENT PRACTICES IN SPECIAL EDUCATION

One might ask how the Amish learn to work with special needs populations. In most cases, the response one will receive is that they will seek information from English neighbors or public school teachers who have some expertise in working with special needs students. They will also indicate that they will consult the numerous books available on the subject. There are also extensive chances for teachers to discuss this subject among themselves. For example, in the Holmes County area of Ohio, there are six-weeks teachers' meetings specifically for special-education teachers. In addition, Amish publications and minutes from summer teachers' meetings indicate that working with special needs students has been a topic of conversation for several years. For example, the minutes of the 1996 midwestern teachers' meeting included the topic of working with special-education students. The 2000 Indiana teachers' meeting included a lecture on slow learners. The six-weeks teachers' meetings may include discussions of special education, especially when an area does not provide specific teachers for this population. In areas where there are special-education teachers, the six-weeks teachers' meetings will have fewer topics devoted to this subject. Over the years the *Blackboard Bulletin* has had numerous articles about working with special needs students.

TYPICAL SPECIAL EDUCATION CLASS SETTINGS AND INSTRUCTION

During my observations of special-education schools/classes in several states, I noticed a distinctive pattern of instruction. The instructional patterns are based on the typical Amish teaching style, with the exception that the teacher works with only one child at a time rather than one grade at a time.

While the teacher is working with one child, all other students are expected to be at work. To begin the day, all the students in a school, including the special-education students, will meet together for the opening exercises. Opening exercises include taking attendance, reciting the Lord's Prayer, a Bible story reading, and singing. Immediately after this is completed, students will proceed to their assigned seats and get busy on the day's work. In schools with special-education teachers, the special-education students will move to a specific part of the room, an annex, the basement, or the second floor of the building. The teacher will then take turns working individually with each child for a short duration, assign a task, and then move on to the next child. This will continue during the entire instructional time, with the teacher taking short breaks to record the progress of each scholar.

It should be noted that the teachers at every school I visited ensure that all students are included in the playground games at recess or before school begins. Running records (observations) will give specific examples of a special needs class so the reader can get an idea of the typical teaching in a special needs class. The first was conducted on a snowy day in Indiana in February of 2005, the second is of a classroom in Illinois during the same time period, and the third is of a school in Holmes County, Ohio, during January of 2005.

INDIANA SPECIAL EDUCATION CLASSROOM

Mary (the teacher) has three special needs students who meet in the basement of the school. There are two teachers who serve grades one through eight on the main floor of the building. Mary has a small, well-organized desk, a map of the United States on her wall, a four × six–foot blackboard, and two carpets on the floor under the students' desks. As is typical of most Amish schools, the room is very quiet, and Mary teaches using a soft voice. The daily work for each of her scholars is outlined on the blackboard and is quoted below. Each column represents that day's assignments for one student.

Special Education Daily Assignments at a School in Indiana*

Arith L. 7	Arith L. 7	Arith L. 17
Voc L. 35 & Quiz	Read story	Voc L. 24 & quiz
Eng. L. 38	Eng. L. 100	Eng. L. 17
Health chap. 1 test	Health pg. 127–130	Health chap. 2, pt. 1

*Arith is an abbreviation for arithmetic, Voc is an abbreviation for vocabulary, Eng. is an abbreviation for English, and L. indicates lesson

After recess (about 10:15), Mary spent about one minute with each student, providing individual help as needed at his or her respective desk. At

10:20 Mary began a reading lesson with Elam; Mary read a paragraph out loud and then he read a paragraph out loud. They continued in this way until they finished the story. Mary then asked him several comprehension questions about the reading. This lesson was over at 10:35, and at this time Mary worked at her desk and then helped students at their desks with their work. At 10:40 Mary helped student Sarah for a bit, and then spent about four minutes with Reuben. He first read his vocabulary words to her, and then they discussed the meaning of each word. At 10:45 she went back to Sarah. At this point a man from the health department came for a water sample. After getting a water sample for him, she continued to circulate around the room to help students and teach in small bits as well as record things at her desk. This continued until it was time for lunch, which was about 11:30. At this point a bell rang, and all the scholars came together for the prelunch prayer. Students were then dismissed one row at a time to wash their hands and get their lunch boxes. All of the children then ate together on the main floor of the building. After lunch all students and at least one teacher went out to play in the snow.

This pattern of instruction will then repeat itself during the two afternoon sessions, which are divided by the afternoon recess. It is important to emphasize that just like all Amish students, special needs students are taught to wait patiently for help from the teacher when she is instructing other students. Special-education teachers usually use the same textbooks as those utilized by other teachers in the community.

ILLINOIS SPECIAL EDUCATION CLASSROOM

As noted previously, in the Arthur, Illinois, community, special-education rooms are provided by building annexes to existing school buildings. These annexes are a smaller version of the typical school. The annex visited contained the teacher's desk, four student desks, a bench for visitors, a bookcase, and a table. The room was large enough that it could easily seat 10 students. The walls of the room were labeled north, east, south, and west.

The room contains two bulletin boards with teacher-made information. The first board has the Lord's Prayer, and the second lists the books of the Bible. I arrived in the room at about 9:05, and the teacher was conducting a reading lesson with one child at the table. The student and teacher would take turns reading paragraphs from the story. After they read the story, the teacher asked the student several questions about the story. Finally, the teacher gave the student the next reading assignment after reviewing new vocabulary for that reading selection. This reading lesson lasted about 15 minutes. After this the teacher helped another one of the students, who was using a ruler to measure things for her arithmetic assignment. The teacher then checked on the progress of each student. Next, the teacher conducted another reading lesson in the same manner as that of the previous reading lesson. The class schedule for the periods of the day was posted on the blackboard and is found a below.

Daily Assigments in an Illinois Special Education Classroom

1st	Reading	Sam
		Sarah
	Arithmetic	Jonah
		Emma
2nd	Arithmetic	Sam & Sarah
	Reading	Jonah & Emma
3rd	English	
4th	Vocab	Jonah & Sarah
	Spelling	Sam
	Phonics	Emma

HOLMES COUNTY, OHIO

This observation occurred at one of the older Amish schools in the area. The school is a one-room school with a full basement. It was a cold and snowy day in the winter of 2005, and many students were warming sandwiches on the coal stove located in a corner of the room. There are three teachers at the school, with one teacher serving first through fourth grades, and the second teacher serving grades five through eight. The senior teacher, Mary, has about 15 years of teaching and works with the two special needs students, John and Barbara, who attend the school. This school is equipped with drapes that may be used to separate the classes during instructional time. Mary has a desk in the back corner of the room. Two student desks are placed directly in front of her desk, and this corner of the room is also equipped with drapes that may be drawn if the teacher wants some privacy from the rest of the school during instructional time. On the afternoon of my visit Mary was seated alongside the desk of John. The teacher was using flash cards of common English words that she would present to the child. If John got the word correct he could place it in the pile on his desk. If he was incorrect Mary would help him sound out the word. She would then place the word back in the stack. After five minutes Mary concluded this portion of the lesson by telling John that he had done a good job. She then showed him how to complete a page in his workbook. Mary went back to her desk for about two minutes to record some information. She then came back and sat by John as he continued his workbook assignment. After he completed his workbook assignment, Mary and John took turns reading paragraphs from the story in the *Pathway Reader.* After they completed this reading, Mary asked the student two questions about the story. She then reminded John of the penmanship exercise he needed to complete next.

Mary now turned her attention to Barbara, who had been working on an arithmetic assignment. Mary moved her chair beside Barbara's desk and reviewed the problems she had completed so far. After checking each problem, Mary said, "Good work, Barbara. All of the problems are correct. Let's practice some addition and subtraction flash cards." Mary presented the flash cards, and Barbara would say the answer as soon as she knew the answer. Every once in a while, Barbara would confuse an addition problem with a subtraction problem, and then Mary would have her say the entire problem and point to the addition or subtraction symbol. This strategy helped Barbara, and in each instance the student stated the correct answer.

At this point it was time for lunch, and Mary rang the bell. After singing a blessing the students were dismissed one row at a time to retrieve their lunch pails. It is interesting to note that every student in this school had a large bottle of hand sanitizer, which each student washed his/her hands with before eating lunch. Students who had sandwiches warming on the top of the stove retrieved them as they went back to their seats. Some of the items wrapped in foil were actually slices of pizza, which the students enjoyed while talking with their friends.

OTHER PATTERNS OF INSTRUCTION FOR SPECIAL EDUCATION

Some Amish communities do not provide extra teachers for the instruction of special needs and learning-disabled students. In this case the teacher will provide extra assistance to the child. One school in central Pennsylvania has several special needs students among the scholars in the school. The teacher assists the students as needed and also elicits the help of older students as tutors. For example, an eighth-grade student who had completed his geography assignment was asked to help the special needs first grader with his vocabulary lesson. The eighth grader, who seemed pleased by the request, knelt down by the first grader's desk and proceeded to help him with his work.

Harroff (2004) found a similar pattern of instruction in Indiana schools that do not provide extra teachers for special-education students. The teacher will seat the special needs students at a desk where they can receive the teacher's assistance more readily. Some Indiana Amish parochial schools will accept assistance from the local public schools and will welcome those teachers into the school to work with the special needs student.

Fisher and Stahl (1986) state that Amish teachers of special needs students are devoted to their students and make every attempt to teach them basic skills in reading, writing, and mathematics. The teachers also make sure the students learn responsibility and patience, virtues that will be essential for their adult life in Amish society.

Another interesting example of the inclusion of a special needs student into the life of the school community was noted in the singing for parents and visitors. In most Amish schools visitors from the community are expected and encouraged. Since this is the case, teachers make sure that each child has a poem or saying memorized to recite for the visitors. Schools may also have special songs they sing as well. At one school in Indiana the special needs student was one of the students given the role of holding up one of the key props utilized during the singing of the song for visitors. In a Pennsylvania school, the students line up for singing in eight columns of three to four students at the front of the room. Lower-grade students are placed in every other column. The upper-grade students hold the songbooks and help the younger ones keep their place in the book. This arrangement worked well at this school, since an upper-grade student could help the younger special needs child.

COMMUNITY CARE AND PROVIDENCE FOR SPECIAL NEEDS ADULTS

Finally, the Amish provide for special needs adults in a variety of ways. For example, a community in Ohio provided the building and financing for a home business, a clock and watch shop, for a man who was bound to a wheelchair. In another instance in Iowa, an elderly gentleman had a home business of cracking and picking black walnuts, which he sold at the local dry goods shop. A family in Ohio has added a bookstore to the back of the house, and their two daughters, one of whom has a handicapping condition, operate the bookstore. In another instance, a couple from the Midwest writes a variety of books, with the proceeds going to a family with a child with Down's Syndrome. A wheelchair-bound individual in Ohio makes beautiful as well as functional handmade baskets. These baskets are sold in a variety of Amish–owned and operated businesses as far away as Lebanon, Pennsylvania.

One of the most interesting examples of community providence is the coloring book program sponsored by an Amish publisher for an adult (Sarah) who was stricken with rheumatoid arthritis at a young age. The publisher asked its readers to provide freehand drawings that Sarah could then compile into a coloring book. Sarah received over 3,000 drawings. She called this a "flood of love." Sarah used many of these drawings to produce five coloring books. One of these coloring books has been printed at least seven times since 1987. All of these examples illustrate the fact that the Amish strive to ensure that everyone is cared for at school and in the community.

10

Amish Communities and Schools in the Northeastern United States and Canada

A mistake is a chance to try harder.

—Aphorism posted at an Amish school in Ohio in 2005

This will be the first of three chapters in which we explore some of the unique characteristics of Amish schools and communities in the United States and Canada. In some cases a history of the local area will be given because of the distinctive nature of the events. In other cases specific interesting events about schools will be provided. These three chapters provide specific information about most of the larger settlements as well as those that present a good picture of the variety of schools and communities in North America. Each chapter will also include a table of some of the unique school names for schools in that region.

In this chapter we focus on the northeastern states and Ontario, Canada. In chapter 11 we spotlight communities in the southeastern United States, and in chapter 12 we focus on midwestern and western states. As we explore these different communities one should remember that all of these settlements, regardless of size, are built around a strong sense of community, with parents and elders taking the responsibility to provide an appropriate education.

Pennsylvania and Ohio are states often associated with the Amish, and there are in fact many communities in these states besides those in Lancaster, Pennsylvania, and Holmes County, Ohio. Lancaster, which is probably the most well-known of all the Amish communities, is within an easy drive of major metropolitan areas of the East Coast including Philadelphia, Baltimore, Washington, D.C., and New York. For this reason the area is a major tourist attraction, with thousands visiting the area on any given day during the spring, summer, or fall. In addition to learning about the Amish culture, many tourists like the fact that they can get a feeling of being in the country when traveling the byways of Lancaster County.

Holmes County, Ohio is the world's largest Amish community and has a good number of tourists, but fewer than the Lancaster settlement. Holmes County is a more rural setting than Lancaster and has fewer tourist-type activities. All Amish communities have one thing in common, and that is that the children in the community will be served by a small school in a rural setting. And because these schools are small, there will be lots of them scattered about the countryside. As we have already seen, both Lancaster and Holmes County have provided much of the leadership for the Amish parochial school movement. Schools with unique names in the northeastern United States and Canada include Chili Valley, Poverty Point, and Fountain Nook. Our journey will begin in Delaware, the home of the first Amish parochial school in the United States.

Unique School Names in the Northeastern United States and Canada

Honeysuckle Knoll	Flat Iron
Cranberry Marsh	Diamond Crossing
Hardscrapple Hill	High Up
Dividing Ridge	Pioneer Trails
Grapevine Creek	Stagecoach Run
Chili Valley	Fountain Nook
Genza Bottom	Paint Valley
Tea Run	Fountain Valley
Four Corners	Thorn Hill
Ore Bank	Little Nittany
Oil Creek	Brick
Cardinal Wing	Frog Hollow
Cream	Two Log
Poverty Point	Rattlesnake Run

(*Blackboard Bulletin*, 2005)

DOVER, DELAWARE

The Amish community in Delaware is located a few miles to the west of the city limits and is the closest Amish settlement to a state capital in the United States. The land in this area is fairly level with some gently rolling hills. Late April is an especially beautiful month because the grass is green and the native dogwood trees are in bloom.

The Amish from several different communities first settled in this region in 1915 (Luthy, 1994). The area is home to ten Amish parochial schools, with the majority being two-teacher schools (*Blackboard Bulletin,* 2005). The average number of pupils per school in the 2004–05 school year was 36, with a teacher-pupil ratio of one to 20. Teachers in this area attend the summer teachers' meetings that are held each year in Lancaster County, Pennsylvania.

There are several unique characteristics about this community. The first and most important is that it is the home to the first Amish parochial school in the United States. As noted previously, Apple Grove was opened in 1925. The school itself has been moved four times but is still situated in the general vicinity of its original location. Today, Apple Grove School has two teachers who share the one-room school. In keeping with its historic tradition, Apple Grove School is the only Amish or Mennonite school I have visited that has a sign inside the building indicating the date of origin. Letters that spell out "Welcome to Apple Grove School" are strung on wire across the room about one foot below the ceiling. The school has a large green chalkboard across the front of the room and has wainscoating about four feet high under the windows on each side of the classroom. The floor is made of plywood and has been painted gray. One bulletin board features a horse head within a horseshoe that each student colored, with the horseshoes listing each month of the school year. This school has a combination of desk types: desks and chairs from the 1950s and metal desks with attached seats from the 1920s. A saying on a teacher-made poster states:

All that you do
Do with your might
Things done by halves
Are never done right

The second unique characteristic of the Dover community is that it holds a communitywide school auction on the third Saturday each October. Items for sale at the auction include furniture, quilts, farming equipment, and household goods. About 2,000 people obtain bidding numbers for this event, and proceeds from the sale are used to help finance the schools in the area.

The third unique aspect of this community is the bike tour that is sponsored by the Kent County Tourism Office. Held each September, the bike tour meanders through some of the Amish farm areas, with bikers riding 15, 25, 50, or even 100 miles. One of the refreshment stops on this tour is at an Amish school.

The fourth distinctive feature about this community is that some horse-drawn buggies have electric turn signals and yellow blinking lights atop the buggy. Furthermore, Kent County and the state of Delaware have erected numerous signs on the roadways in this area warning motorists of buggy traffic, children walking to school, and school areas. In fact, the signage in this area is the most extensive I have observed in any Amish community in North America.

MAINE

This Amish community is distinguished by the fact that it is the northernmost settlement of Amish in the United States. According to the *Blackboard Bulletin* (2005) there is a small community of Amish near the town of Smyrna, Maine. Smyrna is located in Aroostook County, Maine, and is in the northeastern portion of the state along the Canadian border. The Amish school in the area is Smyrna Christian School and was begun in 1996. The school had 23 pupils and two teachers during the 2004–05 school year.

MARYLAND

Maryland is home to two Amish communities. One is in Cecil County, which some might consider a southward extension of the Lancaster, Pennsylvania, settlement, and the other is in St. Mary's County. During the 2004–05 school term there were eight Amish schools in the state and the majority were one-teacher schools (*Blackboard Bulletin,* 2005). The average number of pupils per school is 29.

St. Mary's County

The northern edges of St. Mary's County and southern St. Charles County are home to a substantial number of Amish families. The *Blackboard Bulletin* (2005) indicates that there were seven Amish parochial schools in the area, all being served by one teacher except the school that houses a special education program. The average number of pupils per school is 30. Hammett (1991) indicates that a five-person elected school board oversees all of the schools, employs the teachers, and taxes the Amish community for funds to run the schools. The schools have German lessons one afternoon per week.

St. Mary's County has played a unique role in the history of Maryland, especially its founding as a colony. Governor Leonard Calvert and fellow passengers on the *Ark* and *Dove* founded the colony of Maryland in this area in March of 1634. The immigrants left England in November of 1633, and the ships became separated at sea due to stormy weather. After a layover in Barbados in January of 1634, the ships were reunited and set sail for Maryland, with a stopover in Virginia. For over ten years the colony of Maryland was based in St. Mary's County (Hammett, 1991). Today St. Mary's County enjoys a temperate climate and remains suburban/rural in nature, with pastures, fields, and woods on the rolling terrain encompassing the northwest section of the county. In late April the area is especially scenic because one will see many native dogwood trees in bloom in the wooded areas. The Patuxent River serves as the northeast border of the county, the Potomac River serves as the southeast border, and the Chesapeake surrounds the southeast tip of the county. The county is home to several state parks and the Patuxent River Naval Air Station. Some local English residents are concerned about the eventual encroachment from the urban sprawl of Baltimore and Washington, DC.

The *History of St. Mary's County Maryland 1634–1900* by Hammett (1991) has several pages devoted to the Amish community. The Amish began moving to this area in 1939. An elder in the original group noted that Lancaster County was becoming overcrowded, so St. Mary's County became their destination because it was less crowded and had relatively inexpensive land for sale, and it seemed that the Amish would be able to determine the length of schooling for their children. The farmland was much less expensive than in Lancaster County, and the soil was revived by the farming methods of the Amish. In 1941 the community was quite alarmed when one man died from a tick bite and a woman and her son were hospitalized with tick fever. The county health department was able to inoculate the rest of the community to prevent further spread of this illness.

Hammett (1991) states that school attendance laws proved to be a complication for Amish parents for several years. Amish elders claimed to have a written agreement with Governor Herbert R. O'Connor (in office at the time of their move to the area) that Amish children could leave school after the successful completion of seventh grade. However, the Maryland school laws changed in 1947 and required children to attend school between the ages of 7 and 16. This proved to be a problem. The St. Mary's County School Board attempted to enforce the law, and the Amish peacefully resisted. Both sides in this issue respected the opposing viewpoint, and this prevented many of the confrontations that were occurring and would occur in other states. The dilemma was not settled until 1967, when State Senator Paul Bailey drafted legislation that recognized Amish schools. By 1976 the Amish were operating three schools in this area.

On school mornings one will hear the school bell ring at about 8:00, signaling the beginning of the school day. As the bell rings one will see children scurrying through the fields to get to school on time. Children in this area generally walk to school unless there is heavy snow or rain. A small number of scholars who live a good distance from their school are driven by motor vehicle to school by a local resident. English neighbors indicate that the Amish children know the three Rs and learn the skills necessary to become part of the rural workforce. Residents of the area further indicate that the Amish are good neighbors and that they actively support blood drives and local fire departments, and assist anyone who has had a fire or tornado destroy their home or barn. For example, vanloads of Amish support blood drives in the towns of the area. The Amish interest in literacy is cemented by the fact that on many days one can see buggies parked at the library in New Market. Some of the economic pursuits of the Amish in the area include farming, lumber milling, furniture making, quilting, baking, and welding. Amish school members indicate that they appreciate having their own school and that they have not had difficulty in finding teachers for their schools.

The south central portion of St. Mary's County is home to an Old Order Mennonite Community near Loveville. The area was discovered by two young Mennonite men from Lancaster County (not yet members of the church) on a motorcycle ride to Maryland. The young men had heard about the Amish immigration to the county and wanted to see the area for themselves (Hammett, 1991). Their report to the homefolks must have been a positive one, as the Mennonites began moving to the area in the 1940s.

MICHIGAN

Michigan is home to over 20 Amish settlements, with one of the larger settlements located near Centerville in the southern part of the state (*Blackboard Bulletin*, 2005; Luthy, 1994). Centerville was the first Amish community in the state and was founded in 1910. Michigan has been a popular destination for many Amish families, with over 15 new settlements established since 1972. About half the 52 Amish schools in Michigan are one-teacher schools. The average number of scholars per school is 25, and the teacher-pupil ratio is one to 15. The first schools in the state were opened in the mid-1970s in the Bronson and Mio settlements.

A small community of Amish resides near Bloomingdale, which is a locale that is the recipient of large amounts of lake effect snow. The average snowfall for the area is 70 inches per year, and the community received about 200 inches in the winter of 2001. Evergreen School was opened in 1999 and is a former public one-room school that is now owned by the local chapter of the Veterans of Foreign Wars (VFW). The VFW leases the building to the Amish for $1.00 per year with an option to renew or purchase in the future. The school has the original bell that is used each school day (Miller, 2002a).

The Centerville community is located in St. Joseph County along the Indiana state line. This area is composed of fairly level land with rolling hills. There are large patches of woods in the area, and in the winter it is not unusual to see herds of deer looking for food. Schools in this community are usually two-teacher schools and are of frame construction with white siding.

The first school in the area was Spring Creek School, which was built in 1974 (Miller, 2002a). Overcrowding at this school prompted the residents to build Pleasant View School in 1981. Woodlawn School was built in 1982 and gets its name because the school sits in the woods. During the first winter, pupils at this school spent recess skating on a neighbor's pond, and the next year the parents built a shallow man-made pond for the pupils.

NEW YORK

New York is home to over 10 Amish settlements, and most of the 53 schools in the state are one-teacher schools (*Blackboard Bulletin*, 2005; Luthy, 1994). New York has been an attractive state for new Amish communities, with over 10 new settlements since 1972. The average number of scholars per school is 27 and the teacher-pupil ratio is one to 21. One of the most unusual locations for an Amish community is around the town of Romulus in the Finger Lakes region of New York. This farming area is between Seneca Lake to the west and Cayuga Lake to the east. Cayuga Lake is about 40 miles in length and can get as much as four miles wide. Both lakes are very deep in spots and thus do not freeze over in the wintertime. The land between the lakes is about seven miles wide and is fairly level in the middle until it slopes down to the lake. The topography and climate make this an ideal spot to grow grapes, as evident from the existence of over 15 wineries in this area. These slopes are ideal places for the grapes to grow because the air is always moving and thus will not stagnate. Many of the wineries offer wine tasting so that consumers can try the wine they might like to buy. The views of the lake and the land beyond are very scenic year-round.

Steuben County, New York, is home to three Amish settlements. Steuben County is located in south central New York along the Pennsylvania state line. The largest city in the county is Corning, which is in the eastern part of the county. Steuben County is about 40 miles wide and about 40 miles from south to north. In the last quarter of April one will see the weeping willow trees starting to turn green, the daffodils in full bloom, and the tulips in bud stage. Hardscrapple Hill is located in the Amish settlement near the town of Addison (*Blackboard Bulletin*, 2005). This area is very hilly, and many of the hills and mountains in the area are forested.

The Amish settlement near the towns of Jasper and Woodhull is also fairly hilly, although there are small stretches of level ground in the valleys. Many of the Amish in this area are involved in farming, sawmilling, quilting, making peanut brittle, and managing small stores. The third Amish settlement in Steuben County is located near Prattsburg in the north central part of the county. This area is also fairly hilly, with level ground in the valleys. Amish in this area are employed as farmers, sawmill owners, greenhouse operators, cabinetmakers, and bakers. Most of the roads in this area are gravel. There is a large mountain to the northwest of the settlement. The lone school in the area sits along a gravel road on top of a ridge in the middle of the community, and the view of the hills and mountains from the school is stunning, with vistas for many miles. This school has a nice set of swings, a phone booth on the edge of the schoolyard, and a level play area for the scholars.

OHIO

Ohio is home to the largest Amish settlement in North America: Holmes County. Many of the residents of this community reside in Wayne and Tuscarawas counties as well. Another large community is found in Geauga County, southeast of Cleveland. Schools in these two communities are generally two-teacher schools, but other communities in the state, such as Ashland, Fredericktown, Gallipolis, Kenton, and Quaker City, have one-teacher schools. As of the 2004–05 school term there were 286 Amish parochial schools in Ohio, with an average of 30 scholars per school and a teacher-student ratio of one to 17 (*Blackboard Bulletin*, 2005; Luthy, 1994). Since 1972 Ohio has had at least 19 new settlements founded as the Amish seek affordable land suitable for traditional farming methods.

Geauga County

The Amish settlement in this area is found around the towns of Burton and Middlefield and includes the western portions of Trumbull County. This area is composed of rolling hills with wooded hillsides. The locale is famous for maple syrup made from local trees, and many Amish farmers produce the syrup as well. In the late winter one will see many of the trees in this area with taps and buckets. Since the fresh syrup is so readily available, many community groups have pancake breakfasts on Saturdays in March. The town of Middlefield is a fairly busy town where many Amish do their shopping and banking. The town has a new library that has plenty of business on Saturdays. The library is used by the local Amish population, and it is not unusual to see an entire family driving off in their double-seated buggy with everyone but the driver busy reading their new books. There are two unique characteristics about Amish education in this area. Some Amish parents elect to send their children to kindergarten in a public school setting. The second is that some schools in the area have spelling bees, with students competing from two or more schools at one selected site.

Byler (1997) reports that the first Amish arrived in the area from Holmes County, Ohio, in 1883, and that by 1887 a total of 23 families from Holmes County as well as Lawrence County, Pennsylvania, populated the area. As of

2005 the area was home to over 50 Amish parochial schools, with most of these being two-teacher schools (*Blackboard Bulletin*, 2005). Three of these schools have an additional teacher to work with special-needs students. The Geauga settlement is the fourth-largest Amish community in the United States, with over 50 congregations as of 1992 (Kraybill & Olshan, 1994).

One of the newer schools in this settlement has a movable wooden partition (this is a substantial partition made of 2x4 studs and wood paneling) to separate the two classrooms. The windows on both sides of the school provide plenty of natural light. The school has a full basement, white vinyl siding, and a coal stove, and the basement has coat hooks and a place to put boots for each child attending the school. The basement also has a Ping-Pong table and a foosball table that are used at recess in bad weather. The schoolyard has a set of swings and two outhouses. On the date of my visit in the winter of 2005, the school floor was very clean, even though it was midwinter. The classroom for the older scholars had star charts for spelling for each child. There was also a chart to keep up with attendance, and it looked as if all scholars but one still had perfect attendance. In some schools in this settlement, students who have perfect attendance will receive a reward at the end of the school term.

Holmes County

Holmes County, Ohio, is the center of the largest Amish settlement in the world and includes parts of Tuscarawas and Wayne counties. This area has many tourist attractions, but there are fewer tourists here than in the Lancaster, Pennsylvania, area. The area is characterized by gently rolling hills with patches of level land. The area features several regularly scheduled auctions/sales each week in towns such as Mt. Hope and Sugarcreek. As in Lancaster County the Amish in the area have diversified their economy to include many home-based or rural-based businesses. There are numerous furniture-manufacturing shops in the area, as well as bulk-food stores. One bulk-food store northwest of Berlin serves very large ice cream cones and is a popular destination in the warmer weather.

There are over 140 parochial schools in this area, with most being served by two teachers in a one-room school setting (*Blackboard Bulletin*, 2005). Many of the newer buildings also have a basement. Most schools have some type of playground equipment and a backstop for ball games. Schools, except those associated with more conservative groups, also have a nice sign on the front of the school indicating the name of the school, and some signs also indicate the year the school was built.

A new school in this area costs about $60,000. Since it is a challenge for the people in the area who need a new school to pay for one themselves, the community has agreed to "tax" itself for new school construction. Amish are taxed per family unit once per year and per wealth at another point in the year. This money will be available when a new school needs to be built. Each local board still needs to raise money itself, but additional funds come from the entire settlement. Schools that were built in the last few years will get some funding from this source in the near future to help pay for the expenditures.

Children in this area walk to school or ride bikes, and one will see large groups walking to and from school each morning and afternoon. If the walk to school is very lengthy, some parents may take their children in a buggy or hire a driver to take them in the event of stormy weather. At one school I visited in the winter of 2005, several students had a good 20–25 minute walk to school that included traversing some rather steep hills. Children who go to Amish schools in this area do not ride public school buses. This area is home to the first two Amish schools in Ohio, Maple Grove and Fountain Nook. Most of the scholars at Maple Grove School ride bicycles to school (even in snowy weather), and the bikes are parked under the overhang of the large shed at the edge of the schoolyard.

One of the most distinctive and historic schools in Holmes County is Oak Grove School. The school has a unique bell tower and was built circa 1900. The school is nestled on a wedge of land between a dirt road and a blacktop road. This white clapboard building, which serves about 25 Amish children in grades one through eight, has a combination wood/coal stove, unpainted wood floors, wall hooks on which to hang coats, and four sets of large single-pane windows on the north and south sides of the school. The unheated side porch serves as a site for storing personal belongings, such as boots and lunch pails. Four rows of desks face the front of the classroom and the teacher's desk. In front of the building is a field for recess and baseball. The field is abuzz with activity each Wednesday evening during the summer months, as local residents play a friendly game of softball.

Anderson School is one of the oldest schools in that United States that has been in continuous operation (Lehman, 2004). The school is located on Lautenschlager Road midway between Kansas Road and Carr Road in Wayne County, Ohio. The school began in 1830s and was a public school until July 1959, at which time the school was sold to the Amish, who then used it as a parochial school. While early written records about the schools are incomplete, the school was definitely in operation in 1838. Tradition states that Anderson has been three buildings. The second building burned in the winter of 1914–15. School was then held in a shed until the new building was erected. Anderson School still looks as it did in 1919.

Knox County

Knox County is located to the west of Holmes County and is home to four Amish settlements, with the largest being Fredericktown in the northwest corner of the county; this community includes residences in Morrow County as well. There are 28 schools in the county with most being one-teacher schools (*Blackboard Bulletin*, 2005).

The Fredericktown community is composed of some very hilly sections and some fairly level ground. English residents of the area state that the Amish are good neighbors and that they are very active with blood drives and donations to the fire companies and provided a good amount of labor for the building of the new library in town. Schools in the area are of frame construction with white siding. Schoolyards usually have a swing set and a backstop for ball games. Several of the residents tap the many maple trees on the wooded hillsides of the area and produce fresh maple syrup each spring.

Gallia County

Gallia County is located in southeastern Ohio, and the Amish community is located in and around the small towns of Cadmus and Gage. This is very hilly country with small patches of level land, and in early April the area is still prone to cool temperatures. Residents in the area are engaged in farming, woodworking, and baking. There is a furniture shop in the town of Cadmus and a small bakery near Gage. The bakery has pies, breads, cookies, and doughnuts for sale each Friday and Saturday, and the raspberry pies are especially tasty. Schools in the area are of frame construction with white siding.

Gallia County has six schools, and one teacher serves each school. During the 2004–05 school term there were an average of 21 scholars per school (*Blackboard Bulletin*, 2005). Gage School was the first school in the area and was organized in 1994. The newest school in the community is Pioneer Trails School, which is a unique name for an Amish school.

ONTARIO, CANADA

The province of Ontario is home to nine Amish settlements, with the first founded in Milverton in 1824 (*Blackboard Bulletin*, 2005; Luthy, 1994). The most recently founded settlements are in Parry Sound County and Huron County. There are 29 schools in the province, with a majority having at least two teachers.

Aylmer, Ontario

Aylmer, Ontario, is home to an Amish community composed of three church districts and is located in Elgin County. Aylmer is just north of Lake Erie and is about 100 miles southwest of Toronto. The area is well known as a rest stop for migrating tundra swans that rest in the area each spring. The area is composed of fairly level farmland with very few stones or rocks. Many of the farms also have extensive amounts of forested land that provide plenty of fuel for the woodstoves, which are in use most of the year. Among Amish communities, Aylmer is most noted for being home to Pathway Publishers, which publishes three periodicals, titled *Blackboard Bulletin, Family Life,* and *Young Companion.* It also publishes books such as the *Pathway Reading Series,* an integral part of the reading curriculum of many Amish and Mennonite parochial schools as well as that of many families in the United States that home-school their children.

Aylmer is also home to the Heritage Historical Library. The library, founded in 1972, is owned by Pathway Publishers. The goal of the library is "to collect all materials written by, for, and about the Amish." Materials are also collected about the Old Order Mennonites. The library has accumulated a wealth of information and is well organized, having materials filed in 99 categories. The library contains many centuries-old volumes, such as copies of the *Swiss Froschauer Bible,* the *Martyrs' Mirror,* and the *Ausbund.*

Aylmer is a picturesque area, and by the second week of May one will see the green fields of winter wheat, green pastures, dandelions, daffodils, and tulips in full bloom. Farmers will be busy disking the fields and doing some planting. In the late evening one will see the draft horses in the lush green fields grazing after a long day of work. If one is lucky he may also catch a glimpse of calves in the field scampering about, testing their running ability. Many farms in the area grow their vegetables in hothouses even in the summer months, but most vegetables are grown in the fields. There is a large cooperative in the area where some 40 Amish farmers can sell their fresh vegetables and fruits to be shipped by truck retailers in the Toronto area. The co-op has a man-made pond that freezes in the winter. The ice is cut and stored to be used for cooling of the farm products during the hot summer months. Most Amish homes in the area have a woodstove in the kitchen that is used for baking, cooking, and heating the home. These stoves are produced at an Amish-owned factory in the area and are very functional and energy-efficient.

The Amish community is located east of the town of Aylmer and is bisected by Highway 3. This is a fairly busy road, but especially so on Friday the 13th, which is known as a holiday for motorcycle riders in Canada. Motorcycles will be very plentiful on the roads on that day. Aylmer, which is home to the Ontario Police College, is a prosperous small town of 7,000 and has a thriving main-street area that has numerous restaurants, shops, banks, and a bakery. The town has a farmers' market and flea market each Tuesday. Like most prosperous towns in rural North America, the town will have lots of traffic on a Friday afternoon. Compared to the larger Amish communities in the states, traffic is fairly light on area rural roads.

The settlement has five parochial schools that usually employ two teachers each term (*Blackboard Bulletin*, 2005). The first school in the area was begun in 1953. Teachers in the area have always been involved with the summer teachers' meetings since their inception in the 1950s. Area teachers now attend the Michigan/Ontario teachers' meeting each summer.

PENNSYLVANIA

The commonwealth of Pennsylvania was the original destination of the first wave of Amish immigrants from Europe in the 17th century, with many of these immigrants finally settling in Lancaster County. As noted in chapter 2, the commonwealth of Pennsylvania was founded by William Penn as a haven for persecuted religious groups in Europe and England. As a result Quakers, Moravians, Lutherans, Mennonites, and the Amish populated the state. The Amish are now dispersed among over 30 different settlements, and the commonwealth has 387 schools, which is 100 more schools than any other state or province in North America (*Blackboard Bulletin*, 2005; Luthy, 1994). The majority of schools in Pennsylvania follow the Lancaster model of education, which means that most schools are one-teacher schools. In the 2004–05 school term almost 10,000 scholars attended Amish schools in Pennsylvania, with an average of 25 pupils per school and a teacher-pupil ratio of one to 23. Over 20 new settlements have been founded in the commonwealth since 1972. As in other states, the Amish are continually seeking affordable land suitable for traditional farming activities, and that farmland is quite expensive. For example, one 95-acre farm near Paradise sold for 1.97 million dollars at an auction on December 17, 2005. Furthermore, a farm near Quarryville was listed for sale at the same time for 1.75 million dollars (*Diary*, 2006).

New Wilmington

The Amish community in this area is about 60 miles north of Pittsburgh and surrounds the villages of New Wilmington and Volant. The area is characterized by rolling hills with small stretches of fairly level land west of New Wilmington. Most Amish structures in this area are painted white (homes, barns, outbuildings, and schools), and a substantial number of homes and schools have light blue doors. Many of the farms have several purple martin houses. Most of the Amish in the area are engaged in farming. The area has a large cheese factory, a produce auction that meets four times per week in season, and several small sawmills. There is a local public bus service that serves the area, and one of the bus stops is at the edge of the schoolyard of one of the Amish schools. One of the most distinctive aspects of this community is that the horse-drawn buggies have tops that are an orange/brown color. This is quite unusual given that most Amish buggies in North America have black or gray tops.

Amish families associated with the Byler group in the Big Valley of Mifflin County, Pennsylvania, first settled in this area in 1847 (Scott, 1981). There are 17 Amish schools in the area as of the 2004–05 school term, with all but one having one teacher (*Blackboard Bulletin*, 2005). The teacher-pupil ratio in this community is one to 26. One distinctive school in the area has orange/brown trim around the windows, light blue doors, and a tall swing set in the front yard. The Poverty Point School's distinctive feature is that it is the only one-room school that I have ever seen that has a large bell on a stand in the schoolyard near the front corner of the building.

Somerset County

There are two Amish communities in Somerset County, which is situated east of Pittsburgh in southwest Pennsylvania on the Maryland state line. There are over ten schools in the area, and each is a one-teacher school (*Blackboard Bulletin*, 2005). The average number of scholars per school is 22. The area has rolling hills with a few patches of level ground and a mountain situated between the towns of Pocahontas and Salisbury. Atop this mountain are at least a dozen large propeller-type windmills that generate electricity. In late March one will observe some farmers plowing fields. One Amish community is in the eastern part of the county near the village of Pocahontas. Most of the families in this area are engaged in farming. The second Amish community is located between the city of Salisbury and the town of Springs. This area is very close to Maryland, and some Amish in this community probably own land that crosses the state line. This area has several parochial schools located in wooded areas on the side of a hill, making the walk to or from school harder depending on the location of a home relative to the school. The area has a well-equipped school for special-needs students. One of the most interesting uses of an old school is in evidence in this county. A local farmer has transformed a former one-room school into a garden center that serves as one end of a large greenhouse. Since this is located on a fairly heavily traveled road, one would surmise that a new school was constructed in a more rural setting to replace this school.

The Somerset County Historical Society notes that the Allegheny Mountains separate Somerset County from eastern Pennsylvania, and as a result this area was not heavily settled by those of European descent until after trails and roads were built as avenues for troop movement in the French and Indian War. Thus European settlement of the area began in the 1760s. However, the roads and trails were not easily traveled, and the new settlers were fairly isolated until 1800. An interesting ongoing activity of the Berlin Area

Historical Society is the restoration of the Glade one-room school (circa 1868) as a schoolhouse museum.

Clinton County

The Amish community in Clinton County is located in Sugar Valley, which is in the eastern part of the county. The county is famous for its Pennsylvania State Flaming Foliage Festival, held each October. Many of the Amish adults in the area migrated here from Lancaster County. Residents make their livelihood at a variety of shops, farms, and business activities that include greenhouses, pine crafts, seed sales, kitchen cabinets, chain saws, quilts, lawn furniture, air compressors, honey, sheep, goats, and poultry. One major furniture shop in the area specializes in solid oak and cherry pieces. In late April farmers in the area will be busy in the fields. In good weather students in the area will enjoy playing softball at recess, with their teacher serving as the pitcher. The *Blackboard Bulletin* (2005) indicated that in the 2004–05 school term there were five schools in the area, all of which were one-teacher schools. There were an average of 28 scholars per school.

Lancaster County

The Lancaster County, Pennsylvania, settlement is the most widely known, publicized, and visited Amish settlement in the world. Because of that many tourist attractions have sprung up in the area that have little to do with the Amish and more to do with shopping and recreational activities for tourists. There are also several major highways that intersect the county, which dramatically increases the motor vehicles on highways and county roads in the area. Lancaster County is subject to quite heavy traffic in the tourist season and on any major holiday. For example, Lancaster placed ninth in the United States for the worst traffic jams at a popular tourist destination over the July 4 holiday (AOL News, 2005). The county is also popular for industry and housing, and these interests compete with the farmers in the area for any available land that comes up for sale. Because of the aforementioned problems and the fact that the Amish population in the county has been increasing, many residents of the settlement have migrated to new settlements with available farmland, fewer tourists, less traffic, and more reasonable land prices. Still, the area is a vibrant community that is spilling into the southern portion of Berks County, western Chester County, and even Cecil County in northern Maryland as families have searched for additional farmland. An interesting event occurred at a restaurant in Lancaster in the winter of 2005 as I was dining with some Amish friends. Two men from Montana came in and were asking people about available farmland for sale. This resulted in quite a chuckle by the Amish outside after the meal, for they knew there is little land for sale in Lancaster County.

Many years ago the major occupation for the Amish in Lancaster County was agriculture. Because of the reduced amount of land available for young families, the community has diversified the economy to include many shops that are located on farms. There are a wide variety of shops, with most related to woodworking or aspects of enterprises related to agriculture. Many families have farm stands where the passerby can purchase fresh vegetables, crafts, quilts, and baked goods. Lancaster County is famous for shoofly pie, and most farm stands that sell baked goods will have fresh shoofly pie available each Friday and Saturday except during the winter months. In addition, some of the families run stands at farmers' markets in surrounding cities as far away as Annapolis, Maryland. Lancaster is also home to the Gordonville Print Shop, which provides numerous publications for Old Order Mennonite and Amish communities and schools. The *Ordnung* of the Lancaster community prohibits the use of bicycles and roller blades but does permit the use of scooters.

As noted previously, the first Amish parochial schools in Pennsylvania were begun in Lancaster because of the closing of the rural public one-room schools. These two schools, Oak Grove and Pleasant View, are still in existence. There are over 175 Amish schools in Lancaster County, with an average of 27 scholars per school, and they are almost always one-teacher schools (*Blackboard Bulletin*, 2005). The schools are situated so that the children can walk to school. School playgrounds are usually equipped with swings and a backstop for ball games. In the summer, some schoolyards will have volleyball nets for evening activities for area youth.

The Amish of Lancaster County have always been strong supporters of local fire companies and have assisted with numerous sales for well over 40 years. For example, Kauffman, Petersheim, and Beiler (1992) indicate that the Amish were involved with the first Bart Township Fire Company sale in the 1960s, which netted a profit of $1,800, a sum that made everyone happy. By the 1990s this fire company sale was so successful that two days were needed to sell all the items. The Amish support for fire companies is not unique to Lancaster County; Amish residents in many communities around the United States and Canada actively support the needs of fire companies in their area.

Since most Amish schools, barns, and homes are of wood-frame construction, they are especially vulnerable to fires, with many fires at schools attributed to arsonists. For example, Kauffman, Petersheim, and Beiler (1992) report that the fire at Valley Road School consumed 90% of the building and its contents on an October evening in 1971. Reports indicate that the fire was started on the porch of the school—a clear indication that it was started by arsonists. Once the fire was out, it must have been heart wrenching for the passerby to see the scholars rummaging through the charred remains for personal belongings.

New schools in the Lancaster area are constructed with exteriors that are maintenance free and may even include brick structures, as does a new school near the town of Gap. Most schools will have vinyl siding, with the preferred colors being white or tan.

Big Valley

One of the most distinctive Amish settlements in North America is found in the picturesque Big Valley of Mifflin County. This valley is home to several different Amish groups (Hostetler, 1993). The Nebraska Amish drive white-top buggies and are the most conservative group in the valley. This group was the target of arsonists in 1992, when six barns were burned, a seventh damaged, and over 150 animals killed. The "Byler Church" members drive black buggies with yellow tops while the other Amish in the area drive black-top buggies. There are over 15 schools in this area, and are all served by one teacher except the special-education school, which has two teachers. Nebraska Amish schools are usually white with a blue entrance door and are generally smaller in size than other schools in the area. Schools for other Amish groups in the area are of frame construction with white or light gray siding. Schools in the Big Valley do not have playground equipment or backstops for ball games. Schools in this area have an average of 29 pupils per school (*Blackboard Bulletin*, 2005).

Centre County

Centre County has several communities of Amish, with most located in the eastern part of the county. One group is located in and around the town of

Figure 10.1. Sunnyside School, Mifflin County, Pennsylvania

Rebersburg in the Brush Valley. This community has ten schools, and each school is served by one teacher except the special-education school, which has two teachers. Schools in this area have about 25 pupils per school.

Schools in the Brush Valley are usually of frame construction with vinyl siding. In addition to the usual white siding, schools in this area may have brown or gray siding as well. Many students in the community ride their scooters to school. Some students in the area ride along to school with their English neighbors on public school buses each day.

A community of Nebraska Amish lives in Centre County west of Aaronsburg along State Route 45. There are at least two Amish schools in this area and the schools are of frame construction with white siding. Schoolyards will include a horse shed and outhouses but do not have playground equipment or a backstop for ball games. Both of the Nebraska Amish schools in this area are tucked away in small valleys away from the main road.

Lycoming County

One of the Amish communities in Lycoming County is located in the Nippenose Valley. European settlers first came to this area in 1765, with a large influx in 1769 when the colony of Pennsylvania offered veterans of the French and Indian War land west of the Lycoming Creek at 22 cents per acre (Williamsport/Lycoming Chamber of Commerce, 2002). Bastress Mountain separates Nippenose Valley from the Susquehanna River and the city of Williamsport. Williamsport is home to the Little League World Series, which is held each August and brings tens of thousands of visitors to the area from around the world. Coming across Bastress Mountain from Williamsport, one will get a spectacular view of the valley and the mountains to the south. During the last week of April one will see forsythia bushes as well as the dandelions in full bloom and rich green grass in pastures and yards and along the roadway. Land in the valley is fairly level with a pleasant mix of rolling hills and small creek beds. The area is home to many farms and greenhouses. One can see several mountains to the south of the valley. The west end of the valley is home to a large stone quarry as well as Ravenswood State Park in the Tiadaghton State Forest. There are two Amish schools in this valley, with one being appropriately named Mountain View School.

11

Amish Communities and Schools in the Southeastern United States

For success attitude is as important as ability.

—Aphorism posted at an Amish school in Indiana in 2005

In this chapter we focus on the southeastern United States. The region includes the southernmost Amish settlement in the United States at Beeville, Texas. The Amish reside in nine states in the southeastern United States, including Florida, Kentucky, Mississippi, North Carolina, Oklahoma, Tennessee, Texas, Virginia, and West Virginia. The community in Sarasota, Florida, is a retirement community that is populated by a variety of Amish and Mennonite groups but does not have a school. Schools with unique names in the southeastern United States include Daniels' Ridge, Charity Echoes, and Muckle Branch.

Unique School Names in the Southeastern United States

Daniels' Ridge	Little Bend Locust
Arrowhead Knob	Harmony Echoes
Charity Echoes	Amish Lane
Muckle Branch	Almond
Gulf Breeze	Rustling Oaks
Old West	Blossom Hill
Cedar Bluff	Three Oaks
Mint Springs	

(*Blackboard Bulletin*, 2005)

KENTUCKY

Kentucky is home to 11 Amish settlements, with the first settlement in the state founded near Guthrie in 1958 (*Blackboard Bulletin*, 2005; Luthy, 1994). All of the other communities in the Bluegrass State have been founded since 1972. There are 34 schools in the state, and the majority are one-teacher schools. The average number of pupils per school at the one-teacher schools is 20 (*Blackboard Bulletin*, 2005). There are several two-teacher schools, as well as one three-teacher school in the state. One of the unique features about Kentucky Amish parochial schools is the fact that one school, Blossom Hill, is named after a Jersey cow. The Hopkinsville community decided to build a new school in 2003 (Miller, 2004a). The school was built from lumber harvested from the nearby woods and was situated in the former grazing area for one of the school board member's cows. The cow's name was Blossom, and she roamed the area for fresh grass and came back to her home each morning and evening to be milked. Thus we have Blossom Hill School, which is most likely the only school—public, parochial, or private—in the United States or Canada that is named after a Jersey cow.

Crittenden County

Crittenden County is a very hilly region of western Kentucky and is bordered by the Ohio River to the northwest. The Amish community is located west of the towns of Marion and Mattoon. Marion is the county seat and was named after the Revolutionary War hero Francis Marion. The Clement Mineral Museum is located in Marion and houses thousands of fluorite specimens. Most of the hills are forested in this locale, and in the spring a good number of the trees are tapped to make maple syrup. A small group of Amish visited this area in 1977 looking for land for sale. They must have liked the land and the climate, as the Amish moved to Crittenden County later in that year. All of the initial families were from Dover, Delaware. In later years families from other states joined these original settlers. Natives of the area state that the first group of Amish faced a very hard winter in their first year, since many of their homes had not yet been completed. Most of the roads connecting the Amish settlement are dirt roads, and there are several steep climbs in the area that will pose a challenge to a horse pulling a full buggy.

Many of the Amish farmers in Crittenden County raise produce on a contract basis. In the beginning years they raised pickles, then pimento peppers, and more recently tomatoes (Miller, 2004a).

The area has six schools, with one of the two-room schools being served by teachers who are brothers. The first school in the area was Daniel's Ridge school, which was begun in 1978. It is a two-room school that sits below the top of a ridge and has a nice field for a ball game. Twin Oak school was built in 2000 when the Daniel's Ridge School could not accommodate all the scholars in the area (Miller, 2004a). Meadow Ridge School was built in 1996 and has a full basement. After the foundation was completed, a frolic was held to build the school, which was nearly completed in two days. A school in the area with a unique name is Crooked Creek Valley School, which was built in 1986. The name comes from the creek in the woods below the school. On occasion, the scholars like to play around the creek at recess. Another unique thing about this school is that some students get to school by crossing a hanging bridge that is strung across the creek.

Crab Orchard

Crab Orchard is located in Lincoln County, Kentucky. Lincoln County was founded in 1780 and was named in honor of Benjamin Lincoln, a Revolutionary War officer who was asked by Congress to conduct the war in the southern colonies. Lincoln County is located in central Kentucky about 60 miles south of Lexington and was one of the three original counties in the state. Crab Orchard is a small town, and on summer evenings some non-Amish residents like to sit on their front porches and enjoy the cool of the evening and watch the traffic on the main road through the town. The area has a mixture of hills and fairly level valleys; however, some of the hills in the area are very steep, which makes horse-and-buggy travel both difficult and dangerous. Some English farmers in the area grow tobacco, and the first crop of hay will be cut and baled by the middle of June. The area is home to many species of birds, including bluebirds and cardinals. Some roadsides of the area will be very colorful in mid-June because of the profusion of wild daylilies and trumpet vines. The daylilies are orange, and the trumpet vine flowers are orange and red. Amish residents are engaged in farming, treating lumber for fences, woodworking, and running bulk-food stores.

The Amish first moved to this area in 1994, and, as in most new communities children were home-schooled until there were enough students to begin a school (Miller, 2004a). The community has had three or four schools in operation over the last few years, depending on the number of scholars residing in each section of the settlement. All schools in the area have an exterior of white metal siding. Donald Miller (2004a) notes that Harmon's Lick and Locust Grove schools were built in 1996 and that Harmon's Lick is named after Harmon's Lick Creek, which is just 125 yards north of the school.

MISSISSIPPI

According to the *Blackboard Bulletin* (2005), there were two Amish schools in Mississippi in the 2004–05 school year. The schools are located near Randolph in Pontotoc County. Randolph is west of Tupelo in the northeast corner of Mississippi. Oak Forest School and Pontotoc School are both one-teacher schools and had an average of 16 scholars per school in 2004–05 school term.

NORTH CAROLINA

There was one Amish parochial school in North Carolina in the 2004–05 school year. The school, Whispering Pines, is situated in the middle of the Amish community of Union Grove, which is located in southwest Yadkin County, North Carolina. The area has a nice mixture of fields and forest and is composed of rolling terrain. During the 2004–05 school term the school had two teachers with an average of 11 students per teacher. Whispering Pines is a fairly new structure with white vinyl siding and has two rooms, a coatroom, and restrooms. Funds for the building materials for the school were generated by several construction projects completed by members of the community. For example, a pole building was erected for a local English farmer, and proceeds from the project went to the school fund.

Whispering Pines School has been in existence since 1985, and prior to building the new school classes were held in two nice mobile-unit classrooms at the same site. The school has a spacious grass playground for games of tag or softball. The schoolyard also has a large shed for horses or ponies. Students use a variety of ways to get to school, including pony carts, horse-drawn buggies, scooters, and bicycles. Residents of the area are engaged in farming, furniture making, construction, baking, and retail sales. Shiloh General Store bakes fresh bread each Tuesday through Saturday and bakes a delicious loaf of oatmeal bread.

The community at Union Grove was established in 1985 (Luthy, 1994). It is interesting to note that Luthy (1986, pp. 299–300) reports that a previous and now defunct Amish community in Moyock, N.C., organized a school for the 1925–26 school year. A hotel was built to house Amish settlers in this area, and school was held on the second floor of this hotel. This was the only Amish school ever operated in a hotel.

OKLAHOMA

There are two settlements of Amish in Oklahoma (*Blackboard Bulletin*, 2005; Luthy, 1994). The Mayes County community was founded in 1910 and has three church districts. The Coal County settlement was organized in 1978 and has one church district. Each community has one school, and two teachers work at each school. The average number of scholars per school was 26 during the 2004–05 school term (*Blackboard Bulletin*, 2005).

The Amish community in Coal County has operated parochial schools since the 1980–81 school term. A new one-room school, Elm Creek, was built in 1990; later a barn was built to house the students' horses (Miller, 2000). Later residents moved a small house to the schoolyard for teachers who needed a place to reside. Each fall an auction has been held to raise funds for school operations. On average over 100 quilts are sold each year, and the auction attracts thousands of bidders. Residents of the Coal County settlement make their living as farmers, carpenters, mechanics, and woodworkers. Some of the unique animals in the area include tarantulas, scorpions, armadillos, and seed ticks, which are about the size of a pinhead.

TENNESSEE

Tennessee is home to four Amish communities, and parochial schools in the state are always one-teacher schools (*Blackboard Bulletin*, 2005; Luthy, 1994). The first Amish community was founded north of Etheridge in 1944, and the other three settlements have been established since 1975. During the 2004–05 school term there were 19 schools in the state with an average of 22 pupils per school. The largest community is located in Lawrence County near the town of Etheridge. The first Amish school in the area was opened about 1945.

Some of the first Amish residents to Etheridge emigrated from Ohio because they believed that the Amish in Ohio were adopting too many new ideas. Most residents of the Etheridge community are farmers, with others involved with various aspects of woodworking. The area has several sawmills, furniture shops, and harness shops. The land in the area is fairly level with rolling hills. Many of the farmers in the area have blueberry bushes and/or grapevines and also grow sorghum. At roadside stands one can find fresh peanut brittle, bread, eggs, and baskets. The peanut brittle and bread are quite tasty and are usually freshly made for Friday and Saturday sales. The area is home to lots of red-winged blackbirds, bluebirds, and gold finches, and most homes have purple martin houses.

Schools in this area are small and do not have any playground equipment in the schoolyard. One of the smallest schools in the area is built on a cinder block foundation and has a concrete porch. The roof is covered with tin, and the exterior walls are covered with three-foot-wide asphalt "roll type" roofing. The inside walls and ceiling are made of plywood that has been painted white, and the floor is unpainted plywood. The school has a barrel-shaped woodstove in the center of the classroom and three windows on the east and west sides of the school. The schoolyard has two outhouses, situated on two corners of the property, and an unpainted woodshed.

English residents in the area have established several small businesses marketing the area as a tourist destination. Amish-made wood products are sold at one of the businesses.

A recently established Amish community is west of Summertown, Tennessee. There is one school in this community, Natchez Trace Christian School, for the 20 scholars in the area (*Blackboard Bulletin*, 2005). This community was founded in the fall of 2000, and a trailer has been used for the school (Miller, 2004a). In its first year of operation the school had six pupils. The area has a mix of fairly level land and rolling hills. Residents of the Summertown community are farmers and woodworkers, and the area is heavily wooded.

TEXAS

One of the southernmost Amish communities in the United States is located about 10 miles from Beeville, Texas. This area is home to Gulf Breeze Parochial School, which is a one-teacher school that had 12 students in the 2004–05 school year (*Blackboard Bulletin*, 2005). Prior to construction of the schoolhouse, classes were held on the second floor of a home for two years, given that there were fewer than six students each year. The school was built in the fall of 2001.

Being situated just 50 miles from the coast means that the area enjoys a breeze from the Gulf of Mexico most days of the year (Miller, D., 2004a). Residents in the area are shop owners, farmers, leather workers, and quilters. An English resident of the area provided the community with good firewood for many years and would not take payment because when he was orphaned as a boy, an Amish family cared for him until relatives finally came to get him. During the summer of 2005 farmers in the area grew cotton and corn (*The Diary*, September, 2005).

VIRGINIA

There are two Amish settlements in Virginia; one is located near Cullen and the other near Pearisburg. Each community has a school, with Almond School in Cullen being a one-teacher school and Walker Valley School near Pearisburg being a two-teacher school (*Blackboard Bulletin*, 2005). Almond School is a traditional frame-construction school with white siding and a blue/green door. The Walker Valley School is a unique structure because it is a log building and is double the size of a traditional one-room school. The school also serves as the meeting place for church services since many of the homes in the area are much too small to serve as a meeting place for church, and barns in the area are also much smaller than the traditional bank barns found in Ohio and Pennsylvania.

Cullen is located southwest of Richmond. The area is fairly hilly, with many of the forests in the area having been recently logged. In late April the area is quite picturesque with redbud and dogwood trees in bloom in the woods of the area. Amish residents are primarily farmers, and there was one family operating a sawmill.

Pearisburg is a unique community since many of the residents live on the lower half of Walker Mountain, with garden plots on any available level land on the hillside and some fields east of the creek in the valley. Residents in the area are engaged in farming, woodworking, and raising exotic birds. The aviary has several types of geese, ducks, and swans for sale to the public and also hosts tours of the facility. The views from the front porches of the homes on Walker Mountain are quite beautiful, with a clear view of the entire valley and the mountains to the west.

Reports indicate that a new Amish settlement is starting in Halifax County, Virginia (*Diary*, Nov. 2005 & *Diary*, 2006). A new school will most likely be started in this area once enough scholars reside in the community.

WEST VIRGINIA

According to the *Blackboard Bulletin* (2005) there was one Amish school in West Virginia during the 2004–05 school term. The school was located near Letart, West Virginia. Letart is situated in the hilly country along the Ohio River in Mason County. The school is named Sycamore Hollow School and had 15 pupils and one teacher in the 2004–05 school term. Some residents of this community hunt for deer, and a good deer harvest was reported for this community in the winter of 2005–06 (*Diary*, Nov. 2005).

The Amish traditions of frolics for school funds and to help others are in full force in West Virginia. For example, a wood-cutting frolic for school funds was held in December of 2005 (*Diary*, 2006). In addition, some local residents made the long trek to Pearisburg, Virginia, to help build a new home for an Amish family in that community (*Diary*, Sep. 2005).

12

Amish Schools and Communities in the Midwestern and Western United States

Our life is what our thoughts make it!

—Aphorism posted at an Amish school in Illinois in 2005

In this chapter we will spotlight schools and communities in the midwestern and western United States. The region includes long-established communities near Arthur, Illinois, and Elkhart/LaGrange, Indiana, as well as very new settlements in Colorado. Interesting school names in this region include Mayflower, Eight Square, and Pumpkin Vine.

Unique School Names in the Midwestern and Western United States

Cable Line	Eight Square
Golden Rule	Pumpkin Vine
Tollway View	Coyote Hollow
Echo Ridge	Echo Vale
Friendship	Barnyard Echoes
Norway	Scotland
Missouri	Bright Prairie
Eagles Nest	Ruby Valley
Meadow Lark	Railside
Hay Creek	Hill and Valley
Quaker Valley	Irish Ridge
Mayflower	Horn
String Town	Middle Fork

(*Blackboard Bulletin*, 2005)

ILLINOIS

Illinois is home to eight Amish communities, with the largest near Arthur. The Arthur settlement was organized in 1864, and the remaining communities were all begun after 1987 (*Blackboard Bulletin*, 2005; Luthy, 1994). The state has 28 schools, with the first schools, Plainview (1966) and Prairie Lane (1968), organized in the Arthur area. Most schools in the state are two-teacher schools and have an average of 28 scholars per school with a teacher/pupil ratio of one to 15.

Arthur is the center of the largest settlement of Amish in Illinois and is located in the eastern part of the state about 150 miles south of Chicago. The town of Arthur has a thriving downtown business district that includes two large covered sheds to park horse-drawn vehicles. The sheds are a welcome relief to the horses in cold weather or in the hot summer sun. Arthur is home to several well-known auctions/sales each year, including the Mennonite Relief Sale held each August, the School Benefit Auction held each September, and the Central Illinois Draft Horse Sale held each October. The School Benefit Auction proceeds help fund special-education programs for Amish students in the area.

Several Amish families first migrated to this area in 1864. The community now has a population of about 4,500 people organized into 26 church districts. The land in this area is very level, and the soil is very productive if farmed in an appropriate manner. As in larger Amish communities, many households have home-based businesses in furniture, gazebos, lawn furniture, quilts, bicycles, and other farm-related endeavors.

The Illinois Amish Interpretive Center (2005) estimates that about one-third of the Amish youth in the area attend public schools. Public school staff work carefully with the Amish to provide appropriate curriculum for the pupils, and the public schools will hold graduation ceremonies for the eighth-grade graduates.

The majority of Amish youth in the area attend parochial schools, and Donald Miller (1980) stated that the main reason for leaving the public schools was that the Amish did not feel sex education, physical education, or films were necessary for their way of life. As of the 2004–05 school term there were 16 Amish parochial schools in the area, with five of the schools having an annex to provide instructional space for special needs students (*Blackboard Bulletin*, 2005). The average number of students per two-teacher school is 35, and the average class size for an annex is four students. Most schools in the area have two teachers. The first school in the area was Plainview, which was built in 1966 (Miller, D., 1980). It was a two-teacher school and had 49 scholars enrolled the first year. The first school board consisted of five men from the community. The Amish in Illinois have a state school board to oversee all schools.

INDIANA

Indiana is home to over 10 Amish communities, with the largest in the Elkhart/LaGrange area. Other large settlements are located near Berne, Grabill, Montgomery, and Nappanee (*Blackboard Bulletin*, 2005; Luthy 1994). The Amish have a long history in the state, with the Nappanee settlement, organized in 1839; the Elkhart community, established in 1841; the Kokomo settlement, organized in 1848; the Berne community, established in 1850; and the Grabill settlement, organized in 1852. The state had 153 schools during the 2004–05 school term, with the majority being two-teacher schools.

The Allen County settlement is unique in that it is one of the few settlements in North America that has schools with three to five teachers. Schools in Indiana have an average of 38 scholars per school and a teacher-pupil ratio of one to 17.

Elkhart/LaGrange

The largest Amish community in Indiana is located in northeast Indiana around the towns of Shipshewana and Middlebury. Much of the land in this area is fairly level, with some rolling hills. The area attracts numerous tourists from the Midwest, and the community has attempted to regulate growth in this industry as well as retain its local, small-town atmosphere and its religious heritage. As a result, many of the shops in Shipshewana are closed on Sundays. The area is home to a well-known open-air market that attracts large crowds. The market occurs each Tuesday and Wednesday from May to October. The area holds an antiques auction every Wednesday and a horse auction that happens every Friday. Both of these events are held throughout the year.

Luthy's analysis (1994) of the tourist industry in the area notes that the growth of the tourist industry is linked to the growth of the Shipeshewana Flea Market. The tourist industry in the area began in the 1960s and has had steady growth since that time. Those benefitting from the tourist industry are no doubt pleased with the profits generated each year. However, local residents not involved with the flea market or the tourist industry are no doubt frustrated by the traffic and continued expansion of tourist-related activities and building.

There are more than 60 Amish schools in this community, and all are two-teacher schools; the average number of pupils per school is 36 (*Blackboard Bulletin*, 2005). Many schools have a basement, and some even include space for an apartment for the teachers. Some of the apartments are not used for housing by the teachers. If this is the case, the room is used by the special-education students and teacher.

Some of the first schools in the Elkhart/LaGrange community included Plain View, Pleasant Ridge, Blue Ridge, and Eight Square (Farmweld, 2004). Plainview was built in 1948 and later razed and completely rebuilt. Teacher living quarters were provided above the entrance on the south end. The school is about 1.5 miles east of Middlebury. In 1957 Pleasant Ridge was built due to overflow attendance at Plain View. The school is located northwest of Shipshewana. An entrance and teacher quarters upstairs were added to the structure in 1983. Blue Ridge was built in 1966 and is situated northwest of Shipshewana. The name comes from the two blueberry patches nearby. Eight Square was built in 1967. The original structure was red brick with eight corners, which provided impetus for the unique name. The original building burned in 1961 and was replaced with a rectangular block structure. This school was razed in 2000 and replaced with a new building.

On a visit to this area in April of 1997 I noticed an Amish farmer disking his fields in preparation for spring planting. It was a nice sunny day, and since I had been riding my bike for quite a while, I decided to take a rest. I sat down under a tree and watched the horses as they moved across the fields. It seemed to me that the farmer was taking a short nap as the horses continued across the field. A few minutes later the horses stopped in the field not too far from me, and the farmer came over to chat. I noticed that the farm machinery had what looked like a bucket seat from a 1965 Ford Mustang bolted atop the metal seat. After we exchange greetings I said, "That looks like a comfortable seat you have there."

The farmer replied, "Sure is. It is so comfortable that I sometimes fall asleep while working in this field. The horses know what to do, though. They have worked this field for many years."

As we talked further, I indicated that I lived in North Carolina. He remarked that he had been through North Carolina on several occasions as he and friends from his community took a van to Florence, South Carolina, to get their teeth fixed. Florence is well known for dental clinics that provide dental services for patients from around the United States. At that time some clinics were open 24 hours per day six days per week, and one could get dentures within 24 hours.

Allen County

Allen County had seven schools with an average enrollment of 90 scholars per school during the 2004–05 school year (*Blackboard Bulletin*, 2005). Springfield School, which began in 1959, is the largest Amish school complex in North America and had a population of almost 150 students taught by five teachers during the 2004–05 term.

Harroff (2004) reports that many Amish children in Allen County ride public school buses to school. Amish students are on the first bus run, and thus school starts at about 7:30 each morning. Since the Amish schools are not in the vicinity of the public schools, after transporting the Amish pupils, the buses make another run to pick up public school students.

Harroff (2004) further notes that several Amish schools in Allen County are of brick construction. One newer school in the area has four full classrooms, indoor drinking fountains, wash basins, and a small library. The schoolyard has a medium-size barn, two cement basketball courts, a volleyball net, a large grass area for ball games and tag, and a cement pad for visitor's buggies that is often used by the scholars for in-line skating.

Berne/Geneva

The Berne/Geneva settlement is located in the eastern part of the state and has very level terrain. The community is unique in that residents drive open-top buggies year round, which makes for some cold drives in the winter. As in other communities in the Midwest, snowstorms can become quite treacherous because of the wind often associated with these storms.

Scott (1981) notes that the Amish in the Berne/Geneva settlement utilize a dialect based on their roots in Berne, Switzerland, and thus are referred to as the Swiss Amish. While there are commonalities, the Swiss dialect is different from the Pennsylvania Dutch used in most Amish communities. There are four communities of Swiss Amish in North America and all are restricted to the use of open buggies. Because of this most people have a large umbrella for use in rain or heavy wind. Buggies in this area are not upholstered and do not have backrests.

As of the 2004–05 school term there were 33 schools in this community, and most were two-teacher schools (*Blackboard Bulletin*, 2005). It is interesting to note that many of the schools in this area have names associated with a valley (Hidden Valley, Pleasant Valley, and Swiss Valley) or a creek (Bear Creek, Blue Creek, and Engle Creek).

Daviess County

Daviess County is located in southern Indiana almost directly west of Louisville, Kentucky. The Amish settlement here was founded in 1868 when immigrants from Europe arrived to make this their new home. Daviess County is one of the top five Amish settlements in terms of population in Indiana (Kraybill & Olshan, 1994). The area is home to eleven schools. One of the schools is a three-teacher school, while each of the remaining schools has two teachers, as is the case with most Amish schools throughout Indiana (*Blackboard Bulletin*, 2005). Ten of the eleven schools in the area have at least one male teacher, which makes this community distinctive because female teachers serve most Amish parochial schools. The average number of pupils per school is 54, which means that each teacher serves about 27 scholars per year.

Another unique aspect of this settlement is that most pupils ride pony carts or small buggies to school. The small buggies are actually a reduced-scale version of the buggies used by families for transportation, and three or four siblings will ride to school together each day. The ponies have a shed to stay in during the day, and the buggies will be parked in the schoolyard.

The land in this area is fairly flat, and many of the rural roads are stone or gravel, which makes for a muddy ride in late winter and early spring. One of the schools in the area is a two-room school, with one teacher instructing grades 4–8 and the other teacher instructing grades 1–3. The school also has one helper who alternates between classes every other day.

Boys in this area really like to play basketball, and this school has an outdoor cement basketball court. Girls like to play volleyball, and the schoolyard has a net for these games. Older students have the privilege of playing basketball or volleyball while the younger students play on the swings or play running games. Each school in the area has a school board, and the community also has two representatives on the Indiana State Amish School Committee. This committee meets about three times per year and keeps the local communities up to date on new laws and requirements.

Daviess County was hit by a tornado on the afternoon of November 15, 2005 (*Diary*, Sep. 2005). About 50 homes were damaged with some farmsteads losing all their buildings. Amazingly, none of the Amish residents of the area were killed or suffered serious injuries as a result of the tornado. Amish communities in Ohio, Illinois, and other settlements in Indiana immediately sprang into action and sent work crews to help with the cleanup, roof repairs, and the rebuilding of homes and farm buildings.

IOWA

Iowa is home to 51 Amish schools spread over 13 settlements (*Blackboard Bulletin*, 2005; Luthy 1994). The first community in the state was established in Kalona in 1848, while the settlement near Hazelton was founded in 1914. All the other communites in the state have been established since 1969. Some communities prefer two-teacher schools while others prefer one-teacher schools. The average school has 21 pupils and the pupil-teacher ratio is 13 pupils per teacher. The three largest communities in the state are located in Bloomfield, Kalona, and Hazelton.

Bloomfield

The Bloomfield community is located in Davis County, Iowa, and was begun by former residents of the Kalona, Iowa, settlement. This community is

Figure 12.1. Echo Ridge School, Bloomfield, Iowa. Example of a two-teacher school with a small apartment for teachers over the entrance.

growing at a rapid pace and may soon eclipse Kalona as the largest Amish community west of the Mississippi River. Residents of the community are engaged in farming, woodworking, lumber production, dog breeding, and shop ownership. The area is composed of rolling hills interspersed with stretches of flat land. Most of the schools in the area are two-teacher schools, and they have one large room for instruction and may have large curtains to divide the room as needed. Schools in the area are of frame construction with white siding and include a bell tower. Most schools in the area have a small living space over the entrance for teacher lodging, but few if any teachers live at the school. Schoolyards usually include swings, seesaws, and a backstop for the ball field.

Upper-grade students in this area get to go on a field trip each spring. For example, one year the seventh and eighth graders visited the John Deere plant and the next year they visited schools in Kalona. During the 2004–05 school term there were 10 schools in operation in this area, with about 22 students per school and with each teacher responsible for about 11 students. Echo Ridge School is built on the top of a hill, having an expansive schoolyard and a very nice view in all directions. The schoolyard has lots of playground equipment, including six swings, a large sliding board, a basketball hoop, and a backstop. Since most of the scholars at this school drive pony carts to school, there is a large red horse shed on the school grounds.

Kalona

The Kalona, Iowa, settlement is noted as being the largest Amish community west of the Mississippi River and is located southwest of Iowa City in Johnson and Washington counties. Twin County Dairy is a popular destination for locals and tourists because of the fresh cheese curds and cheese for sale. The area is also known for the large quilt show and sale held each April. The area is composed of gently rolling hills and large stretches of fairly level land. The black loam soil is free of rocks and stones. Residents of the settlement are mainly farmers. Many farmers in the area are engaged in goat milk production, with the milk being shipped to Wisconsin. Additionally, some residents sell produce and crafts at roadside stands while others are engaged in quilt making and woodworking. There is an especially refreshing drink served at some produce stands in the area. It is a mixture of rhubarb juice and 7-Up and is a nice treat on a hot day, especially if one has been traveling many of the dusty gravel roads in the locale.

The Amish first moved to this area in the mid-19th century, with the first congregation established in 1851. The area has nine schools with an average of 24 students per school. Most schools in the community are two-teacher schools, and the teachers divide teaching responsibilities by subject rather than grade. Thus, one teacher might be responsible for teaching arithmetic while the other will be responsible for reading. Two of the schools in the area have an additional teacher for special-education students. Schools in this area are of frame construction with white metal or wood siding, and most have indoor plumbing. Schoolyards in the community usually include swings, seesaws, and a backstop for the ball field. In addition to the schoolhouses, this community has several Sunday school buildings, which are used for German language Sunday school. Worship services are held in the homes on a rotating basis every other Sunday, alternating with Sunday school.

One of the unique characteristics of the Kalona area is the Middleburg Parochial School. The history of this school dates back to the 1830s, but it is not known if the present building dates to that time. However, records do indicate that this building has continuously served as a school for a long time. This school has been in operation as an Amish school since 1972. The classroom is quite large and has 11-foot ceilings and a hardwood floor. The building has a full basement and was purchased from the local school district once it was closed as a public school.

Lamoni

The Lamoni Amish community is located in south central Iowa along the Missouri/Iowa border. Lamoni is the home of Graceland University, which was founded in 1895 and is associated with the Community of Christ Church. The Amish community in Lamoni is a fairly new settlement founded in 1998, and some of the residents actually live in Missouri. The community has three schools with an average of 29 pupils per school (*Blackboard Bulletin*, 2005). The schools in this area are all small plain frame structures with white siding, black metal roofs, and a small bell tower. Schoolyards have a horse shed and two outhouses, but do not have any playground equipment.

Figure 12.2. Amish School, Lamoni, Iowa

Buchanan County

The Hazelton Amish community is located in Buchanan County, about 20 miles east of Cedar Falls, Iowa. The area is most known for the Amish school controversy in the 1960s, as documented in chapter 4. The area has large stretches of level land with gently rolling hills. The Amish first moved to this area in 1914, with several families moving from Kalona. Most of the residents make their living as farmers or shop owners.

The first Amish schools in the area were Limestone View and Hickory Grove, both of which opened in 1946 when the public school system decided to close all the country schools in the area (Miller, 2004c). Limestone View was the old Charity Flats public school and was purchased after it was closed. The Amish moved the school, using horses, about 1.3 miles to its present location. Hickory Grove was a public school and was purchased by the Amish when it closed; the school is still located in the same area. The Amish hired certified teachers to teach in their parochial schools until 1962. At this point the Amish decided to hire teachers from their community who were not certified to teach in public schools in Iowa. The hiring of uncertified teachers was part of the cause for the controversy in the 1960s. The Amish currently have five parochial schools in the area, with all schools being one-teacher schools and with most having an assistant at each school. The average number of scholars per school in the 2004–05 school term was 16.

In an effort to prevent the problems that occurred with Amish parochial schools in the Hazleton area, the Jesup and Wapsie Valley school officials worked with the Amish to set up seven one-room schools in recently closed public schools. The Amish agreed to the arrangement after a traditional curriculum for the students was arranged. This agreement is still in effect today, with the school district providing certified teachers. One of the seven schools burned down several years ago; the district supplied architectural plans and the materials, and the Amish provided the labor for the new school. Before building commenced, the Amish asked the teacher for her input on aspects of the building. As a result the building turned out like a traditional one-room school in spite of the architectural plans.

KANSAS

Kansas is the home of only one Amish community that has established parochial schools for its children (*Blackboard Bulletin*, 2005; Luthy, 1994). The community is located in the Haven/Hutchinson area about 30 miles northwest of Wichita and was established in 1883. This community has two schools that are both two-teacher schools. During the 2004–05 school year the average number of pupils per school was 20. Residents of the area have several vocations, including farming, carpentry, mechanics, quilting, and factory work.

Amish parochial schools in Kansas have kindergarten, which is unique since Amish schools rarely have kindergarten students in attendance (Miller, 2000). The most recently built school is Whispering Pines. This school is a 28-by-44-foot building and includes a full basement, and the schoolyard includes a corral and a barn that can accommodate 10 horses and a buggy. There is also a trailer on the property for teachers who need a place to board. This school was built in 1997 after local residents became dissatisfied with public schools in the area. The residents received help in planning this school from ministers and school board members from Kalona, Iowa, and Arthur, Illinois.

Frolics are held in this area to support their school. For example, the men of the community got together in December of 2005 for a wood-cutting frolic, with proceeds going to the school fund (*Diary*, 2006).

MINNESOTA

Minnesota is home to five Amish communities, and as of the 2004–05 school term there were 23 parochial schools in the state with an average of 17 scholars per school (*Blackboard Bulletin*, 2005; Luthy, 1994). All Amish communities in the state have been started since 1972, and the largest community in the state is in Fillmore County in the southeast portion of the state. All schools in Minnesota are one-teacher schools, and the first school in the state was opened in the 1970s.

As in most states, Amish schools in Minnesota are white, the one exception being Meadow View School west of Harmony, Minnesota, which has light blue metal siding. Most of the residents of the Harmony/Granger community are farmers. This settlement straddles the state line between Minnesota and Iowa, so some of the residents live in Iowa.

Andrew Kinsinger (1997) notes that the early immigrants to Minnesota found it difficult to abide by Minnesota school law and requested his assistance. Kinsinger, who was a leader in the Amish parochial school movement in Lancaster, agreed to visit the state. Before he left Pennsylvania, a meeting was scheduled with the governor's assistant on education. Upon his arrival in the state, he met with several Amish elders and then the next day went to the capital to meet the governor's assistant. Kinsinger writes that the result of the meeting was that the Amish were allowed to have their own schools.

MISSOURI

Missouri is home to many Amish settlements, and one of the most populous is located in and around the town of Jamesport in Daviess County. Jamesport is in northwestern Missouri, due south of Des Moines, Iowa, and northeast of Kansas City. The first person of European descent to purchase land in the area was Jesse Harris, and the log cabin he built in 1836 is now located in the Jamesport City Park (Jamesport, Missouri, 2006). The Amish first moved to the area in 1953 and now number about 150 families. The Amish in the area are involved in farming, along with numerous business ventures. These businesses include a lumber mill, bakery, furniture shop, harness shop,woodstove shop, quilt shop, and bulk-food store. Flea markets are held in Jamesport on Mother's Day weekend in May and the last full weekend in July. Residents of the area have many positive comments about the Amish schools in the area. For example, one resident stated, "It is really amazing how quickly the first graders learn English." The resident further stated, "The children are well educated and learn to respect their elders."

As of the 2004–05 school term there were over 20 Amish communities in the state and 60 Amish parochial schools (*Blackboard Bulletin*, 2005; Luthy 1994). The earliest Amish settlements were in Bowling Green, organized in 1947; Jamesport, organized in 1953; Clark, organized in 1954; and Anabel, organized in 1957. Amish schools in Missouri have an average of 24 scholars per school and a teacher-student ratio of 18 to one. The first schools in the state, Maple Branch (1948) and Shady Creek (1950), were in the Bowling Green community in Pike County.

MONTANA

There are four Amish settlements in Montana, with Rexford, the first settlement, beginning in 1975 (Luthy, 1994; Miller, 2002b). This settlement is sometimes referred to as the West Kootenai and is bounded on the north by the U.S.–Canadian border and to the east by the Lake Koocanusa Reservoir. Wildlife in the area includes deer, elk, moose, bear, coyotes, wolves, and mountain lions. The snow-capped mountains and clear mountain streams serve to enhance the beauty of the rugged terrain. Residents in the area make their living in log-home and rustic-furniture manufacturing. Gardens require special care given the short growing season and the cool night temperatures in the summer. The second Saturday in June is the annual auction and marks the beginning of the tourist season in the area. Many Amish residents of Montana hunt for antelope, elk, and deer and were quite successful in that endeavor during the 2005–06 fall and winter hunting season (*Diary*, 2006).

Mountain View School has served the community since 1975 and had 13 scholars in the 2004–05 school term (*Blackboard Bulletin*, 2005). School was first held in the old Tooley Lake Schoolhouse, which had served as the public school in the area for many years (Miller, 2002b). The school was not in use when the settlement was founded, so the Amish leased the building and all the supplies in the school. By 1976 the community had built a school in a more central location, and the school supplies and playground equipment were moved from the Tooley Lake School before it was razed. In the fall of 1998 fire consumed the entire building, including all the supplies; the community quickly pitched in to build a new log schoolhouse. The school was completed in four weeks, and instruction began anew. Donations for the new school came from numerous sources, including the Eureka School District. From the schoolyard one has a great view of Mt. Robinson, which is snow capped at least nine months of the year. As of the 2004–05 school term there were five Amish parochial schools in Montana, with an average of 23 scholars per school and a teacher-student ratio of 13 to one (*Blackboard Bulletin*, 2005). The first school in the state was Mountain View in the Rexford community in Lincoln County.

WISCONSIN

Wisconsin is home to over 25 Amish settlements, with the largest community near Cashton (*Blackboard Bulletin*, 2005; Luthy, 1994). There are 27 Amish settlements in Wisconsin, with the first organized in Medford in 1925. Wisconsin has been an attractive state for Amish migration, with 21 new communities started since 1970. As of the 2004–05 school term there were 134 schools, and the majority of these schools were served by one teacher. For example, most schools in the Cashton area are one-teacher schools. One exception is the school in the Shawana County community, which is a two-teacher school. It is interesting to note that Shawana County has an estimated deer population of 16 deer per square mile (Miller, 2002b). It is not unusual to see deer in the area, and the community's school is aptly named Deer View. The average number of scholars per school in Wisconsin is 22, and the teacher-pupil ratio is one to 18 (*Blackboard Bulletin*, 2005).

Historically speaking, Wisconsin played an important role in the Amish parochial school movement. As noted in chapter 3, the Amish community near New Glarus was the site of the Amish school controversy that eventually led to the Supreme Court ruling of *Wisconsin v. Yoder,* which resulted in the court's guaranteeing the Amish the right to organize and staff their own schools on the grounds of religious freedom.

Cashton

The community in Cashton, Wisconsin, is located in the western part of the state and was begun in 1966 when several families from Geauga County, Ohio, and Buchanon County, Iowa, purchased farms in the area (Miller, 2002b). This area is very hilly, and farms in the area are termed two-step farms, meaning that they have some valley land and some fairly steep ridge land.

The area is very scenic, with nice views of the rural landscape from the top of the many ridges in the area. In winter the landscape is beautiful after a fresh snowfall. The primary vocation of most of the early residents was farming. As of 2005 many residents were sawmill operators, shop owners, woodworkers, quilters, dry goods store owners, basket makers, and harness shop proprietors (Miller, 2002b). The area has lots of wildlife, including beaver, coyote, deer, fox, grouse, raccoon, and turkey. Making maple syrup is an early spring activity because of the numerous maple trees in the area.

Kingston

The Kingston, Wisconsin, settlement is in Green Lake County, and the occupations of the residents include baking, carpentry, farming, and woodworking (Miller, 2002b). Milk produced by the farmers is placed in cans and cooled in water-filled tanks before being taken to the local Amish-owned cheese making facility, which specializes in producing blue cheese. The area has six schools, with most of the schools being served by two teachers. Most of the schools include living quarters for the teachers. A humorous event occurred at the North Scott School—humorous to all in the community except the teacher. A frog found its way into the drain before it was closed. Later that day the teacher was quite surprised to see a pair of frog eyes looking up at her from the drain as she attempted to use the sink! Amish school board members have lots of duties, and on this day a school board member was summoned to free the frog (Miller, 2002b).

COLORADO

According to the *Blackboard Bulletin* (2005) and W. Sherman (personal communication, September 2005), there is a small community of Amish in Colorado. Mountain View School, which was begun in 2003, is located in Rio Grande County, Colorado. The school had one teacher and 24 scholars during the 2004–05 school year.

As in other Amish communities, the residents of Colorado are fond of the outdoors. For example, during the winter of 2005–06 the young people enjoyed ice skating. In addition, bird watchers reported that the bald eagles were back in the area for the winter months and everyone liked seeing their white heads and tails in vivid contrast to the Colorado sky (*Diary*, 2006).

The Amish traditions of school programs and frolics for school funds also continue in Colorado. Thus, the community enjoyed the Christmas program held at the school on the evening of December 22 (*Diary*, 2006). In addition, residents of the settlement worked together on the third cutting of hay for the season, with proceeds going to the school fund. It must have been an interesting sight as forty draft horses working in teams of four were employed to mow the hay that day (*Diary*, Sept. 2005).

13

Community, Literacy, and Responsibility Revisited

The secret to happiness is helping others to find it.
—Aphorism posted in an Amish school in Iowa in 2005

In this concluding chapter we will revisit literacy, community, and responsibility as they relate to Amish education. We will then explore some of advantages as well as the problems related to Amish education in the 21st century. Finally, we will explore the future of Amish education in North America and show how their educational system is a viable educational alternative that will remain in North America for many years to come.

LITERACY

As we discovered in previous chapters, Amish schools provide a firm foundation of an eighth-grade education in subjects such as reading, arithmetic, and writing (penmanship). My recent observations in Amish schools affirm the writing of previous authors such as Hostetler and Huntington (1992), who have noted the positive aspects of Amish education in these core subjects. Visits to Amish homes and businesses have confirmed that the Amish are certainly proficient in these subjects for running home businesses, farms, and small retail establishments. In addition to proficiency in these core subjects, all Amish children learn gender-specific skills that will enable them to provide for the needs of their families as they enter adult life. While it is true that the Amish children do not learn science, computer science, or advanced mathematics, they do learn what I might argue is more important for their culture, a work ethic that is centered on getting the job right the first time and getting the task done on time. This approach to education has served the Amish well, as they run successful farms and small businesses. Their work is often prized by the non-Amish because of quality workmanship and attention to detail. Many American businesses tout their use of Amish-made products as a testament to the quality workmanship in the final product. For example, numerous English-owned furniture shops advertise Amish-made products and use the horse and buggy as a symbol to identify their company with the Amish. Other companies, such as The Original Mattress Factory in Charlotte, North Carolina, advertise Amish-built wood frames in all of their radio advertising.

Literacy encompasses all aspects of Amish life and is stressed in schools. In the early grades teachers strive to make sure all students receive a firm foundation in reading and writing. Younger students see reading modeled for them each day by the upper-grade students. At home children see their parents reading numerous Amish-produced periodicals as well as farm and garden periodicals. Literacy is part of home and school life. By third grade most students have a basic understanding of reading and, more important, like to read. My observations in Amish schools revealed that children like to read a library book when they have completed their work for the day. Some students, to the consternation of their teachers, may even be reading a library book when they are meant to be doing their assignments for the day. In addition to free reading, Amish students spend a great deal of their regular classroom time reading class assignments. Since teachers typically spend only about 10 minutes per grade level per hour with their students, the rest of the time students must read their textbooks to learn information to complete their assignments. After eighth grade, Amish students who live in states with the vocational plan must keep a journal of their learning activities during the week. A good number of Amish adults also keep journals of their activities, and some of these journals can be quite detailed.

Another factor that leads to the focus on literacy in Amish culture is that homes do not have television, video games, radios, or other electronic devices designed for entertainment. Thus, reading becomes a much more prevalent activity in an Amish home. Amish homes also do not have telephones, so written letters become an important way to communicate with relatives and friends who live in distant communities. Amish children also like to write letters and enjoy having pen pals who have the same birthday. In fact, *The Diary* usually publishes at least 25 written requests from children who are seeking pen pals in each month's issue.

Finally, since the Amish value their history, they spend a good deal of time reading about that history. In addition, almost every community has a scribe who writes to Amish publications each month telling of the important events in that community over the last month. Many times these scribes are also engaged in keeping a written history of their community and/or family. These histories are often published by Amish printers.

The Importance of Oral Literacy

As noted in chapter 6, Amish teachers speak much less than their public and private school counterparts. This is because teachers spend much less time giving directions since students know the routine of each lesson. When teachers do give directions, students learn early in their school life that they must listen carefully because the teacher will not repeat directions. Since this is the case, Amish children learn that when their parents or teachers speak they are to listen and follow the directions. And since teachers use few words, those words then become more important and more powerful. For example, most of us have had the experience of a teacher or politician who has talked too long. Because of this the speaker's words have less meaning. The power of Lincoln's Gettysburg Address is in the fact that he used a few carefully selected and ordered words to make his point. Another reason that the spoken word becomes more important in an Amish school is that the Amish teachers generally speak in soft and low tones. Thus, children must listen carefully so that they do not miss directions or the instructions for how to complete a problem.

COMMUNITY

As we have seen in previous chapters the Amish build community through their approach to education. Before beginning formal schooling Amish children learn about the community in their family. They learn that everyone has chores to do and that successful completion of these jobs is important for the well-being of the family. Children also learn that the animals they care for depend on them for food, water, and shelter. In all cases, to miss a chore has ramifications for others in the family or animals on the farm. Before going to school, children also learn about the community of their extended family and how the members of that extended family count on each other when major chores need to be accomplished. Chores such as butchering, harvesting, or canning several pecks of peaches require many people working together to accomplish one task. Children learn that their community values manual labor and that group work is a time for fellowship. Before formal schooling begins, children also learn about their church family and how members of that community support each other in times of joy and need.

Once children begin school they learn about the community of the school. Amish schools are structured around the good of the community rather than individual accomplishments. One of the most important lessons children will learn in the first weeks of formal schooling is that they must wait their turn for assistance from the teacher. They learn that the community of the school revolves around a clear pattern of instruction. As we have seen in chapter 6, this pattern includes a short time of instruction and recitation with the teacher followed by a longer period in which the student completes his or her assignments and studies for upcoming lessons. Since Amish schools have all eight grades, the younger students quickly learn the community mores of the school by watching the behavior of older students.

Students soon learn that the work of children is to learn academic skills during their time in the classroom. They also learn that recess is a time to play. As discussed earlier in chapter 4, recess is an important time because it is here that children also build friendships with their peers that they will carry on into their adult lives.

Schools also build community by the fact that older students help younger students accomplish their schoolwork. Scholars thus learn that community is centered on helping all gain important life skills.

Finally, we have seen that students in Amish schools are rarely singled out for awards of any kind. This sends a clear message to all students that community good is more important than individual accomplishment, recognition, or placement at the head of the class.

Once formal schooling ends at eighth grade, students learn about the work community from learning by doing. Students learn gender-specific skills by working with their elders on various work-related tasks on the farm, in the home, at the home-based business, or with a parent who has a business, such as a carpenter who serves the needs of the community in jobs away from the home setting. This period of vocational training comes at a pivotal point in the life of an adolescent. The vocational training is of critical importance because it prepares young people with the ability to provide for their families as Amish adults. So while young people have a chance to develop their sense of self, they do so in the context of the adult Amish world during the working hours of the day. During the evening hours adolescents spend time with their peers and sometimes "sow their wild oats" but usually do so within the community of other Amish adolescents.

To conclude, a sense of community is built throughout Amish children's lives with critical aspects of community building occurring during their time at school and within the vocational training that all students receive from parents and elders.

RESPONSIBILITY

Amish children learn at an early age that they are responsible for their own learning at school. For example, when a teacher is teaching the sixth graders arithmetic, she will not be able to address questions from pupils from the other seven grades in the school. Students thus are more inclined to reread the difficult passage or rework the arithmetic problem on their own. And if they do not do this, they will learn the value of patience. Additionally, Amish teachers do not use excessive individual positive reinforcement to get students to do their work. Students are held responsible for getting their work done. As one teacher stated, "We expect work to be done on time and in an accurate manner."

Another responsibility shouldered by the Amish scholar is the cleanliness of the school. Pupils are responsible for the general cleaning of the school each day and clean up in a cheerful manner. This general cleaning usually occurs each day at the beginning of the afternoon recess. As noted in chapter 4, it is not unusual to see Amish pupils staying after school to help the teacher with a special cleaning project.

Upper-grade students are also responsible for helping younger graders with their academic work and do so as directed by the teacher. This responsibility is shared by male and female students.

Amish schools are a vivid example of how the community takes personal responsibility for all aspects of the school. The community builds, remodels, and maintains the school in the same manner that it cares for its individual homes, barns, and sheds. The school board, which is elected by the families in the area, is responsible for finding a good teacher, providing adequate books and materials, and providing fuel for the stove or furnace. The school board is also responsible for fixing minor structural problems at the school. Additionally, the school board is responsible for smoothing out any problems that may appear at the school that the teacher is unable to handle.

Teachers have the responsibility for planning and implementing the daily academic work of the scholars under their tutelage. Teachers understand the importance of this task and do not underestimate the enormous responsibility they shoulder each day. Remarks by teachers in the *Blackboard Bulletin*, the Amish journal of education, often mention the prayerful approach teachers take in meeting their responsibilities as teachers.

THE ADVANTAGES OF THE AMISH EDUCATIONAL SYSTEM

A clear advantage of the Amish educational plan is that students learn the skills of manual trades under the tutelage of skilled craftsmen. Adolescents learn the trade of carriage making by working with a carriage builder. They learn all aspects of the trade in a supportive setting. For example, a carriage maker has two adolescent sons learning the carriage-building trade in his Lancaster County, Pennsylvania, shop. The oldest son recently was given the responsibility of taking the lead on an important restoration project for an

East Coast museum. The son's restoration was a work of skilled craftsmanship truly worthy of museum-quality work. The younger son's role in another restoration project was the polishing of the recently painted buggy. The smoothness of the finish was as good as that of any luxury automobile. This system of vocational training is not limited to one skill, as all Amish children learn the skills of animal husbandry, gardening, and home maintenance.

Another distinct advantage of Amish education is that the schools are small, with the average Amish school serving less than 30 students. This smallness ensures that all children receive attention each day. No child can be ignored, avoided, or forgotten, and neither can the child be unimportant or fail to be recognized as a member of the community. This quality of Amish schools was once the norm in public education in the United States, as well over 100,000 one-room schools served the needs of students in the early 1900s. The Amish have continued this pattern of education and have added their own unique style over the years.

Another important advantage to Amish schools is that students hear much of the material they will need to learn on at least three occasions. Younger students hear much of the teaching of older students; thus after first grade, students have some recollection of the material they will study in second grade and beyond. In some cases students in eighth grade may have heard the history lesson for the day while they were in each of the prior seven grades. Finally, older students will hear the lessons of younger students, which will bring back the memory of that lesson.

Noted Amish authority Donald Kraybill was interviewed in January of 2005, and he indicated that there were several advantages to the Amish education system. The first advantage of Amish schools is that with small teacher-pupil ratios students receive lots of personal attention. This personal attention is also increased because students and teachers interact with one another outside of the classroom. The second advantage is peer tutoring. Older students help younger students on a daily basis, and this has four benefits: Peer tutoring helps the teacher meet the needs of all students, younger students benefit from the extra assistance and from the fact that older students may use different ways to explain things, peer tutoring benefits the older students because teaching helps them remember the skills they teach, and peer tutoring benefits future teachers because it gives the tutors practice at teaching. The third advantage of Amish schools, as noted by Kraybill, is that the students learn a good work ethic. Students learn early that they are responsible for getting their work done in an accurate manner and on time. The last advantage noted by Kraybill is that students learn a basic management style that is needed to run a business, farm, or home. My observations and interviews confirm all of the advantages noted by Kraybill.

The January 1985 edition of the *Blackboard Bulletin* shared advantages of the Amish parochial school from the perspective of the readers. One advantage noted was that in many cases children have the same teacher for several years. Thus teachers know the needs and abilities of all their students quite well. The second noted advantage was the summer teachers' meetings, where information is shared with teachers, school board members, elders, and parents. Thus, not only do the meetings share important information for teachers, but all stakeholders in the educational process hear the same information as well. This works to build a strong sense of community and further illustrates the importance of education.

The *Blackboard Bulletin* is an advantage for Amish education in a similar manner to the summer teachers' meetings. The journal offers timely articles and school-related ideas and strategies that are read by the entire community, not just the teachers. This makes it more likely that all stakeholders in the educational process know the same important information, which improves both the school and the community.

The fact that the community builds the school with its own funds and its own labor makes it more likely that the community will take care of and even cherish the school. There is intrinsic value for a person when the individual is involved in the actual labor of building a school. The individual gets the feeling that "this is our school" and is thus more likely to be involved in the educational process that occurs there.

A further advantage of Amish education is that parents are expected to visit the school. This is a clear sign to the children that what happens here is important and should be respected.

Another distinct advantage of Amish schools is that students do not expect to be entertained at school, and teachers do not try to entertain students. As mentioned previously, in the Amish culture school is the work of children, and work is to be enjoyed. Thus, the Amish do not view work as something to be avoided so that they can purchase entertainment. Amish children learn this at an early age from their parents, siblings, extended family, and church community. Furthermore, since Amish schools and homes do not have electricity, they do not have the entertainment of television, radio, and video games. As Postman (1985) postulated in *Amusing Ourselves to Death*, entertainment has changed the American culture in negative ways. The American culture spends an inordinate amount of time being entertained by TV and video games. This takes time away from other activities, and one current concern of health professionals is that our population is becoming more obese each year. There is a clear difference between Amish pupils and public school students. Public school students expect to be entertained at home and at school and avoid manual labor. Amish students see manual labor and work as something to be enjoyed.

Another clear advantage of Amish schools is that they have three recesses per day. Few would argue against the fact that children need a chance to play and get some fresh air. Having three recesses per day with a long recess at lunch allows the Amish scholars to intersperse the work of school with the play of recess. This allows them to come back to the classroom refreshed both physically and mentally. This reduces the amount of misbehavior in the classroom and increases the time-on-task behavior of Amish students. The fact that most Amish students also walk or ride a bike or scooter to school, combined with three recesses per day and with chores each evening, means that Amish children are usually not overweight.

Another advantage of Amish education is that unsuccessful teachers usually do not remain in teaching because there are plenty of employment opportunities in the Amish community. There are two ways teachers leave the field of education. The first and most common is that the teacher leaves education after realizing that he or she does not have the skills or personality for teaching. The second way is that school boards do not invite the teacher back the next year. In either case, ex-teachers can find work within the community.

The last distinct advantage of the Amish parochial school system is that the schools teach virtue. This virtue is based on what C. S. Lewis, as cited by Markos (2000), terms a virtue based on goodness defined by the teachings of Jesus. While it is true that Amish schools do not teach religion, they do teach a model for life, a model that focuses on kindness, gentleness, humility, and the joy of work. Thus Amish schools and communities teach the three Rs and at the same time teach virtue. Lewis believed that the teaching of virtue is the key to the educational process because if we teach virtue, then children grow up to be caring, responsible adults.

Advantages of Amish Education

- Low teacher-pupil ratios
- Peer tutoring
- Small schools ensure that each child is valued
- Success of the group is valued more than individual success
- Builds community
- Three recesses per day
- Instills positive work ethic in all students
- Students hear the lessons for other grades
- No electronic entertainment
- Teacher continuity from year to year
- Teaches virtue by example
- Learning by doing
- Summer teachers' meeting attended by all stakeholders
- Parents expected to visit the school

- *Blackboard Bulletin*—read by teacher and parents
- Unsuccessful teachers do not remain in the classroom
- Teaching viewed as a calling
- Community labor builds the school

PROBLEMS WITH THE AMISH EDUCATIONAL SYSTEM

There are several clear problems with the Amish educational system, which the Amish themselves have identified in numerous Amish publications over the years. For example, the September 1972, September 1982, and January 1985 issues of the *Blackboard Bulletin* discussed some of the problems of Amish schools. Topics discussed included problems in two-teacher schools, the teacher shortage, the mentoring of new teachers, there being too many young teachers, and parents who do not visit the school.

We will explore the teacher shortage problem first. Like many public schools, Amish schools have a problem finding good teachers to staff their schools. Reasons for this problem include low teacher salaries compared to other employment opportunities in the community, teacher turnover, and in a few areas a lack of cooperation of one or two families in the community. As with public schools, the teacher salary issue is not easy to solve given the finances required to address the situation. School boards are aware of this problem and have increased teacher remuneration in several communities.

Teacher turnover is also not easy to solve given the fact that most Amish teachers are young, unmarried females. Once these women marry they leave teaching to take on the difficult and labor-intensive job of managing a household. Most teachers teach for about three years before they marry. Thus, a school board must on average replace a teacher every three to five years. Some would argue, however, that even if the teacher only stays three years that is much more continuity than in other types of public and private schools in the United States and Canada.

The problem of having many young teachers also means that many Amish teachers are not much older than their pupils. This problem can be exacerbated by a school board that is not as helpful as it should be. Fishman, as cited by Kilmuska (1989), argues that having young teachers is not a problem because teachers teach in ways that are similar to ways they were taught in school and the way the Amish raise children in their home. Furthermore, Kraybill, as cited by Kilmuska (1989), feels that the majority of Amish teachers are doing a very good job.

Amish leaders do struggle with curricular issues, and this is most often noticed in discussion about textbooks. Key questions include the price of the textbook, appropriate content, and the perceived strengths and weaknesses of the textbook. Given that textbooks produced for public schools do not often meet the needs of the Amish school and are quite expensive, the Amish and Old Order Mennonites have taken on the task of writing and producing their own textbooks.

Problems in Amish Education

- Young teachers
- Teacher shortage
- Teacher turnover
- Low teacher salaries
- Parents who do not visit the school
- Parents who do not respect the teacher

THE FUTURE OF AMISH SCHOOLS

A review of research by Myers (2000) found correlation evidence for several variables associated with happiness. Happiness has less to do with age, gender, and income and more to do with three factors. The three factors positively associated with happiness are the quality of one's work and leisure activities, having a supportive network of close relationships, and having a "faith that encompasses social support, purpose, and hope" (Myers, 2000, p. 65). Given this research and the fact that the Amish way of life values work as something to be enjoyed, values community over individual accomplishment, and provides a faith system that has a clear network of social support, purpose, and hope, it is no wonder that Amish individuals are happy. Not surprisingly, Myers further points out that the Amish of Pennsylvania experience a very low rate of major depression.

In my interactions with Amish individuals I have always perceived them to be happy individuals who are content with their way of life. Since the future of Amish schools is tied to the existence of the Amish community, I would suggest that barring unforeseen government intrusion the Amish population will continue to grow and thrive in North America.

The rapid increase in the Amish population (Kraybill and Bowman, 2001; Luthy 1994), which has resulted in migrations to numerous new settlements, bodes well for the future of Amish schools. This, coupled with the fact that the Amish have built a successful educational program that has to this point ensured that Amish adults are gainfully employed, only serves to validate the Amish educational system.

The Amish belief system, a belief system that shapes all aspects of one's life taken in context with their traditions, serves to mold the way the Amish view education. While they realize that reading, writing, and arithmetic are important, they believe that a sound education is more than learning the 3 Rs. Education is about preparing one for a life of separation, humility, and service among a community of believers. A life based on their belief system and their historical heritage. A heritage that values manual labor in the farming tradition as something to be cherished, not avoided. The Amish believe that the one-room schoolhouse located in a rural setting was and remains an ideal setting for one to acquire these skills and values.

Appendix A

Research Procedures

The data and observations in this book describe Amish educational practices across the United States and Canada. A variety of data sources were used, including in-depth interviews, primary source documents, secondary source documents, and ethnographic observations. Structured interviews were designed to collect information from a variety of individuals in Amish communities. Because the Amish do not want their names publicized, I have not used the names of Amish informants in this book unless they have given me permission. In addition, names of schools that I have visited are not revealed in this book. I am deeply grateful for the time and energy devoted by the Amish to allow me to gather the information required to make this book a reality.

Many primary source documents were reviewed at the Heritage Historical Library in Aylmer, Ontario, and at the Lancaster Mennonite Historical Society in Lancaster, Pennsylvania. A good portion of the data and observations in this book were collected between January and June 2005. During that time I visited Amish schools and communities throughout the United States and Canada. I was fortunate to be able to interview many people from the Amish community, including teachers, bishops, ministers, school board members, oversight committee members, deacons, historians, former teachers, textbook writers, workbook writers, bookstore owners, parents, and grandparents. In addition I also interviewed individuals who are not Amish but who have close contact with members of the Amish community. These individuals include neighbors, friends, librarians, receptive operators, information-center personnel, drivers, and owners of establishments frequented by the Amish, such as hardware stores, lumber yards, drug stores, and small grocery stores. I am deeply indebted to all of these wonderful people who have been gracious with their time and information.

Rigor has been incorporated into this project by having drafts of each chapter in this book reviewed by an Amish teacher and/or an Amish elder. Once the chapter was read each person suggested changes that were then incorporated into the final version of the book. I am deeply grateful to these individuals for their assistance. In addition, several colleagues have reviewed drafts of this manuscript and have offered numerous suggestions and questions that have led to changes that have made the text more relevant and readable.

Specific information related to the Iowa school controversy was collected in structured interviews with three individuals who had firsthand information about the disagreement. The three structured interviews were held in Des Moines, Iowa, in October of 2004. Those interviewed included Attorney Harlan Lemon, Gene Raffensperger, and David Bechtel. Attorney Lemon was the prosecuting attorney in the case against the Amish. Gene Raffensperger was the reporter for the *Des Moines Register* who discovered and then chronicled the events surrounding the controversy. Both individuals were present at many of the major happenings in this controversy. Mr. David Bechtel was the administrative assistant to the State Superintendent of Instruction. Mr. Bechtel was involved in reviewing all materials related to the compromise legislation and overview of the eventual school plan.

While a good portion of the information for this project was collected between January and June of 2005, it should be noted that I have been conducting research related to one-room schools and Old Order Mennonite and Old Order Amish education for over 20 years. Visits to Amish communities in previous years add to the empirical data gathered in 2005. Additional empirical data sources include national surveys to each state Department of Education conducted in 1989 and 1997 and 2004 to document the number of public and private one-room schools in each state. Appendix B lists the numerous Amish communities visited and dates of those visits.

Appendix B

Amish Communities and Dates of Visits

Community	**State**	**Dates Visited**
Dover	Delaware	January, February, and April, 2005
Arthur	Illinois	February, 2005
Berne	Indiana	March, 2005
Daviess County	Indiana	February, 2005
Elkhart/LaGrange	Indiana	April, 1997; February, 2005
Fountain City	Indiana	March, 2005
Nappanee	Indiana	March, 2005
Bloomfield	Iowa	March, 2005
Hazleton	Iowa	October, 2000 and 2004; March, 2005
Kalona	Iowa	June, 2002; March, 2005
Lamoni	Iowa	October, 2004; March, 2005
Riceville	Iowa	March, 2005
Crab Orchard	Kentucky	February and June, 2005
Marion	Kentucky	February, 2005
Garrett County	Maryland	March, 2005
St. Mary's County	Maryland	January, February, and April, 2005
Harmony	Minnesota	March, 2005
Jamesport	Missouri	March, 2005
Romulus	New York	April, 2005
Addison	New York	April, 2005
Jasper/Woodhull	New York	April, 2005

(*continued*)

Community	State	Dates Visited
Prattsburg	New York	April, 2005
Union Grove	North Carolina	Numerous visits since 2000
Ashland	Ohio	June, 2003; February, 2005
Gallia County	Ohio	April, 2005
Geauga County	Ohio	February, 2005
Holmes/Wayne County	Ohio	Numerous visits since 1991
Knox County	Ohio	April, 2005
Licking County	Ohio	April, 2005
Centre County	Pennsylvania	January, 2005
Danville	Pennsylvania	January, 2005
Juniata County	Pennsylvania	January, 2005
Lancaster County	Pennsylvania	Research conducted in this community at least once each year since 1984
Lycoming County	Pennsylvania	January, 2005
Mifflin County (Big Valley)	Pennsylvania	Numerous visits since 1988
New Wilmington	Pennsylvania	March, 2005
Shippensburg	Pennsylvania	July, 1997; July, 1998
Snyder/Union	Pennsylvania	Numerous visits since 1986
Somerset County	Pennsylvania	March, 2005
Etheridge	Tennessee	April, 1998; February, 2005
Cullen	Virginia	January and April, 2005
Pearisburg	Virginia	January and May, 2005
Cashton	Wisconsin	March, 2005

Appendix C

Tag Games

A popular tag game in the Arthur, Illinois, area is "21 skip to do." In this game several children serve as "taggers" or "itters" and chase the other students about the schoolyard. When children are tagged they must go to an area enclosed by a rope on the ground. They remain here until there are 21 students tagged. Once this occurs they shout "21 skip to do" and scatter about the schoolyard to start the game anew.

A similar game in Holmes and Wayne counties of Ohio is called "22 Eskimo." In this game there will be a square base marked off in the middle of the playground guarded by four "itters." When tagged by the fifth "itter" or any of the four "itters" guarding the base the pupil must step into the base. This student will then stretch out his/her hand until a free person touches it and counts to 22 and says "Eskimo." This person will then be free. Sometimes a free runner pretends to be tagged or caught, steps into the box or base area, counts to 22, and says "Eskimo," and everyone in the box will now be free again. The "itters" are on the lookout for this and try not to let it happen. The game is over when all the runners are caught. In the Bloomfield, Iowa, area the game requires that one count to 23 and is called "23 × ado."

Another tag game is called "circle base." In this game there will be two, three, or four long boards, which will serve as bases. Some children will begin the game as "taggers," while the others will be chased. The children will then try to circle all the bases while the taggers chase them. When one is tagged he/she must go stand at a certain spot. If a person is successful in running around all the bases, then all the children who were tagged become free.

"Grade base" is a commonly played game that begins with all of the students on the base for their grade. For example, first graders will be on one base, the second graders will be on another base, and so forth. Bases may be small boards, a post of the swing set, or the corner of the school. Children then run around and try to tag other students. If they do tag a student, that student has to stand at that grade's base until he or she is freed. To free a student or students, a person from another grade must touch that team's base without first being tagged. Students are free to run around as they wish and can take breaks at their base to chat with their fellow students. On a cold day during the winter of 2005 I watched a group of children and their teachers play this game for 40 minutes during the noon recess. Teachers and students alike report that grade base is an enjoyable game, especially on cold winter days, because it requires lots of running and is a big challenge to complete. This game may take the entire 45-minute noon recess period to complete.

A game similar to circle base is called "single base," where two to four boards serve as bases, depending on the number of scholars in the school. Every person on the base is a tagger. For example, Peter comes off base #1 and one minute later Sarah comes running from base #3. Sarah is off last, so if she tags Peter, he will be on Sarah's team the rest of the game unless a person from another team or base tags him. In the meantime, two careful watchers from base #4 see that both Peter and Sarah have left their base and see that Sarah is trying to tag Peter; they will then try to sneak up on them and tag them both, thus gaining two more people for base #4. Also if anyone (let's say Vernon) from a base runs around another base one time without being tagged, he has circled that base one time. If Vernon can circle the same base three times, everyone on that base is now on Vernon's team. The game is over when everyone is finally on the same team.

Prisoners base is another popular game, and students in Ohio like to play this game as boys versus girls. There will be a base at opposite ends of the playground, one for the boys and one for the girls. Each team secretly selects a captain. As in other tag games, the last person off a base can tag anyone who was off before him or her. If persons are tagged (caught) they are prisoners and must go to the other team's base and stay there until they are freed. To free a member of a team a player must touch him or her before being tagged. If a captain is tagged by her team and she is a prisoner, then all the girls are free.

Another well-liked tag game is called "jail" and is an interesting game to watch. The game is usually played with a baseball and a "jail." The baseball bat will be propped up on a pole or tree. The jail will be made using a rope or sticks to outline a rectangle on the grass or snow. Children who are tagged must stand inside the jail until another student knocks down the bat without first being tagged. Students are then free to flee the jail. As with other tag games, several students serve as "taggers" and attempt to tag as many people as possible. All of the above-described tag games have some strategy involved with the game, and it is very interesting to watch the ways students free their classmates. For example, in the jail game a student may pretend to be deep in conversation with another child but be carefully watching the students who are guarding the jail. Once they see an opportunity they will dart to the base and knock down the stick. Other students will devise ways to have several students dart for the base at one time. This makes it more likely that at least one of the students will not be tagged.

Appendix D

Chronology of Anabaptist and Amish History

1455	Gutenberg publishes the first printed Bible
1517	Luther posts Ninety-five Theses on church door at Wittenberg
1519	Zwingli begins preaching in Zurich
1521	Luther is condemned as a heretic, goes into hiding at Wartburg Castle
1522	Luther completes translation of Bible into German and returns to Wittenberg
1524	Peasants' War in Germany begins; executions of Anabaptists in Switzerland begin
1525	First adult baptisms in Zurich mark beginning of the Swiss Brethren
1527	Anabaptist leaders agree on seven principal beliefs in *Schleitheim Confession of Faith*
1530	Anabaptism spreads to the low countries
1531	First Dutch Anabaptists are executed
1534	Luther publishes complete Bible
1535	Group of Anabaptists jailed in Passau castle and begin writing hymns—these hymns eventually form basis of the *Ausbund*
1536	Menno Simons is baptized and denounces violence
1555	Peace of Augsburg—territorial princes choose whether their territory will be Lutheran or Catholic
1562	Massacre of Vassey begins French Wars of Religion
1568	Dutch revolt under William of Orange against Spain
1579	Union of Utrecht establishes the Dutch Republic
1598	Edict of Nantes ends French Wars of Religion

1614	Swiss authorities end public execution of Anabaptists and instead jail, fine, or exile them
1618	Beginning of Thirty Years' War
1632	*Dordrecht Confession* outlines Mennonite doctrine and ends division over social avoidance in northern Anabaptist groups
1634	Colony of Maryland founded
1648	Thirty Years' War comes to an end
1660	*Martyrs' Mirror* first published
1680	William Penn receives grant of land west of the Delaware River
1693–97	Split over social avoidance between Hans Reist and Jacob Amman; later efforts to reunite groups fail and followers of Amman are eventually labeled Amish
1737	*Charming Nancy* arrives at Philadelphia with several Amish aboard
1748	*Martyrs' Mirror* begins to be published in Ephrata, Pa.
1772	Somerset County, Pa., settlement founded
1779	Amishman Issac Kauffman jailed in Reading, Pa., for failure to give up his horse to Colonial militia officer
1791	Mifflin County (Big Valley), Pa., settlement founded
1808	Holmes County, Ohio, settlement founded
1839	Adams County, Ind., settlement founded
1840	Elkhart County, Ind., settlement founded
1850	Garrett County, Md., settlement founded
1852	Allen County, Ind., settlement founded
1861	Civil War begins
1862	Annual Ministers meeting (Diener Versammlungen) begin. Ends in 1878
1865	Arthur, IL, settlement founded
1865	Splits between tradition-minded Amish (Old Order) and change-minded Amish (Amish Mennonites) begin
1869	Davies County, Ind., settlement founded
1886	Geauga County, Ohio, settlement founded
1901	Mass production of automobiles
1910	Peachey Amish withdraw from Old Order over practice of strict shunning and use of telephones in the home
1915	Dover, Del., settlement founded
1925	Apple Grove Parochial School begins and is first Amish parochial school in U.S.
1938	Oak Grove School and Esh School established in Lancaster County: first Amish schools in Pa.
1940	St. Mary's County, Md., settlement founded
1944	Maple Grove School and Fountain Nook School established in Holmes/Wayne County settlement: first Amish schools in Ohio

1944	Lawrence County, Tenn., settlement founded
1957	*Blackboard Bulletin* begins publication
1965	Amish school controversy in Hazleton, Iowa, results in AP photo of children running into a nearby cornfield
1965	*Blackboard Bulletin* publishes special edition devoted to 40-year anniversary of the opening of Apple Grove School
1967	National Committee for Amish Religious Freedom is organized
1969	*The Diary* begins publication in Lancaster County, Pa.
1972	Supreme Court decision in *Wisconsin v. Yoder* upholds Amish parochial schools

Appendix E

Aphorisms Posted in Amish Classrooms

DELAWARE

If you want to feel rich just count the things you have that money can't buy.

All that you do
Do with your might
Things done by halves
Are never done right

GEAUGA COUNTY, OHIO

A mistake is a chance to try harder.

Each new day brings another chance to try.

The secret of happiness is in helping others find it.

LAGRANGE, INDIANA

One school had two very nice teacher-drawn bulletin boards with winter scenes. The first bulletin board included this saying:

The future lies before us like a sheet of fallen snow. Be careful how you tread it, for every step will show.

The second bulletin board had this saying:

> Whatever thy hand findeth to do
> Do it with all thy might.

Another saying posted in the room:

> For success attitude is as important as ability.

Another school in the LaGrange area had this aphorism posted on the bulletin board:

> Character—it's how you live your life when no one is watching.

ILLINOIS

> It is the voice you use
> And the smile on your face
> That makes our school
> A pleasant place

> A smile adds a great deal to your face value.

> If you aren't big enough for criticism
> You are too small for praise.

> Our life is what our thoughts make it!

> Stretching the truth won't make it last any longer.

> A thing done right today means less trouble tomorrow.

IOWA

> The best way to cheer yourself up is to find someone else to cheer up.

References

Amish lose fight for old schools. (1938, June 28). *The New York Times*, p. 22.

Amish pupils back in 1-room school. (1938, November 29). *The New York Times*, p. 25.

Amish school controversy in Nebraska. (1982, January–February). *Liberty*. Washington, DC. p. 19.

Amish school may be closed. (1965, January, 14). *The Budget*, p. 2.

Amish seek relief form teacher law. (1978, February 2). *Lincoln Star*, p. 5.

Amish threaten school succession. (1938, July 21). *The New York Times*, p. 23.

Amish told to obey order or close school. (1965, October 7). *Toledo Blade*, p. 4.

Amish win reprieve for one-room school. (1966, November 30). *Ann Arbor News*, p. 3.

Ammon, R. (1994). Observation of a first-year Amish teacher. *Multicultural Education, 12*(2), 6–10.

AOL news. (2005). Retrieved June 30, 2004, from http://aolsvc.news.aol.com/news/article

Avenatti, L. (1991). Qualitative study of an Amish school. *Contemporary Education, 62*(3), 199–201.

Beiler, A. (1956). Statement of principles of a church vocation in agricultural practice by the Old Order Amish Church in Pennsylvania.

Blackboard Bulletin. (1957–2005). Aylmer, Ontario: Pathway Publishers.

Bontrager, J. (1989). In J. Hostetler (Ed.), *Amish roots: A treasury of history, wisdom and lore*. Baltimore, MD: Johns Hopkins University Press.

Brubaker, S. (1979). *Feed my lambs*. Goshen, IN: Pilgrim Publishers.

The Budget. (1965, May 27), p. 1.

The Budget . (2000, June 21), p. 1.

Byler, J. (1997). *Early Amish settlers of Geauga County, Ohio*. Gordonville, PA: Gordonville Print Shop.

Byler, U. (1969). *School bells ringing*. Aylmer, Ontario: Pathway Publishers.

Byler, U. (1989). An idea is planted. (pp. 132–133) In J. Hostetler (Ed.), *Amish roots: A treasury of history, wisdom and lore.* Baltimore, MD: Johns Hopkins University Press.

Cary P. (2004). *Luther: Gospel, law and reformation.* Chantilly, VA: The Teaching Company.

Church and family directory of the Old Order Amish: Dover, Delaware. (2000).

Dean, T. (1978, January 15). Newcomers to Nebraska continuing the old-time lifestyle. *Sunday Journal and Star,* p. 5

Dewalt, M. (1997). One-room schools: Current trends in parochial education. *The Lutheran Educator, 38*(1), 12–20.

Dewalt, M. (1989). One-room schools in the United States. (ERIC Document Reproduction Service No. ED306062)

Dewalt, M., & Troxell, B. (1986). Case Study of an Old Order Mennonite one-room school.

The Diary. (2005, September). Gordonville, PA.

The Diary. (2005, November). Gordonville, PA.

The Diary. (2005, December). Gordonville, PA.

The Diary. (2006, January). Gordonville, PA.

Die Botschaft. (1993, August 18), p. 44.

Die Botschaft. (1993, August 25), p. 11.

Die Botschaft. (1996, December 25), p. 32.

Die Botschaft. (1999, March 17), p. 51.

Egerton, J. (1967, January). One-teacher schools are still around. *The Education Digest, 33,* 12–14.

Esh, C. (1986). *The beginning and development of parochial special schools.* Gordonville, PA: Gordonville Print Shop.

Farmweld, D. (2004). *History and directory of Indiana Amish parochial Schools.* Topeka, IN: Study Time Publishers.

Fisher, G. (1978). *Farm life and its changes.* Gordonville, PA: Pequea.

Fisher, S. & Stahl, R. (1986). *The Amish school.* Intercourse, PA: Good Books.

Fishman, A. (1988). *Amish literacy: What and how it means.* Portsmouth, NH: Heinemann Educational Books, Inc.

Fuller, W. (1982). *The old country school.* Chicago: University of Chicago Press.

Good growth guide. (2004). East Earl, PA: Schoolaid.

Gordonville Print Shop. (1973). *Pennsylvania Amish directory of Lancester and Chester County church districts.* Gordonville, PA.

Gray, W. (1956). *The new basic readers.* Chicago: Scott Foresman and Company.

Greogory, B. (2001). *The history of Christianity in the Reformation era.* Chantilly, VA: The Teaching Company.

Grove, M. (2000). *Legacy of one-room schools.* Morgantown, PA: Masthof Press.

Gulliford, A. (1984). *America's country schools.* Niwot, CO: University Press of Colorado.

Hammett, R. (1991). *History of St. Mary's County, Maryland, 1634–1990* N. p.: R. C. Hammett.

Harroff, S. (2004). *The Amish schools of Indiana: Faith in Education.* West Lafayette, IN: Purdue University Press.

Hayes, D. (1972). *The Iowa Amish and their education.* Unpublished master's thesis, University of Iowa.

Heritage Historical Library. Documents in archives. Aylmer, Ontario.

Hershberger N. (1985). *A struggle to be separate: A history of the Ohio Amish parochial school movement.*N. p.

Hostetler, J. (1989). (Ed.). *Amish roots: A treasury of history, wisdom and lore.* Baltimore, MD: Johns Hopkins University Press.

Hostetler, J. (1993). *Amish society* (4th ed.). Baltimore: Johns Hopkins University Press.

Hostetler, J., & Huntington, G. (1971). *Children in Amish society.* New York: Holt, Rinehart and Winston.

Hostetler, J., & Huntington, G. (1992). *Amish children: Education in the family, school and community* (2nd ed.). Fort Worth, TX: Harcourt Brace Jovanovich College Publishers.

Hughes, W. (1986). *The one-teacher school: A disappearing institution.* Washington, DC: Center for Education Statistics.

Huntington, G. (1994). In D. Kraybill & M. Olshan (Eds.), *The Amish struggle with modernity.* Hanover, NH: University Press of New England.

Illinois Amish Interpretive Center. (2005). Exhibit. Arcola, IL.

Jamesport, Missouri. (2006) Internet site. Retrieved 1 April 2006 from http://www.jamesport.net.

Kauffman, Petersheim & Beiler. (1992). *History of southern Lancaster County.* Elverson, PA: Olde Springfield Shop.

Kilmuska, E. (1989, May 24). Plain teachers: They are young, Christian role models who teach only a few years then leave to marry. *Lancaster New Era*, pp. A1, A15.

Kinney, J. (Ed.). (1996). *The Amish of Holmes County.* Orrville, OH: Spectrum Publications.

Kinsinger, A. (1997). *A little history of our parochial schools and steering committee from 1956–1994.* Gordonville, PA: Gordonville Print Shop.

Klein, S., & Hoogenboom, A. (1973). *A history of Pennsylvania.* New York: McGraw Hill.

Kraybill, D. (1989). *The riddle of Amish culture.* Baltimore: Johns Hopkins University Press.

Kraybill, D. (Ed.). (1993). *The Amish and the state.* Baltimore: Johns Hopkins University Press.

Kraybill, D. (1994). The struggle to be separate. In D. Kraybill, & M. Olshan (Eds.), *The Amish struggle with modernity.* (pp. 1–17). Baltimore: Johns Hopkins University Press.

Kraybill, D., & Bowman, C. (2001). *On the backroad to heaven.* Baltimore: Johns Hopkins University Press.

Kraybill, D., & Olshan, M. (Eds.). (1994). *The Amish struggle with modernity.* Baltimore, MD: Johns Hopkins University Press.

Kreps, G.M., Donnermeyer, J.F., & Kreps, M.W. (1997). *A quiet moment in time: A contemporary view of Amish society.* Sugarcreek, OH: Carlisle Press.

Lapp, C. (1991). *Pennsylvania school history: 1690–1990.* Elverson, PA: Mennonite Family History.

Lehman, J. (2004). *Anderson school district #6.* Harrisonburg, VA: N. p.

Lindholm, W. (1989). An act of self-preservation. In J. Hostetler (Ed.), *Amish roots: A treasury of history, wisdom, and lore.* (pp. 140–141). Baltimore: Johns Hopkins University Press.

Luthy, D. (1985). *Amish settlements across America.* Aylmer, Ontario: Pathway Publishers.

Luthy, D. (1986). *The Amish in America: Settlements that failed, 1840–1960.* LaGrange, IN: Pathway Publishers.

Luthy, D. (1994). Amish migration patterns. In Kraybill, D., & Olshan, M. (Eds.), *The Amish struggle with modernity.* (pp. 243–260). Baltimore: Johns Hopkins University Press.

Luthy, D. (1997, October). The beginnings of the *Blackboard Bulletin. Blackboard Bulletin.*

Luthy, D. (2003). *Why some Amish communities fail: Extinct settlements, 1961–2003.* LaGrange, IN: Pathway Publishers.

Lyndonville, NY (2005, September). *The Diary, 37*(8), 28.

Markos, L. (2000). *The life and writings of C. S. Lewis.* Chantilly, VA: The Teaching Company.

Meyers, T. (1993). Education and schooling. In D. Kraybill (Ed.), *The Amish and the state* (pp. 87–108). Baltimore: Johns Hopkins University Press.

Michigan moves to bow to Amish education. (1965, January 21). *The Budget.* Sugarcreek, OH.

Miller, D. (1980). *The Illinois Amish.* Gordonville, PA: Pequea Publishers.

Miller, D. (Ed.). (2000). *Kansas-Oklahoma Amish directory.* Millersburg, OH: Abana Books.

Miller, D. (Ed.). (2002a). *Michigan Amish directory.* Millersburg, OH: Abana Books.

Miller, D. (Ed.). (2002b). *Wisconsin, Minnesota, and Montana Amish directory.* Millersburg, OH: Abana Books.

Miller, D. (Ed.). (2002c). *Iowa Amish Directory.* Millersburg, OH: Abana Books.

Miller, D. (Ed.). (2004a). *Kentucky and Tennessee Amish directory.* Millersburg, OH: Abana Books.

Miller, D. (Ed.) (2004b). *New Order Amish directory.* Millersburg, OH: Abana Books.

Miller, D. (Ed.) (2004c). *Iowa Amish directory.* Millersburg, OH: Abana Books.

Miller, J. (1995). *Indiana Amish directory: Elkhart, La Grange, and Noble counties.* Middlebury, IN.

Miller, L. (1983). *Our people: The Amish and Mennonites of Ohio.* Scottdale, PA: Herald Press.

Morton, R. (1958). *Marking sure of arithmetic.* Morristown, NJ: Silver Burdett Company.

Myers, D. (2000, January). The funds, friends, and faith of happy people. *American Psychologist,* 55(1), 55–57.

Mykrantz, S. (1994, Winter). Preparing Amish students for the adult world. *Holmes County Traveler,* p. 34.

Nebraska Amish Plan to operate own school. (1979, August 12). *Mennonite Weekly Review,* p. 2.

New Amish school strike looms in Pennsylvania. (1938, September 5). *The New York Times,* p. 13.

New Friends. (1977). LaGrange, IN: Pathway Publishers.

Nolt, S. (1992). *The history of the Amish.* Intercourse, PA: Good Books.

Pathway Book Catalog. (2004). LaGrange, IN: Pathway Publishers.

Payne, J. (1970). Analysis of teacher student classroom interaction in Amish and non-Amish schools using the Flanders interaction analysis technique. Dissertation, Penn State University.

Peters, S. (2003). *The Yoder case: Religious freedom, education, and parental rights.* Lawrence, KS: University Press of Kansas.

Plain people win right to their own schools as well as own way of life. (1938, December 12). *Newsweek,* 32.

Postman, N. (1985). *Amusing ourselves to death: Public discourse in the age of show business.* New York: Penguin Books.

Raffensperger, G. (1965a, November 7). Amish in daily drama of mirth, steadfastness. *Des Moines Register,* p. 1.

Raffensperger, G. (1965b, November 20). After tears, anguish, Amish attend classes. *Des Moines Register,* pp. 1, 6.

Raffensperger, G. (1965c, November 23). Amish children cry, sing to thwart officials again. *Des Moines Register,* p. 1 & 3.

Richardson, H. (2005). Creating pathways: A comprehensive study of children's literature in Amish parochial schools. Unpublished Senior Thesis, College of Wooster.

Rod and Staff Catalog. (2005). Crockett, KY: Rod and Staff Publishers, Inc.

Rodgers, H. (1969). *Community conflict, public opinion and the law: The Amish dispute in Iowa.* New York: Merrill Publishing Company.

Schwieder, E., & Schwieder, D. (1975) *A peculiar people: Iowa's Old Order Amish.* Ames: Iowa State University Press.

Scott, S. (1981). *Plain buggies: Amish, Mennonite, and Brethren horse-drawn transportation.* Lancaster, PA: Good Books.

Seitz, R. (1991). *Amish ways.* Harrisburg, PA: RB Books.

Sherman, W. (1967, September–October). The Amish exemption from school standards. *Midland Schools,* pp. 24–27.

Sherman, W. (Ed.). (1998). *Iowa's country schools: Landmarks of learning.* Parkersburg, IA: Mid-Prairie Books.

Smucker, M. (1988). How Amish children view themselves and their families: The effectiveness of socialization. *Brethren Life and Thought, 33*(3), 218–236.

Snyder, T. (1987). *Digest of education statistics.* Washington, DC: Center for Education Statistics.

Snyder, T., & Huffman, C. (1995). *Digest of education statistics.* Washington, DC: National Center for Education Statistics.

Spangler, D. (1994). *Good morning teacher Daisy.* Gordonville, PA: Gordonville Print Shop.

Staff. (1999, November). School directory. *Blackboard Bulletin,* pp. 9–28.

Staff. (1986–2005). *Blackboard Bulletin.* Alymer, Ontario: Pathway Publishers.

Teacher talk. (1973). Ontario: Pathway Publishers.

The Amish of Holmes County. (1996). Orrville, OH: Spectrum Publications.

The Standards of the Old Order Amish and Old Order Mennonite parochial and Vocational Schools of Pennsylvania. (1969). Gordonville, PA: Gordonville Print Shop.

Tips for teachers: A handbook for Amish teachers. (1977). Ontario: Pathway Publishers.

Troy, T. (2000, October 24). Mt. Hope school ranks first. *The Blade,* pp. A10 & 11.

Troyer, E., & Stoll, J. (1965). Apple Grove Mennonite School first of its kind. *Blackboard Bulletin*, 37–39.

Urban, M. (2005, May 30). Amish to build one-room school in Tulpehocken. *Reading Eagle*, p. B1.

Weaver, W.M. (1997). *Dust between my toes: An Amish boy's journey.* Wooster, MA: Carlisle Printing.

Williamsport/Lycoming Chamber of Commerce. (2002). History of Williamsport and Lycoming County [Pennsylvania]. Our towns, 2010. Retrieved March 31, 2006, from http://www.williamsport.org.

Wisconsin v. Yoder et al., 406 U.S. 205 (1972).

Wittmer, J. (2001). *The gentle people: Personal reflections of Amish life.* Minneapolis, MN: Educational Media Corporation.

Yoder, E. (1990). *I saw it in the budget.* Hartville, OH: Diakonia Ministries.

Yoder, P. (1991). *Tradition & transition: Amish Mennonites and Old Order Amish 1800–1900.* Scottsdale, PA: Herald Press.

CPSIA information can be obtained at www.ICGtesting.com
Printed in the USA
BVOW08s0232050116

431810BV00001B/25/P